19.95

Country Lawyer:

An Autobiography

By

Fred Whitaker

Country Lawyer:

An Autobiography

By

Fred Whitaker

Best of East Texas Publishers
P.O. Box 1647 • Lufkin, Texas 75901

Best of East Texas Publishers
515 South First • P. O. Box 1647
Lufkin, TX 75901
(409) 634-7444

To my mother, Annie Lucy English Whitaker,
in gratitude for her loving encouragement and belief in me.

And special thanks to my daughter, Jennifer,
for the long hours she spent checking facts, reading the manuscript
and gathering photographs to make this a historically accurate book.

Table of Contents

Foreword

I wanted to read what my old law school classmate had to say about his career and, on a Saturday, when I gave this book full attention, I became so absorbed in the account that I finished shortly before daylight Sunday.

The ability to marshal resources and use what is available to overcome the obstacle confronted has always been considered a mark of great talent, even genius, whether in battle or peaceful pursuits. This account of Fred Whitaker's career indicates an enormous capacity for hard work and a touch of genius in its execution.

The account of his early life in East Texas lifts an unspoken paean of praise to the glory of East Texas and the fortitude and resilience of its people. In the world as it was known to us when Fred and I were boys, he in Panola County and I in Wood, East Texas was that "other Eden," and his book refreshes my memory of those untroubled days.

Country Lawyer should be a widely-read book because it details much of interest about East Texas, whether the reader is an old acquaintance, as I am, student, or someone seeking literary entertainment.

T.C. Chadick
Retired, Associate Justice
The Supreme Court of Texas

Introduction

It has been said that the most beautiful music flows from the forest as the wind blows through the East Texas pines.

As I reflect back through the years, I think about my life growing up among the pine trees of East Texas in this gorgeous setting. People familiar with the landscape in this part of the United States say, without exception, that they find it the most beautiful part of our country.

As a boy, I had the privilege of going among the trees where only the sounds came from small animals, the birds in the trees, an occasional owl, or the howl of a wolf in the distance.

Always the wind sang in the trees and its music had the effect of making everything right. Here I meditated, reviewed events in the past, and called upon my fantasy world to imagine my life in the future.

During these growing up years, I visualized myself becoming a lawyer as I gained an education and made my place in life. I wanted to contribute and, maybe, just maybe, influence my community to benefit people with whom I might come in contact as I became a part of the society.

I am so indebted to the many people who gave me words of encouragement throughout my life. Without them, it might have been impossible, under the circumstances of my youth, to have gained an education and had the finances to live, buy books, pay for tuition, and room and board. Survival stayed constantly on my mind as I worked through the years to obtain a license to practice law in the State of Texas.

I owe debts of gratitude to the many other people who encouraged me even as I succeeded as a lawyer and an independent oil and gas operator.

My story began, in so many ways, as I hoed cotton in the fields of East Texas and tried to imagine life beyond the small farm where I lived with my parents and five brothers and sister. Sometimes the obstacles seemed impossible to overcome. It never occurred to me that some day I might share my story to encourage others to dream the impossible dream.

Chapter One

The Rights Between Men

Irecall distinctly, as I hoed cotton in the middle field with my younger brother, Travis, that I had reached the age of thirteen years and twenty-seven days in the year 1922.

On that quiet, sunny day, we suddenly heard loud voices of several men on horseback galloping toward our father plowing near where we hoed. I heard them shout, "The nigger Zack King just killed Park Rayburn." They wanted Papa to join them to scour the countryside.

We knew that if they caught Zack King, they would hang him then and there without a trial.

Papa unhooked the horse from the plow, walked back rapidly to the plow shed, changed the harness to a saddle, and rode off with the men in just a few minutes from the time these people invaded our lives, the lives of Travis and myself.

We didn't feel like continuing our work, and, more or less, stood there in a daze. We wondered why they would take after a man who may or may not have committed a crime, run him down, and take his life by hanging him on the limb of a tree without so much as a hearing before a court of law. We knew about hangings. We'd heard the grownups talk about them.

On June 14, 1922, *The Panola Watchman,* owned and operated by

R.M. Park and his son, published an article that nearly filled page one. It described the killing. At that time, *The Panola Watchman* had the largest circulation of any weekly newspaper in Texas. They maintained their office in Carthage, the seat of Panola County, a community of two thousand about 170 miles east of Dallas, or forty-two miles west of Shreveport, Louisiana, and thirty miles south of Longview, Texas. Carthage had served as county seat since 1848 when Jonathan Anderson, my great-great grandfather, donated one hundred acres of land for the site in Panola, an Indian word for *cotton*.

The article itself best portrays the times and what the people of Panola and surrounding counties believed. The headline read:

"Park Rayburn is Killed By Negro
"One of the saddest tragedies to occur in the history of Carthage was that of last Saturday morning about six o'clock, when a negro by the name of Zack King shot and almost instantly killed Park Rayburn, one of the most prominent and popular young farmers in Panola county.

"From the best information The Watchman can gather, the trouble arose over practically nothing. Park Rayburn lived with his father on their farm about three-quarters of a mile from town, and the negro, Zack King, lived in a tenant house on the Rayburn farm, and helped the Rayburn's (sic) in their farm work. Friday night a party was given by the negro at his home, and it is said some bad booze found its way into the party, and that during the party some window lights were broken out in the negro's house.

"Early Saturday morning young Park Rayburn went down to the negro's house to remonstrate with him concerning the roughness of the night before. The negro, it seems, still had some of the booze in him, and grew impudent toward Mr. Rayburn, causing Mr. Rayburn to strike him in the face. The negro grabbed Mr. Rayburn and in the scuffle got him down. One of the negro women grabbed a butcher knife and made a slash at Mr. Rayburn's throat, when by a superhuman effort Mr. Rayburn warded off the blow and managed to break loose from the negro's grip and made a dash for the door. Reaching the door he started for his home (only a few hundred yards away) called for someone to bring him his gun, that the negroes were trying to murder him. Mrs. Rayburn (wife of the slain man) started toward her husband with his shot gun and had almost reached him, both running toward each other, when the negro, Zack King, stepped to the door with his shot gun and fired at Mr. Rayburn, striking him in the back but not felling him.

Before the negro could fire again, Mr. Rayburn had gotten his gun, and as he turned to fire on the negro, the negro emptied his remaining load, striking Mr. Rayburn squarely in the breast, killing him almost instantly. About a dozen of the shots from the last charge struck Mrs. Rayburn in the shoulder and face, painfully wounding her.

"Seeing that he had killed Mr. Rayburn, the negro stepped back into his house, secured a lot of shells for his shot gun, got a big Colt's pistol which he had and a lot of cartridges, and made a dash for the back door, passing on through the field and made a good getaway.

"Neighbors phoned Sheriff Matthews of the shooting, and in a short time, he, together with several deputies, was on the scene. In giving attention to the murdered man, some little time was lost before the trail of the negro was taken up, who was evidently running the race of his life, for in a short while the Sheriff called for volunteers to run down the negro. The entire town responded almost instantly. Business houses closed and armed posses began to scour the country in every direction for some trace of the negro. In less than an hour the word had been telephoned over the entire county, and armed posses started out from the smaller towns in the direction thought most likely the negro would take.

"In the meantime, Sheriff Matthews seeing that the negro's escape was very likely, telephoned to Shreveport for blood hounds to assist him in the trailing of the negro. The dogs arrived about noon, and immediately took up the trail, but shortly after their arrival a heavy rain began to fall, which greatly hindered their work. However, the dogs trailed the negro to a point on the Santa Fe Railroad track, near town, and followed the trail on down the track toward Gary for a distance of some two or three hundred yards, when the trail abruptly stopped, and the dogs laid down-- as much as to say, we can go no farther, there is no trail to follow.

They were carried back to the starting point, took up the trail again and run (sic) it to the same place on the railroad track and could go no farther.

"Now, a short time after the negro had killed Mr. Rayburn, a motor car belonging to the Santa Fe Section crew was heard to come up the track from the direction of Gary, and in a short time it went back in the same direction, having two negroes aboard the driver and a passenger. As it came up only the driver was aboard, so The Watchman is informed. It is said this motor car passed through Murvaul and on to Gary, reaching Gary with only the driver, where it turned around and returned to Carthage, however, this information has not thus far been verified, but Sheriff Matthews is looking into it, as well as every other bit of information he can secure, besides wiring officers of other places a description of the negro, and to be on the lookout for him, and offering a reward for his capture. For the present, however, it seems that he has made a good temporary getaway, and the majority of our people believe he had assistance in doing so.

"There was never at any time any danger to the negro race of Carthage as a result of the killing, although reports to the contrary were current throughout the State. Negroes came and went, as was their usual custom, during the day of Saturday, and were in no way molested by anyone. Carthage has some of as good negroes as are to be found anywhere, and the negro race generally of Carthage deplores and condemns the work of the negro, King, and many offered their services in any way they could be used toward effecting the capture of the fugitive.

"Very few funerals in our city have been more largely attended than that of Park Rayburn, Sunday afternoon. The presence of the entire townspeople and many from the surrounding communities expressed the deep sympathy our people feel for Mrs. Rayburn and for the father, mother, and sister.

"The funeral procession was led by the American Legion bearing the honored flag over the casket of the one of their number who had paid the price of death. At the Odd Fellows Cemetery, Rev. Egbert Jimmerson of Tatum spoke the words that touched the hearts and minds of each listener. He could not benefit the life that had gone out but expressed the desire to better the lives of those left yet to pay that inevitable debt. The funeral services were concluded with services by the American Legion. They sang "Onward Christian Soldiers" and when the mound was covered with beautiful flowers and a fitting prayer by Judge R.W. Priest was said the former comrades sounded 'taps.'

"Park Rayburn was born near Clayton in 1898, and at the age of 17 years enlisted in the U.S. Navy, trained at the Great Lakes Training Camp. At the close of the World War he returned home with an honorable discharge and soon afterward married the young woman he had met and loved while in training at the Great Lakes Training Camp. Since that time Mr. and Mrs. Rayburn had spent part of their time in our city and part in Chicago.

"Park had united with the Christian Church about seven years ago.

"Our lives are touched with tenderness and sympathy when we think of this young wife so untimely left to battle in the world without her loved companion. To her we express as best we can our most earnest sympathy, also to the father and mother, and to the sister, Zuma, we wish to extend our sympathy in this their great grief."

In the lower right corner of the story appeared a comic "Hambone's Meditations," which read: "Hit don' take long fuh a 'chip' on yo' shoulder t' turn t' a 'knot' on yo' haid!"

A cartoon at the end of the story showed a black man smoking a corncob pipe as he watched whiskey pour from a barrel into a jug. The cartoon would take on great irony when the truth of the killing emerged twenty-eight years later.

On July 20, 1922, W. Henry Matthews, Sheriff, and J. Brassell, Deputy, filed a complaint charging Zack King with murder.

Later, during the July term of court, an indictment was returned by the Grand Jury that reads as follows:

"In the name and by the authority of the State of Texas: The grand jurors, for the County of Panola, State aforesaid, duly organized as such at the July Term A.D., 1922 of the District Court for said County, upon their oaths in said Court present that ZACK KING on or about the 10th day of June, A.D. anterior to this

indictment A.D., one thousand nine hundred and twenty-two, and the presentment of this indictment, in the County of Panola and State of Texas, did then and there unlawfully and with his malice aforethought, kill and murder Park Rayburn by then and there shooting him with a gun against the peace and dignity of the State.
Signed,
T.J. Wooten, Foreman of the Grand Jury."

For months, then years, after this occurred, I heard the older people talk about the killing, and I read articles in *The Watchman* to the effect that regardless of the search made by the good citizens of the community, and law enforcement officers, they simply could not apprehend and arrest this man and bring him back to Panola County, Texas to face trial.

Over the years, this indictment, the basis in which a man may be charged, tried and convicted, or acquitted, became part of the political life of the county. As different men campaigned for sheriff of Panola County, they pledged that they would apprehend Zack King, and bring him back for trial in Panola County.

This series of events happened in such a way that it left an indelible impression on my mind, and I thought about it from time to time for many years. It did not occur to me that this man might be brought back to Carthage for trial, and that I would grow up, obtain a license to practice law, and represent Zack King, as he faced trial in the District Court of Panola County.

Zack King returns

No one in our county forgot the Zack King case. In the late 1940s, the county elected a very capable and vigorous sheriff, Corbett Akins. Sheriff Akins somehow located Zack King in the state of Arizona. Arizona authorities placed Mr. King in custody, but he refused extradition.

In the early part of 1950, Sheriff Akins instigated proceedings to extradite Zack King from one state to another.

The proceedings for the extradition read:
March Fifteenth 1950
Honorable Wesley Bolin
Secretary of State
Phoenix, Arizona

Mr. Bolin:
The Secretary of the State of Arizona respectfully requested
to authenticate papers authorizing Mr. Corbett Akins, Sheriff of
Panola County, as Agent of the State of Texas, to receive into
custody from the authorities of Maricopa County, State of Arizona, a fugitive from justice by the name of Zack King, who stands
charged with the crime of Murder with Malice Aforethought, a
felony.
The necessary instruments accompany this Extradition.
Sincerely,
Governor

After a hearing in Arizona, Dan E. Garvey, Governor of Arizona,
signed the extradition papers and, within a short time, authorities transferred Zack King from custody in Arizona to Carthage, Panola County,
and placed him in jail without bond.

Within two days after Mr. King arrived in Carthage, Mrs. Zack King,
who had not seen her husband for twenty-eight years, came to my office
with two men and arranged for me to represent the defendant. They had
difficulty getting the money together to pay my fee, but they made a
payment on the fee at the time they requested my counsel. From time to
time, they made additional payments with money the colored Masonic
Lodge members raised.

I conferred with my client, who was not only in jail, but in a dark, small
section of the jail used to keep people charged with heinous crimes so they
would not escape.

When I went to the sheriff's office, Sheriff Akins promptly informed
me that the State, through its district attorney, Emmett Wilburn, would
insist that bond be denied. He gave as a reason that the defendant would
likely escape again and go beyond the jurisdiction of the court.

On March 22, 1950, I signed a sworn application as attorney for Zack
King. This application, a writ of habeas corpus, requested the Honorable
District Judge S.H. Sanders, to bring this man before the court for a
hearing on whether bail could be granted, and if so, in what amount.

The use of a writ of habeas corpus grew out of an old English common
law which provided that if a person was unlawfully detained, or confined,
the King would issue a writ. The writ ordered the body of the person

unlawfully detained brought before the King, or his representatives, to determine if he was unlawfully detained.

The proceeding before Judge Sanders grew out of the old common law, which has been the basis of our laws in Texas. Upon hearing the testimony and arguments of counsel, Judge Sanders set bond in the amount of $7,500.

I prepared the bond and, after the defendant signed his name, I and about ten others signed and obligated ourselves to guarantee that Mr. King would present himself in court from day to day and from term to term until the case had been tried or disposed of.

After the sheriff released Mr. King from jail, he came directly to my office, located about one block from the jail. For the first time, I had an opportunity to discuss with him what had happened on June 10, 1922.

The true facts

First, I wanted to know how he got away, escaped, when so many people had tried to catch him after the killing took place. I first told him I wanted him to tell how he actually got away from the scene so fast. Then I told him, in capital letters, that he had to have had someone help him, that I almost knew that the sheriff in his car had helped him.

He remained silent for a minute, then he smiled and told me that I had it figured out right; that the sheriff had picked him up within a few minutes after the killing had happened. They headed west of Carthage on the Henderson Highway, and the sheriff let him out under a bridge over Murvaul Creek.

Zack King worked his way on foot thirty miles north to Longview, Texas, by traveling at night, and hiding among the trees and undergrowth during the day. I asked him how he had survived without food. He said he ate, from hour to hour, wild fruit and berries, but he finally became so weak that he simply had to have something more substantial to eat during the fifteen days he survived on this thirty-mile trip to Longview.

He said he would spot a house near the creek bottom, and would walk up to the back door and ask for food. The lady of the house, without exception, always fed him.

I wondered, and asked Mr. King, if the women who helped him in this manner knew he was a fugitive. He said they had to have known, and they fed him because he was dying of hunger. He said that more than ten women fed him from time to time. I agreed that the women must have known or had a strong suspicion that he was the very man authorities were looking for throughout East Texas.

When he arrived in Longview, he caught a freight train going west. It took him three months, traveling entirely by freight, to reach Phoenix, Arizona. After he arrived, he worked odd jobs to buy food to regain the twenty-five pounds he had lost in his sojourn from East Texas to Arizona.

The true facts about the killing slowly emerged. There had been no party the night before the killing at Zack King's house. Park Rayburn had been paying Sheriff Matthews to allow Park to maintain and operate a whiskey still in the rear of his home located about one mile south of Carthage on the Gary Road.

Park Rayburn had actually called upon Zack King the morning of June 10, 1922, to order him to start operating Rayburn's whiskey still. Mr. King informed his employer that he no longer would work at the whiskey still because it violated the law. However, he offered to continue working on Mr. Rayburn's farm for the meager salary the Rayburn family paid him.

Park Rayburn then accosted Zack King with his gun and, in self-defense, Zack King drew his pistol and killed Mr. Rayburn before Rayburn could kill him. Less than five seconds lapsed between gun shots fired by the two men. Zack King acted in self-defense and would have lost his life had he not shot and killed Park Rayburn.

I believe that Sheriff Matthews primarily carried out his duties to prevent a mob from taking the life of anyone under his care and custody. And, it just might be true that by not arresting Zack King, Sheriff Matthews saved himself from being arrested or embarrassed. Zack King might have talked about the payments made to Sheriff Matthews by Park Rayburn to carry on the elicit business maintaining and operating his whiskey still, a very strict violation of the law. At the time it was a violation of law to even have whiskey in your possession.

We often refer to the rights between men as justice. If Park Rayburn had killed Zack King, it is unlikely an article would have appeared in *The Watchman*. At that time, no one cared when a white man killed a black man, regardless of the circumstances surrounding the killing.

Zuma tells the truth

Only one person, Zuma Rayburn Herring, still lived who had actually witnessed this killing that occurred twenty-eight years before. I went to the home of Zuma Rayburn. She first refused to talk with me about the facts as they occurred on the day her brother died.

A few days after Zuma refused to talk with me about this case, her husband, Mr. Herring, came into my office to engage me to represent him against an insurance company in Houston, Texas. He said he had come to me because I was known as the best lawyer who could best represent him against an insurance company. I accepted his case, and, during the conversation, I related to him how I had attempted to talk with his wife, who would be a witness for the state when the case was tried against Zack King for the offense of murder.

He informed me that he would talk with his wife and try to prevail upon her to let me interview her in my office. I wanted to go over the testimony that she would be expected to give during the trial of the Zack King case. She did appear in my office with her husband. Then I learned for the first time that she would testify to the true facts surrounding the killing, even though people had been led to believe that Zack King had killed Park Rayburn without cause or justification.

I became excited, then thrilled, that we could defend Zack King successfully. I thought we might even prevail upon Judge Sanders to instruct the jury to acquit the defendant for lack of sufficient evidence after the State had attempted to prove its case. Without her favorable testimony the State would be unable to prove its case. If the State attempted to prove its case by this witness she would testify truthfully that Zack King killed her brother in self-defense and would have been killed himself if he had not acted in self-defense.

At the conclusion of my interview with Zuma Herring, she dictated her statement to the secretary in my office. Under oath she then swore that the content of the written statement was true and correct. This became my defense that would assure us of an acquittal if the case went to trial.

On a Friday before the case was scheduled to be tried on Monday morning, during the May term of the court in 1950, I received a call from District Attorney Emmett Wilburn. He asked me if I would come to his office to discuss with him the Zack King case. I immediately went to his office in the old Panola County Courthouse.

During our discussion, he asked me if we could agree upon a short or light term in the penitentiary by pleading guilty. This was not exactly a plea bargaining situation, but somewhat similar to the cases worked out before trial by the defense attorney and the state's attorney as practiced to a large extent in present day jurisprudence.

Mr. Wilburn said he would recommend to the court that the defendant serve only five years in the penitentiary for the crime he had committed. When I rejected his offer and refused to enter into such an agreement for my client, he finally stated that he would agree that the defendant receive a five-year suspended sentence. Mr. King would not be required to serve any time in the state penitentiary provided he would then be a law abiding citizen and not violate any of the laws of the state of Texas during the five years he was under this suspended sentence.

I then knew that Mr. Wilburn had talked with the only witness and that she would testify, if required to do so, to the actual facts as they transpired at the time of the killing.

Later, on Monday morning, the case was called for trial. Spectators completely filled the courtroom. When Judge Sanders called the case for announcement, Emmett Wilburn asked for permission of the court to approach the bench. Before we had a chance to state that we were ready for trial, District Attorney Wilburn presented the court with the following document:

IN THE DISTRICT COURT OF PANOLA COUNTY
STATE OF TEXAS

STATE OF TEXAS   NO. 6690
VS
ZACK KING

Charge: Murder

Now come the District Attorney and moves the court to dismiss the above, entitled and numbered cause for the reason of the insufficiency of the evidence. In this connection the state would show the court that this alleged offense occurred on the 10th of June, 1922, that no witnesses are available to the state except a sister of the deceased who was but a child at the time and who has earnestly urged the State's attorney to dismiss this cause. The State feels that all the facts and circumstances connected herewith including the age of the defendant which is past 70 and the fact that he has apparently been law abiding since the time of the alleged offense, all taken into consideration makes it in the public interest as well as the interest of all parties to this transaction, that this case be dismissed.

Emmett Wilburn
District Attorney
123rd Judicial District of Texas

District Judge Sanders promptly acted upon this motion and dismissed the case. Judge Sanders asked the defendant to rise. A moment of suspense caught the spectators. The judge informed the defendant that the case was dismissed and Zack King would be allowed to be free and clear of all charges that had been lodged against him, that he would go hence without delay. The court then adjourned.

Within moments the spectators, the witnesses, and all present in the courtroom rushed forward with congratulatory remarks. I do believe that the acclaim bestowed upon me as defense counsel was as great or almost as great had I tried the case before a jury with the jury returning into open court with its verdict of, "Not Guilty."

It became a time for rejoicing in a very quiet and joyful way. The defendant, his wife, and close friends walked across the street to my office where we all sat in silence for a long time. Finally, we commented to each other that the case had ended. Zack King could return to his wife and family as a free man, to try to forget the horror and suffering that he had undergone throughout the years while living in Arizona.

We simply put our arms around each other as tears filled our eyes.

How I have enjoyed seeing prejudice reduced or completely eliminated against a black person who comes into our halls of justice. No doubt the poverty and prejudice I experienced growing up in rural East Texas inspired my later defense of people, whether white or black, unjustly accused and mistreated.

Chapter Two

Hoeing Cotton and Dreaming

Our family first lived some four miles north of Carthage on a farm we later referred to as the Oscar Johnson place. I hadn't quite reached three years of age and, because I was still the youngest, Mother let my hair grow into long, blonde curls that came down to my shoulders. This I considered a handicap. My older brothers, W.B., Clarence, and Herbert, known as Tony, began calling me a girl even though we already had a girl in the family, Evie May, always known as Sue.

The long hair caused other problems. The house sat on a slight hill that provided a perfect slide. I'd roll down the bank as we played rough and tumble games. After I'd return to the house, Mother always admonished me for getting so many cockleburs, trash, and twigs in my hair.

All this changed when we moved from the Johnson place to the old original family house, built in about 1880 by Grandfather John Whitaker, and located on the Marshall Highway two miles north of Carthage. Grandfather had constructed the house of rough, unpainted lumber. We referred to the house as a "dog trot." A long hallway connected the front door to the back door and people could go from the front to the back without having to open a door.

After we moved into the house, our father, whom we called *Papa*, closed the dog trot and made part of the hallway into a dining room, and built a wooden table and chairs that had rawhide leather covered bottoms. On the backside of the table, he placed one long bench where we children sat and ate.

In the cold weather we would come to the table shivering so much we could hardly hold our knives and forks. Mother always warmed us with the hot biscuits she prepared on the wood-burning stove, and served them with butter and cane syrup that provided us with a wonderful and sustaining breakfast. On certain occasions, she cooked bacon or sausage to eat with our biscuits.

The house had been built without the overhead roof being sealed. When the cold wind blew, it felt like we lived in a tent because the wind swept the heat from the house. We'd warm ourselves by standing or sitting close to the fireplace, but that meant cooking one side and freezing the other.

Of course we had no indoor plumbing and no telephone until 1918 when a company installed party lines throughout the Mitchell community where we lived. The Lacy girls in Carthage operated the central station. We'd ring the telephone with a hand crank, then pick up the receiver and ask "central" to ring a neighbor to whom we wished to talk.

We had no secrets. Once we started a conversation on the telephone, we'd hear a "click" and know other people on the line now listened. Since we had so few interests or amusements, we oftentimes followed the party line conversations. I can almost hear Mother talking to Aunt Sally, Aunt Rodie, and Ola Biggs, and feel the love and affection these women had for each other.

Going to the All-Day-To-Do

The height of our social activities revolved around going to the church's annual All-Day-To-Do, an all-day gathering of people who lived in the surrounding communities. We always planned far in advance for this special event. In about 1919, we had planned for two months to go to the Methodist Church in the Rockhill community, located about ten miles north of where we lived on the Marshall Highway.

We had gone to the Naylor Dry Goods Store in Carthage to buy our new clothes for this great occasion. As we attempted to select a hat for me, I decided that none of them looked good. I certainly refused to choose any of the hats that Mr. Naylor showed me. Papa became impatient with me and took the worst hat on the rack and put it over my head and ears, and said, "We'll take this one."

We bought new shoes, short white sox, pants and coat. Even though I've purchased clothes at Neiman Marcus many times years later, I'm sure I never dressed so well in my entire life as I dressed for this occasion, regardless of the unattractive hat my father made me wear.

We children became so excited about attending the All-Day-To-Do that we slept very little the night before, and were up with our parents by daylight arranging our Easter clothes, packing lunches, hitching up the horses to the wagon. It took us about three hours to make this trip by wagon, and, when we arrived, we saw all the people in their Easter bonnets, and their finest clothes.

When the preaching ended at twelve noon, we took our lunch and began to spread our picnic on the ground. Out of nowhere, it seemed, the largest black cloud that I had ever seen began approaching us from the southwest. So many people had come to the All-Day-To-Do that we knew it would be impossible for all the people to crowd into the church and protect themselves from the approaching storm.

Papa said he had a great idea. He knew by the way the clouds were forming and moving toward us that he could hitch up the horses and we could get ahead of the storm. We could reach safety by going back in the direction of our home.

We got into the wagon with Mama protesting, as she climbed onto the spring seat in front with Papa, that we would never make it. We children sat in the back of the wagon on the rawhide bottomed chairs we'd borrowed from home. Papa treated the horses differently this time as we raced the storm. Previously, he'd let the horses trot sometimes, but most of the time they walked or hurried along in a fast walk. On this occasion, however, Papa held the reins in one hand and a whip in the other, whipping the horses into a run.

We had gone only about a mile when Papa's weather prediction proved incorrect. It became so dark it seemed like night, and long strings of lightening streaked the sky. When the rains came the constant lightning lit the blackened sky, and the roar from the thunder and rain nearly deafened us. I believed the storm had put its wrath upon us.

At first, we children tried to get under the spring seat to stay out of the rain, but the rain swept over us in a tide. We got so drenched that we might as well have been swimming in the river wearing our clothes.

As suddenly as the storm had come, it ended. The sun and a warm breeze began to dry our clothes and, except for that catastrophic event, within a hour we wouldn't have known it had rained. As our clothes dried, they begin to shrink. I didn't mind my hat shrinking because I didn't like it anyway. But, when I looked down to see what had happened to my new white sox, to my consternation, I had no sox. As my sox had dried, they had shrunk below my shoe tops. When I couldn't find my new sox, I cried and cried, until I discovered I still had sox even though they had shrunk so small no one could see them.

You must know we had our fun. Even with the drawbacks of near-poverty and the weather, we never stopped going to the all-day To-Do's held not only in our community, but in nearby communities we visited from time to time.

"We need a lawyer in the family"

During the evenings, I would sit on the front porch of our farm house with Mother who talked with me for hours at a time, telling me about her childhood days, and her family who had been early settlers in East Texas. Her grandfather had been a surveyor, as had her own father who worked as a surveyor and a civil engineer with his four brothers who assisted him in his work. Her grandfather had first worked for the Spanish government before Texas won its independence from Mexico. For his work, he received title to land, and a small amount of cash. Her grandfather, my great grandfather, William English, owned the land given, or paid, to him through Spanish Land Grants, and later through patents through the state of Texas. A portion of his land lay in the great Spindle Top Oil Field.

Mother told me we had to have, as her father told her, a lawyer in the family to recover and take possession of all the lands owned by William English, lands which included great wealth from oil in the Spindle Top Field discovered at the turn of the century. His land grants had amounted to tens of thousands of acres. Little did she know that the land her family had owned had later been claimed by people who settled on these properties and had established, or perfected title, in their names by the statute of limitations.

The state of Texas made rigid rules and laws concerning the statute of limitations. The government desired for people to settle on lands. In order to prevent carpetbaggers from obtaining patents to the land, then returning to the East Coast and selling the properties later for a profit, the government enacted into law that people who patented land in their name must live on the land. They must occupy the land to the exclusion of other people, enclose it, pay taxes on it each year, and only then would finally the land belong to them.

At that time, however, neither Mother nor I knew anything about statute of limitations or land. I found Mama an unusual person. Even though we lived in an unpainted frame house, she maintained the house immaculately.

She assigned me, among other work, the job of scrubbing the dining room and kitchen floors once each week. I used a stiff broom and soapsuds, and then rinsed the floors with clear water.

It was while Mama and I cleaned house that she first started talking with me about getting an education. She wanted me to be Somebody. We discussed the different professions and decided that it would be too difficult for me to become a doctor since medical school required long hours, lab work, and I would have a more difficult time getting a job, working parttime, to pay my way through school.

We thought that the next most prestigious type profession would be a lawyer. I might not have such a difficult time getting a license to practice law, as compared to medicine. We decided the benefits I could give people might not be as great as a doctor who saved lives. I could, though, see justice done and see that property rights were not invaded.

At that time Mama had a brother named H. English. He had no children and he often visited our home. I can hear him and Mama speaking now, as he repeated that he wanted to help any one of us children obtain an education. I knew at the time that they had picked me to gain a college education. First I would complete the grades in our country school, then transfer to Carthage High School before going on to college.

Somehow, I did not want anyone to help me. I wanted to pay for my own education. The very day I graduated from Carthage High School, Uncle H. came to me and said he wanted to send me to school. I could go to any school of my choice in the country; he would defray all expenses. I refused to accept his offer, and told him I preferred to make my own success.

Today, I'm sure I made a mistake because he would have received great pleasure in doing this.

Mother, whose full name was Annie Lucy English Whitaker, had a profound influence on my life. She had had a limited formal education, but was a knowledgeable person. She helped me plan how to overcome the difficulties I would encounter as I made my way through school. The finances needed to get an education seemed almost insurmountable.

We planned our strategy to save money, eliminating cost. We would eliminate any use of tobacco, and I must deny myself any form of refreshment, including Coca Cola.

The Mitchell School

Our school, Mitchell School, lay one mile north of our home. The school looked like the usual Early American schoolhouse with its two-story white wood frame structure. It had two rooms downstairs, and one large room upstairs used mainly for community gatherings and for staging plays that the school provided.

Finally, I reached six years of age in May and became eligible to attend school; the school allowed me to start in October. Our parents provided the textbook, called the Primer, that the other children had used and it looked somewhat worn. This book excited me and in a short time I had memorized the contents from beginning to end. When the teacher called on me to recite, or read a portion of the book, I would stand and read from memory.

At that time, teachers and parents considered math an important subject. I had already memorized all the multiplication tables, learned to add and subtract, and worked arithmetic problems done only by adults before I attended school. The art of learning so excited me that I started to read books that the older children read. Many times I did not understand a word in the text, but if I kept reading I oftentimes got the meaning of the word in context. Today it offends me when I see someone abuse a book, something I consider should be loved and cherished.

My reverence for books did not always translate to discipline. The teachers exercised strict discipline and punished any student who violated the rules. One day someone broke a windowpane. To break the monotony of the day, we students would put our heads out the window, clear our throats, and spit.

Not long after this, a self-made carpenter arrived after school and replaced the windowpane. I did not know the glass had been replaced, so when I hurried to the window and stuck my head out, I broke the windowpane again. I should have felt lucky I didn't cut my head, but the kids screamed and laughed for what seemed like hours. This embarrassment stayed with me for years. Throughout my life I have wondered how I missed seeing the glass. I still find little humor in that mortifying experience.

During my second year in school, at age seven, I had a teacher named Ida Ray, who would later play an important part in my political life. This large, attractive woman took great delight in finding some of us daydreaming instead of studying. We oftentimes put our hands on our desks and drifted off into our imaginations. She walked the room with a hardwood ruler and when we least expected it, hit our hands. The whack caused excruciating pain.

One day as I dreamed of beautiful faraway places, she came along and hit my hands. I screamed with great pain, got up out of my seat and started swinging my fists, hitting her on the knees and thighs as hard as I could hit. This startled her and she began to get me quieted. From that time on, she never hit any child or punished a child without proper cause.

The lure of the carnival

No amount of punishment could stop my daydream of leaving the farm and the hard life in East Texas. I looked for people who had managed to escape, and studied how they had made their way out. Such a family lived near our farm. The father, Marion Chadwick, we used to joke, got a haircut once a year whether he needed it or not. His hair would grow down to his shoulder and give him a distinguished appearance.

Marion Chadwick married Miss Lelia Westmoreland, and they had six children: Pagie, the oldest child, Hollis, Hugh, Joe Ed, the youngest brother, Eva Mae and LaRue who later married Sheriff Akins. Joe Ed grew rather large and he didn't like to wear shoes. I can remember one day he came to school barefooted when snow covered the ground. This always stayed with me, that anyone could withstand such cold.

The family member I admired the most, Hollis, I found the most interesting. As boys often do, when he reached eighteen years of age, he left home. He tried to catch a ride on a freight train, had an accident and lost one of his legs. Of course, from that time on, we knew him as Peg Chadwick. His family provided him with a cork leg, and this slight handicap did not keep him from roaming.

He traveled throughout the United States and finally joined a small carnival where he learned one act. He learned to swallow a sword, and he could eat fire. When he came back to our community with his family in a caravan of three trucks, they put on a show for us. I found it wonderful to see actors who could perform such unusual things. Hollis' stepdaughter, Janette, was a contortionist. She could stand on her flat feet, lean backward and pick up a handkerchief on the floor with her mouth.

I had such admiration for Hollis Chadwick and his family that I began to say that I planned to join a carnival and travel the world. I didn't know what act I might perfect, but I did start practicing, trying to do the split with my legs. That didn't work. Then I tried bending over backward to pick up something on the floor. That didn't work either.

I did know that I must develop some unusual act to attract people to watch me. I did know that I had to develop my muscles and my body to perform. I tried all kinds of exercise, torturing my body during the free time we had from the hard work we performed on the farm. I just knew I had to develop an act that didn't resemble any of the acts Hollis and his family had perfected. I knew they had lots of money because, when they came back to Carthage, they lived during the winter without doing menial work that other people did to survive in East Texas.

Savings begin early

At about this time, when I had reached fourteen years, Miss Vallie Baker came to teach in the Mitchell School. She encouraged me to obtain an education so that I would enjoy life in an unlimited way, and perhaps contribute a great deal to the society in which I might play an important part.

She realized that finances would be important, and decided to pay me, out of her own pocket, three dollars a week if I drew water from the well to supply the water cooler, and if I started the fires in the large wood stoves to heat the classroom. This meant I had to go to the schoolhouse at least thirty or forty minutes before classes began to get the fire started in time to raise the temperature to a comfortable level for the students.

Each week she paid me by check. After each payment, I immediately hurried to the bank to deposit the money. The first time I arrived at the bank barefooted and, in order to endorse the check, and look at the cashier, I had to stand on my tiptoes.

Years later, Mr. Cooke, who owned the bank, told me that he and the other officers of the bank used to seclude themselves in the back of the bank and watch me deposit my check. Oftentimes I brought my dog, Shep, with me.

My account eventually built up to around one hundred dollars. I never withdrew any of these funds because I knew they would help defray the tremendous expenses that would confront me when I got a college education. The thrill I received making these small transactions never exceeded the importance and satisfaction I received when I made transactions involving millions of dollars years later.

Miss Vallie Baker became the first person who paid me for doing work. I had worked and slaved on the farm for years to benefit our entire family, but no money was ever exchanged. Miss Baker later became County Supervisor of Schools. She used to tell students that she had encountered two outstanding students in her years of teaching. She named a girl from Gary in Panola County, and Fred Whitaker from the rural Mitchell School.

Our school was so rural that one day Vernon Barton came to school with his face swollen and bruised. Vernon explained to the teacher that he made the mistake of telling his father again that the world was round. His father had warned him once before to never again make such a preposterous statement when he, the father, knew that the world we resided on was flat.

At age twelve, I violated some rules in the classroom and another teacher punished me by forcing me to sit under her desk. The situation excited me. The first thing I thought of doing was exploring and attempting to see part of my teacher that might not have been available had I not been placed under her desk for punishment.

I found, to my great surprise, that she wore red panties. The color contrasted with her anatomy and made a beautiful color combination. She had probably knitted the panties herself because they were oversize and drooped somewhat. The other pupils in the room could see me under her desk, and, as I explored, they began to laugh. Finally, a girl by the name of Lois Allums went up to the desk and whispered something in the teacher's ear.

My little escapade ended when the teacher began kicking me to get out from under her desk, but I started laughing so much with the other students that the teacher had difficulty establishing any kind of order in the classroom.

Pony Joe

The custom and practice of people who lived a rural life in East Texas usually provided boys, when they attained the age of fourteen or fifteen, a horse. The boy either owned the horse outright or shared it with other members of the family to provide transportation at all times.

Joseph Calvin Whitaker, my father, purchased a small pony, Joe, from the Charlie Capps family who lived about five miles south of Carthage. We called the horse Joe-Joe, and within thirty days from the time we purchased him, Joe-Joe and I had raced every pony in Mitchell community. Everyone declared Joe-Joe the fastest horse in the Mitchell School locality.

He could jump, too, if the fence wasn't too high. We'd urge our ponies to jump logs fallen across the ground. Many times we didn't take the time to put a saddle on the horse and simply rode bareback. I'd grab Joe-Joe's mane with my right hand and hold the reins in my left.

The more Joe-Joe and I rode together, the more familiar we got with what each wanted to do. He had his own way, and I had ways of improvising that he sometimes agreed to perform. Joe, a small pony, weighed no more than seven hundred to seven hundred and fifty pounds. He had the most beautiful buckskin coloring, somewhere between a yellow, brown and beige.

As Joe-Joe and I rode about the countryside, my mind wandered, thinking about the books I read, some purchased by older members of my family, but more frequently books borrowed from neighbors and acquaintances. Some of the books were too far advanced for me to understand completely, but I read them carefully from front to back. I had certain favorites, like *Ben Hur*, and O'Henry's book of short stories.

The most interesting books I read were the Horatio Alger novels and the western novels by Zane Gray. The hero of the Horatio Alger books always started out as a young man with a lot of ambition and, by the time he reached thirty or forty, he had become a millionaire. He always used his own initiative and efforts and whatever was available to him in the society in which he lived. I simply worshiped these characters, and knew I would be exactly as Alger had described his characters. Zane Gray also described his main characters as heroes in everyday life.

From time to time, different neighbors would call and say they had a book Fred could borrow if he picked it up. Day or night, I'd put a bridle on Joe-Joe and we'd head for the neighbor who had this wonderful gift waiting for me. On different occasions, clouds hid the moon and it seemed so dark you couldn't see your hand. I'd point Joe in the right direction and relax the reins. He'd walk or gallop until we located the house sometimes only visible by a dim light in the window. The light signaled for me to approach the house. I'd drop the reins and tell Joe-Joe to wait for me until I got my book. When I returned with the book, I'd tuck it up under my arm because I needed both hands to hang on to Joe-Joe's reins and mane as he raced back to our home.

We used kerosene lamps for light in those days. We'd place the lamp on a table near the chair in which we wanted to sit so that the light would shine over our left or right shoulder and onto the print. I'd sit there for hours at a time with the lamp light shining over my shoulder reading those books, imagining myself as the principal hero.

The trouble with daydreams

Little did I know at the time that these books played a large part in my education, and became the basis for much of the courage and ambition that I maintained throughout my life. I'd read at night, then during the day I'd often stop work, relax, and lean my weight on the hoe handle and daydream about the interesting life I would lead with beautiful cars and clothes. Never, however, did I feel that material things provided advantages that afforded great happiness, or the attainment of a beautiful and contented life. The early teachings of Mother and my Sunday School teacher, Mrs. Lelia Chadwick, saw to that.

The daydreams sometimes brought me trouble, too. I began to tell people that I would become a lawyer. Many people laughed and sometimes I felt humiliated because I knew, too, that we lived on a farm that produced meager income that made it impossible for me to finish high school, attend a university and obtain a license to practice law.

On one occasion as I hoed cotton in the field north of Carthage, my older brother, W.B., told me that if I ever mentioned again that I would be a lawyer that he would kick my little butt completely out of the cotton field. I listened to him. I didn't get especially mad because I knew he was telling the truth. But he did inspire new determination in me and I repeated over and over, "We'll just see about it. We'll just see about it."

I particularly remember a cousin, Jimmy Whitaker, who used to sneer when he'd tell people that his cousin, Fred, was going to be a lawyer. At age twenty-three, when I returned to Carthage with a license to practice law after I'd been gone five years, I'd look at Jimmy from time to time with a pleasant smile on my face. He never again made a disparaging remark about his ambitious cousin, Fred.

The daydreams always returned, no matter the consequences. One day as my brother, Clarence, and I rode our horses to the field, I told him that I would get off the farm and have nothing in my life except excitement. When I said that, he said, "Why don't we just have excitement now?"

He reached over with his short whip and hit Joe-Joe on the rear. Joe-Joe leaped into a dead run and nothing I could do could stop him. I had only one rein, but even if I'd had two, I could not have stopped him. It had rained, and the dirt road, made of East Texas clay, became as slippery a surface as is known to man. As Joe-Joe ran, he slipped and slid all over the road. I hung on to his mane for dear life.

Joe-Joe carried me to the fence around our old home place where he planted his feet in front of the fence to stop and skidded up to the fence. Over the top of the fence I went into the mud. Clarence came running up and asked me if this fulfilled the excitement I wanted when I left the farm.

Family influences

Though we had our quarrels, the people who most influenced me were in my immediate family. My father, Joseph Calvin Whitaker, did not believe in an education, and thought hard work made a man out of you. My mother, whom everyone called Miss Lucy, believed the opposite.

My oldest brother, W.B. (Willie), helped me fulfill my education ambition even though my daydreams annoyed him at times. Clarence took care of me as a child and would help me take a bath in the evening in an old washtub that we used for washing clothes. Mother insisted that we regularly take baths whether or not we needed one. Herbert, known as Tony throughout his life, was a happy-go-lucky sort of person who never took anything seriously. He had one ability in which no one else excelled: he could squeeze a pair of pliers with his left hand so hard the pliers could never again be used.

One day we walked into a filling station and, for some reason, Tony asked the owner if he would allow Tony to show him a little trick. I told the owner that if he allowed Tony to perform his trick, he'd ruin the merchandise on sale in the filling station. The owner answered, "If the son-of-a-bitch can do that, I'll take the loss."

Tony took the pliers, squeezed them together, and pitched them to the owner. Tony became known in the community as the strongest man on anything he undertook. He proved himself in very public ways.

My uncle, H. English, was the Cotton Weigher of Carthage and had been duly elected to this important job by the voters of Panola County. A greater portion of Panola County's economy depended upon the cotton crop. At that time, cotton and timber ranked as the major agricultural crops that provided the main source of income in Carthage and Panola County. As we scratched out a living on our cotton farm, we instilled pride in ourselves by remembering a story told frequently. A bale of cotton produced in Carthage, Panola County, remained continually on display in the London Cotton Exchange.

The citizens of Panola County created the position of Cotton Weigher and built a receiving station for the yearly cotton crop. They rented a large tract of land, adjoining the Santa Fe Railroad tracks, that had a large loading platform used to load the box cars with cotton sent on its way to the Galveston seaport where it made its way to England. Every two years, the people elected an individual to serve as the Cotton Weigher to oversee the weighing of cotton. H. English got paid twenty-five cents for each bale weighed. This resulted in his being paid as much or more than any other county official.

Of course, H. English wanted to help our family, and gave Tony a job unloading and moving cotton bales throughout the cotton yard. This type of work required a strong person with a strong back to do this kind of heavy manual labor.

A black man, Dan, who weighed over two hundred pounds, had worked in the cotton yard for many years and had the reputation for being the strongest man in Panola County. When Tony came along, Dan became known as the second strongest man.

Tony could take the small hook, used to grab a bale of cotton, in his left hand and start whirling the bale of cotton. He'd swing the cotton until he worked it up and on to his back, and then he'd walk more than a hundred feet forward, then back, with a five-hundred pound weight on his back. People came for miles around to watch him do this.

Rural entertainment

Tony had a fast curve ball, too, and pitched left-handed for our rural baseball team. He struck out the best batters in our league. The many rural teams in the area made up our league. People came miles to watch Tony pitch. Fans yelled from the sidelines, "Hey Tony, the alligator boy." Our team became so successful that we rose to the top of our league and played Marshall, Texas. We beat them, too.

We entertained ourselves, growing up in East Texas, and without doubt, none of the kids today could possibly have had any more fun than we had. Our father encouraged us to enjoy ourselves, and gave us something to look forward to. He always told us that as soon as we laid-by our crops, usually in early July, that we could go fishing and spend the night on the Sabine River, about five miles from where we lived.

We fished with a cane pole and line, and caught white perch, what some call brim. We worked pretty hard catching these fish because without them our vittles would have been spare. We brought our staples, like bread and seasoning, to the river with us to eat with the fish. After we caught the fish, we cleaned them, and cooked them in a large, black skillet with lots of fat. We believed this meal the most delightful thing anyone ever ate.

We played and worked so hard that when night came we spent very little time around the bonfire, and slept on the ground on quilts or pallets without protection from the mosquitoes. Our rest during the night enabled us to get up early and start the whole process over.

The time spent on the Sabine River served as our payment for working in the fields seven months a year. In the fall, I picked cotton before I went to school, and, in the spring, I dropped out of school to plow the soil. I only went to school five months out of the year.

Overcoming handicaps

Our two teachers at Mitchell School didn't know the rules of grammar and they were not well-educated people, but had managed, somehow, to get a teaching certificate to teach school. This handicapped my knowledge of the English language, and when I transferred to Carthage High School, I had a further handicap. I had been going to school only five months a year, and Carthage was a nine-month's school.

In order to attend high school, I found it necessary to work to pay expenses. I worked for my brother, W.B., in his service station and averaged working about eighty hours a week. W.B. paid me fifteen dollars a week, plus room and board with him, Joyce his wife, and their daughter Melba, who lived in Carthage.

Not many customers came to the station nights, which I worked, and this allowed me to study and prepare for classwork the following day. Changing oil, changing tires, and repairing tires proved the most difficult thing in working in a service station and doing my studies at the same time. I got so much grease on my hands that I cleaned my hands dozens of times each evening. I never had enough time even though I tried to stay meticulous, neat and orderly. That first year I dropped out of school before the term ended so that I could work in my father's fields planting crops.

The second year, I talked the superintendent of schools into letting me skip a grade; that is, go from tenth to the eleventh grade. I promised to study on the job. Through sympathy, I did get my high school diploma, but I really didn't have a high school education. I didn't have the foundation to go to college. I did save enough money to get myself started. When I received my high school diploma in 1927, one of forty students, I finally had a bank account totaling five hundred dollars, an amount that included the money I had earned for taking care of Mitchell School.

Uncle H. English came to me again and said he would pay all my expenses to any school I wished to attend. By then, H. English owned a sawmill and planer mill near Carthage and served on the board of directors for the First National Bank. We considered him wealthy. I told him I preferred to do it on my own. I did not want to feel obligated to anyone.

My friend, Buck Park, had already convinced me where I should attend college.

Chapter Three

"Fred, get your hoe, and come vith me."

Georhge Buck Park's family of Carthage owned the weekly newspaper, *The Panola Watchman*. At the time I graduated from high school, the Park family had moved to Fort Worth to allow their daughter, who suffered from arthritis, access to the doctors who specialized in the illness. George was about three years older than I was, and knew I was considering going to school in the fall.

The Park family lived only two blocks from Texas Christian University in Fort Worth. George had attended TCU the previous year and knew everyone. George told me that this was not only an excellent school, but it provided jobs for people to work and help defray at least part of the expenses while attending the university.

The last week of June finally came that summer when I planned to start college in September. George had promised to take me to Fort Worth and introduce me around campus. Maybe, just maybe, I could get a job on campus to get credit on the tuition I had to pay that fall.

The Park family, who visited Carthage regularly, had a Model-A four-door sedan. On this particular weekend, the Park family of six piled into their car, and decided the car would be too crowded with me. We arranged that I drive a separate car, a Chevrolet Coupe, as far as Dallas. Jessie

Chadwick, Peg Chadwick's first cousin, owned this car, and Jessie traveled, selling lumber from a sawmill that his family owned. Jessie asked me to drive his car, and as we arrived in Dallas I got so excited that my heart started pounding because I had never seen so many people in such a large place. It simply frightened a boy like myself who had hardly been off the farm during his lifetime.

I'll never forget the time we walked up the steps in front of the Adolphus Hotel with its brass rail that still exists today. We walked into the lobby, and Jessie told me I should sit and wait for the Parks who would arrive in about thirty minutes or so. I waited and I waited, and I waited and the Parks did not appear. The longer I waited the more frightened I became. I knew they had forgotten me or something terrible had happened.

I remained in the lobby for three hours, keeping a constant watch on the front entrance. I do not recall whether I left the chair long enough to even wash my hands in the men's room. I certainly didn't want to miss them and get left in the big city where I didn't know anyone, or know where or how to go anywhere. I stayed there, frightened but excited.

When they arrived, they told me that instead of coming right behind us, they had decided to go to church in Carthage, then make the trip to Dallas. I've never been so glad to see anyone in all my life as when Buck Park walked up those steps and smiled and told me about their delay.

We drove on to Fort Worth where I spent the first night in their home. We decided we should clean up and take a bath that evening. The only bath I'd even taken in my life had been in the large tin tub on the farm. I found taking a bath in a bathroom that had bathroom facilities very unusual, to say the least.

I was so shy that, after running the water in the tub, I simply could not take my shorts off. I sat down in the water, took my bath, wrung out my shorts after I completed the bath, put on new clothes, then felt ready to face the world.

"Fred, come with me"

On Monday morning, in 1928, we went to the TCU campus. I looked around and saw the large buildings, which excited me, and then I became somewhat frightened by all the buildings that made up the campus. Buck first introduced me to Fred Erisman, a senior who had worked at odd jobs, paying his expenses. Fred's father, who owned and operated a small hamburger stand on Magnolia Street in Fort Worth, had saved money for years to send Fred to College. Fred told me it wouldn't be difficult for me to earn my expenses, and took me to meet the superintendent of the grounds, Mr. Dees. Mr. Dees looked me over and asked me to report to him, wearing my work clothes, for work the next morning at seven o'clock.

I'm sure there's not one foot on the TCU campus that I have not covered at some time since Mr. Dees put me in charge of keeping the yards and campus mowed with a large gasoline powered lawnmower.

Mr. Dees had a German foreman, Mr. Fred Dees used to keep us working. Mr. Fred spoke with a decided German accent. For some reason, he expected me to do more of the hard manual work than anyone else because I had physically matured more. In his German accent, he'd say, "Fred, git your hoe and come vith me."

A friend, Jimmy Pate of Alpine, Texas, who worked on the grounds with me, always greeted me, "Fred, git your hoe and come vith me." We worked the entire summer, making two dollars a day, but no cash exchanged hands. They gave us credit for our room and board and tuition for the ensuing year.

When the first week of September came, I went to the dean's office to register and learn if I could enroll and continue to work on campus, but work less than the ten hours a day I had been working. After I enrolled in the courses I wanted to take, someone told me I needed to speak with Butler Smiser, the business manager.

I walked into Mr. Smiser's office, and he told me to have a seat. I felt very tense and wondered if I could afford to stay in school even though I had some credit from my work that summer. I told Mr. Smiser that Mr. Dees had promised me a job that year. Mr. Smiser asked me how much money I had and I told him I had one hundred and fifty dollars, instead of the five hundred dollars I'd saved from the work at the service station and at Mitchell School.

Mr. Smiser said, "Then give me a check for the hundred and fifty dollars."

I told him that if I wrote him the check for one hundred and fifty dollars, I wouldn't have any money left. Then he said, "Just give me a hundred dollars." This I did. I spread that money so thin that I had about one hundred dollars left of the original five hundred when I went to Austin five years later to take the Bar examination.

Collecting hard knocks

While attending TCU, it became necessary at one point that I deliver the Fort Worth Star Telegram each morning and afternoon to subscribers in a certain part of the city. The circulation manager of the newspaper held a meeting with students interested in working and, after the meeting, about thirty-five students accepted employment. In a few days we started delivering the paper on a route assigned to each of us, with names and addresses.

A large number of the subscribers were friendly, and, in some instances, got personally acquainted with us. They accepted us and knew we were working our way through TCU. On occasions they invited us into their homes for refreshments. We were always in a hurry, but we'd accept this hospitality and stay a few minutes.

One of my customers owned and operated a bakery shop just off University Boulevard. When I first became acquainted with him, he invited me to have some hot rolls that he had just taken out of the oven. This happened about five o'clock in the morning, and we chatted a few minutes, eating two or three rolls while we talked. He seemed to look for me each morning, and, I certainly wanted to see him for a little company at that hour of the day, and for the wonderful rolls he provided.

A few subscribers, however, did not treat us in a friendly manner. Some refused to pay us once each month for delivering their paper. My alarm always got me up at three a.m. One morning as I struggled to put my clothes on as I went down the long stair steps in Good Hall where I lived, I noticed that a freeze had come during the night. Ice and sleet covered the steps. About the second step I made, I started sliding on my back all the way to the street below. I don't believe I've ever felt as much pain in my body before or after this happened.

I lay there for a few seconds and thought about all the horrible things that had occurred in my life. One person who occurred to me was the man who lived just two blocks from where I lay and who had not paid me for three months. I got back up off my rear and carefully walked up the steps, got to the telephone and called this customer who refused to pay.

The telephone rang for a long time, but finally someone answered as though half asleep.

"Have you seen the conditions of the weather outside?" I asked him.

"Hell no!" he said, "and I'd appreciate it if you would let me go back to sleep."

"This is Fred Whitaker and I want you to go look outside, and remember that I get up this hour each morning to deliver your newspaper. Don't you think I should be paid?"

The next afternoon, when I delivered his paper, he walked out of the house with a smile on his face and said, "I believe I ought to pay you each month."

We both laughed and became good friends after this occurrence.

But a very prominent and successful lawyer who lived on this route, Wild Bill McLane, acted differently. Apparently I made a big mistake one day in the late afternoon as he and his wife sat in their courtyard in front of their palatial home.

I walked up to him and said, "Could you pay me for the newspaper? You haven't paid for the past thirty days."

This infuriated him. He told me, "If you expect to receive any money at all, you'll have to come to my law office in downtown Fort Worth."

I knew that this would not be practical because the twenty-five or thirty cents profit I made each month for delivering his paper wouldn't pay the streetcar fares, much less the time spent in my making the trip once a month to collect for one newspaper customer.

I attempted to explain why his request would not be practical, but he came up from his lawn chair like a tiger and backed me all the way to the street, calling me every word of profanity known to man. When we got to the street, I felt like we had reached neutral territory. I told him I didn't like being called a sonovabitch, and that he was a sonovabitch and a bastard; then I called him all of the things I knew to say. I told him I'd wipe the surface of the earth with his body. He backed down and slowly went back to his repose and comfort.

I didn't feel any satisfaction from this encounter. I first reported it to my circulation manager, and he, in turn, reported it to Amon G. Carter, the owner and editor of the newspaper. Mr. Carter called me personally and said I had his support and that everyone would be instructed to never again deliver the *Fort Worth Star Telegram* to Mr. McLane at his residence.

Bill McLane, Jr., also a very successful lawyer, lived across the street from his father, and, even though I collected from him, it took extra effort.

He, too, thought his bill should be paid out of his office and not by him or his family at his place of residence. We worked this out, and each month he paid me. Neither of us could have known that we would face each other in court some day as opposing lawyers. The outcome, which still brings me satisfaction, lay three years in my future.

English as a foreign language

I studied hard at TCU, but my lack of education in Mitchell School and Carthage proved a serious handicap. My freshman English Professor, Miss Spragins, who lived in Dallas, didn't discuss or teach the fundamentals of the language in class. I remember her using the term, *split infinitive.* "My gosh, what foreign words," I thought. She lost me as much as if she were speaking a foreign language. Years later I laughed and told her that I majored in freshman English because I took it two years. Finally, I got out of freshman English and passed sophomore English where I studied Victorian English literature.

I found it difficult to write themes, to originate the subject matter and get started. I just didn't have anyone to help me. In my conversations, I used words and phrases that I'd learned on the farm in East Texas. Other people didn't understand me when I said, "I'd just live do this." I meant, "I'd rather do this." Nor did they understand when I said, "We laid by our crops." I meant, "We completed cultivating our crops."

Then one day, a young woman who had a class with me said she noticed my English wasn't very good. She said she'd like to be my tutor. I remember her as a beautiful woman from some town in West Texas. We had a room set aside for us where she taught me English.

After she had taught me for a while, she told me about herself, that she had convulsions, and that she might have a convulsion while we studied together. One day she fell and completely passed out. I caught her before she injured herself, and lowered her onto the floor, gradually moving her into a sitting position until she became conscious. I began having a feeling of sympathy for her. She had helped me and had been very kind and beneficial to my life.

I attempted to study Spanish, but I had no background for a foreign language, but I did study hard and try. The Spanish teacher talked about verbs and adverbs, and, damn, I didn't even know those in English.

My run on the bank

I did know about saving money, and, in 1930, the Depression took its toll on all of us. Depositors in Fort Worth made a run on the First National Bank of Fort Worth where, just prior to the run, I had deposited about three hundred and fifty dollars. That sum consisted of a greater portion of my worldly goods. Bank funds were not guaranteed by the federal government as they are today.

We had heard the rumor on the TCU campus that the First National Bank would go under. I hurriedly took a streetcar downtown and, within thirty minutes, helped form a line that reached about three blocks from the entrance of the bank. I intended to withdraw my funds, if there was any money left to do so.

After I stood in line for a couple of hours, a gentleman whom I knew slightly from Carthage, Mr. Ross, came up beside me and attempted to tell me that the bank would not go under. He assured me all of the Waggoner wealth stood behind the solvency of this institution.

I informed Mr. Ross that should I lose this money I would fail, and would not be able to continue or finish my education at TCU. In a like manner, he advised me that if I would feel better, I should simply follow him. We went into the bank through the back entrance. I signed a check, and he delivered to me the amount of the check in cash. I felt such a relief.

Then I became so frightened that I might lose this money that I failed to sleep at all during the next night. It was too much money to have on my person, and so I ventured back downtown the following day and learned that the scare, or rumor, that had caused the run in the first place, was not well-founded. I saw the bank operating in a normal manner. I ventured up to the cashier's window and redeposited my funds.

Several years later, I became acquainted with Earl Barber who, at the time of the scare, had been working at the First National Bank as a bookkeeper, or cashier. He told me that I should not have worried about the solvency of the bank. He knew it was solid, because the bank paid their employees such a small amount for the work that they performed. Mr. Barber said that on one occasion the employees received slips asking them not to divulge the small salary they received. He told me that he replied by saying not to worry, that he was just as ashamed of it as they were.

Father charged with murder

In my junior year, 1930, I received a letter from Carthage, telling me that my father had killed a man, Bobby Pierce. The authorities had charged my father with murder. At the time I received the letter, he was free on bond. In fact, my father spent very little time in jail immediately after this occurred.

L. M. Hunt served as sheriff at the time, and he allowed my father to remain downstairs where the sheriff and his wife lived while Sheriff Hunt maintained and kept incarcerated prisoners in the jail.

At the time I received the information about Papa, I wanted to go to Carthage, but decided to wait until I went home during the Christmas holidays. Then I'd talk with my father about the difficulty he had had with someone, resulting in this tragedy. On December 20, as soon as I reached Carthage, I went to his home where he lived alone two miles north of Carthage. Even though we were not a demonstrative family, I put my arms around my father and told him to tell me about the difficulties he had had with this man Bobby Pierce. Mr. Pierce had had, since I could remember, a reputation for being a tough, unscrupulous type of man who bullied a great number of the people he encountered, especially when he was intoxicated.

My father related to me what had happened leading up to the shooting just off the public square on the Mount Enterprise Road. In front of Beall's Department Store in Carthage, Bobby Pierce and his friend, Neil Davenport, accosted Calvin Whitaker without any provocation. Bobby Pierce hit my father about the face and body, resulting in severe and painful wounds.

But Mr. Pierce did not seem satisfied at getting the best of the fight, and decided to use his knife to kill my father. As Pierce came at my father with his knife drawn, my father reached into his inside pocket and brought out a .32 caliber pistol and shot Pierce, defending himself from Pierce. The grand jury investigated this matter and indicted Calvin Whitaker for the unlawful death of Bobby Pierce.

My father stood trial in the district court of Panola County. To defend himself, he had to hire two lawyers. To defray the cost of hiring lawyers, it became necessary that Papa make a conveyance to his sixty-one-acre tract of land that he owned two miles north of Carthage. The lawyers charged twenty-five hundred dollars, but my father had no money to pay the twenty-five hundred dollars. As a result, the attorneys had the right to take title and possession of the property in payment of the attorneys' fees.

It was not only necessary that my father, Calvin, sign this deed, but the lawyers also required that the children of age, at the time, sign the deed since they had an interest in the property. We all signed it, except Travis who was a minor at the time.

All of us children were very supportive of our father and attended the trial from day-to-day. We had seats inside the bar, sitting near our father and his attorneys in close proximity to the jurors selected to try the case. The jury knew that we were responsible people. We were well-dressed. Word circulated around the courthouse at that time that Fred Whitaker, Calvin's son, was actually in law school and maybe one day would be an outstanding person in the community, even though we were only known as farm people making a living growing cotton and other by-products we might need to survive.

The jury acquitted our father of the offense. The trouble ended except that my father had overwhelming economic problems. About two years later, I returned to Carthage with my license to practice law. On one visit out to the farm to see my father, he asked me if I would try to save the farm and keep it in the family. He especially didn't want one of his neighbors, a man by the name of Hubert Mitchell, to ever own this property. I did not reply to my father at the time. But he did know that I knew in my own mind that I would save this property for him, and did so at a later date. I obtained title to the property in my name some two years after our conversation took place.

I still remember standing in the front yard, in front of the house, when he asked me if I would try to save the farm so that it would not be taken by the attorneys, who were entitled to do so if the attorneys' fees were never paid. I had a lot of compassion and a great feeling for my father but failed to put my arm around him and tell him I would do this. I remained silent. This I've always regretted. Somehow, I believe he must have known that I would fulfill his request. It has always been sad that he did not live long enough to have realized that after I started practicing law that I had sufficient income to pay off this indebtedness. I have since owned the property. Never, in any way, will I forfeit it during my lifetime.

My father and mother had always dreamed about their having wealth at some time, because they believed oil would be discovered on this small tract of land in East Texas. After a rain they could see skims of an oil-appearing substance on small pools of water. This substance, of course, had nothing to do with what might lie a mile beneath the surface of the earth. It somehow gave them hope that oil would be discovered.

Years later, one of the largest gas wells in Texas was discovered on this very land upon which we had hoed, chopped and picked cotton. Since that time, this land has paid me, over periods of years and months, millions of dollars.

Choose another profession other than law

During my senior year at TCU, I took a course in public speaking under Dr. Katherine Moore. I was so shy and downright timid that I couldn't make a talk in her class that would enable me to pass the course. I finally came up with the idea of taking a stimulant. The first drink of whiskey that I ever took consisted of about half of a Coca Cola glass filled with whiskey that George Buck Park gave me to settle my nerves in order to make the thirty-minute talk.

I made the talk and did very well, perspiring all over my face, my clothes. The other members of the class were overwhelmed because they'd never heard me talk before.

After this, Dr. Moore said that she wanted to talk with me about something very confidential between the two of us. We went into the chapel, or assembly hall, and sat down. She put her arms around me and tears began to roll down her cheeks. She said that this was one of the hardest things that she'd ever had to do in life. She wanted me to choose another profession, and not become a lawyer.

She urged me not to become a lawyer because I would not be able to make a speech, or become a trial lawyer in any manner. As I recall, I cried a little, too, but I told her I was going to attempt it anyway. Dr. Moore had taught me one semester and knew how very timid and shy I felt around her and the students, but she didn't realize that I might overcome this weakness after getting interested in cases or lawsuits with which I would become engaged during trial work.

Law school beckons

I knew just where I wanted to go to law school. A friend of mine, Tom McMurray, had just recently obtained his license to practice law in Fort Worth. Tom advised me that a school, Cumberland University, in Lebanon, Tennessee, just outside of Nashville, covered a three-year law course in one year.

Dr. Moore had taught at Cumberland University before coming to TCU to teach public speaking. Dr. Moore said she would help me in any way she could if I was determined to go to law school. She said she would write a letter introducing me to Dr. Stockton, president of Cumberland.

I knew Fred Erisman made excellent grades at TCU. He told me he thought it was foolish for me to spend three more years in law school to obtain a law school degree. He said he'd passed the state bar by obtaining law books for his use to study the law in order to take the state bar examination. However, he said that he attributed a quizzer — a condensed question and answer text that covered all the principles of law — for preparing him for the examination more than anything he had done. Little did I know that Fred's shortcuts to goals would spill over into other aspects of the law and eventually affect me.

At the time, Dr. Moore's offer to write a letter to the president of Cumberland University was just what I needed because I had been at TCU for so long — four years — until I did not have the patience to go three more years to a regulated law school, such as The University of Texas, Baylor University or Southern Methodist University in Dallas. I didn't have the money, either, but I did have a lot of nerve and determination. When I left TCU, I lacked a few hours of completing the required hours to receive a bachelor's degree. I had run out of time and money, and when I heard of the one-year law school in Tennessee, I took off.

The first week of September, 1932, I packed a small suitcase made of cardboard and set out to hitchhike to Lebanon, Tennessee. As I caught rides with different people, I'd oftentimes crowd myself into the seat with my head bowed, wondering why I had undertaken this journey in the first place. I had been deeply in love with Gladys Simpson of Fort Worth. I knew I must become a lawyer, or succeed in some manner, because if I did not I would not be worthy of her devotion.

For hundreds of miles I rode in a daze, my mind churning with thousands of thoughts. At first, I resisted the temptation to cry in the way one resists a complete falling apart. But my situation bore in on me, and at last my spirit broke.

I would then slump forward, or twist into a ball, and tears would flow like a river. Sometimes my face would become twisted, and then I would cry inside and sometimes in a low audible manner. The driver, or other occupants in the vehicle, would come to my rescue, but I would be unable to explain why I felt such desperation.

As my journey proceeded, I simply let my heart bleed, sobbing as I had done so many times in my early life on the farm in East Texas. It has been said that a grown man should not cry, but I sincerely believe that had I not been able to cry during this period of my life, I would not have had the courage to go forward or survive.

In a small satchel, I carried the letter written by Dr. Katherine Moore of TCU, addressed to President Stockton of Cumberland University. I held it close to my person. Without it, I would have been doomed. Two nights after having left Fort Worth, I arrived in Lebanon, Tennessee.

I learned the location of the university from people in the downtown area, and walked several blocks to where I found an unattended dormitory. On the third floor, I found a room with a clean bed, removed my clothes, got comfortable, and slept about eight hours. On Sunday morning, I hurriedly bathed, shaved, and put on my best clothes to go talk with Dr. Stockton.

At about eight o'clock that Sunday morning, the day before school started, I knocked on the door of Dr. Stockton's elegant residence, a two-story wood-frame home. I had little time. Dr. Stockton invited me in and, as he read the letter of recommendation written by Dr. Moore asking him to do whatever he could for me, I noted the many antiques that filled the house, giving it the character of a classic Southern home. Dr. Stockton seemed touched by the letter as it brought back memories of this fine person. His faced softened and tears came to his eyes.

Creating jobs that pay

He did not hesitate to tell me, though, that it was impossible to get a job in Lebanon in order to pay for my school expenses during the Depression. I insisted that he give me some idea of what had been done in the past. He told me that Mrs. Burge, who owned a boarding house about a block away, had used a student the previous year to wait tables and fire the furnace to pay his room and board.

Then he told me a men's clothing store downtown, McLane and Smith, had used a salesman in the afternoons. He further explained that they had decided not to hire anyone this year because business did not justify it.

I hurried to the home of Mrs. Burge after thanking Dr. Stockton for the information and telling him that I would talk with him later. Mrs. Burge came to the door, and I told her why I had come. She said that I need not talk with her because she couldn't use anyone this year. As a matter of fact, she said, school started tomorrow and she didn't have anyone signed up to room there, even though she had room for about eight people to live in her two-story home.

I thought for a second, and asked her if I could help her, since I knew several men from Texas who would arrive, by train and by bus, later during the day. I asked her if she would direct me to the bus station and train depot. "Let me see if I can't do something," I told her. She said if I filled her house I wouldn't have to work, that she'd just give me free room and board. By seven o'clock that evening, I had all the roomers she needed. She promptly gave me the job of waiting tables and firing the furnace.

I moved in with my small cardboard suitcase and slept well that evening. The next day, however, I had further difficulties because I had to go through Cumberland University's business office where a Mr. Cash told me that in no way would I be able to go to school without giving him at least two hundred and fifty dollars in advance.

I said I did not have the money at this time, but I was going to get it, that I would get a loan from my brother who lived in Shreveport, Louisiana, and I already had a job in Lebanon. He reluctantly let me sign in without paying him anything. At that time I had less than a hundred dollars.

The next afternoon, after attending classes and getting registered into law school, I went to see McLane and Smith. They reiterated emphatically that they could not use anyone since business simply did not warrant it. I made them a counter-proposal. I asked them if they would let me work two weeks without pay and, then, if I produced for them, they could put me on the payroll.

Mr. Smith, I can see him now, a man of about forty who stood about medium height. He said he didn't have anything to lose, and he would just take me up on the proposition. I started to work immediately, worked two weeks, and got paid by the store for the first two weeks, which I believe amounted to fifteen dollars per week.

Riding in style with Johnny McLane

In the first few weeks at Cumberland, I met about thirty or forty different students from Texas. After I had been there about thirty days, I met Johnny McLane, son of Wild Bill McLane, who had backed me off his property when I tried to collect for delivering his *Fort Worth Star Telegram* two year before.

Someone was giving a party in a small hotel in Murfreesboro, Tennessee, some thirty or forty miles from Lebanon, but I had decided not to go because the cost of transportation did not fit into my budget, nor did the cost of attending this dance. After the bus had gone I happened to be in the drug store in downtown Lebanon, a meeting place for students, when Johnny McLane came up and said he'd just missed the bus.

"Damn it," he said, "I want to go anyway," and asked the druggist to call a taxi. He insisted that I go with him, and, since some of my obstacles had been eliminated, I enjoyed the taxi ride.

The taxi fare seemed enormous to me, but Johnny not only paid the fare, he gave the driver a five dollar tip. We got to the party a little late, and gin was being mixed in the bathroom. Someone served us small cups of strong gin on the balcony side of the hotel. For some reason, Johnny and I stood in the midst of about one hundred people from school. We had a round of drinks and into our midst came an attractive girl from Alabama who attended Cumberland University. I had heard her say this more than one time, but after she had a drink or two, she reminded everyone that she had graduated from the State University of Alabama.

I told her she shouldn't throw up her hat, that, "Hell, we came in a taxi ourselves." She realized she had bragged too much this time when we got a laugh. We never heard her again say she had graduated from another school before she entered law school at Cumberland University.

Like myself, a large number of these students took the direct route to qualify themselves to take the bar examination without having attended a three-year law school, which, at the time, most states required. Texas made no such requirement. If we could pass the bar examination, that's about all it took to get a license to practice law.

During the early part of December of that year, I thought about how I might travel back to Fort Worth to see my girl friend, and from there get to Carthage to be with my family at Christmas. While talking with a friend in Nashville, I told him about my predicament. He said he might be able to help me because he knew a man in charge of passenger service for a railroad company.

My friend introduced me to the gentleman with the railroad, but he could not think of a way for me to obtain free passenger fare to Fort Worth. I then suggested an idea to him.

"I could introduce you to other students at Cumberland University, just before classes end for the Christmas holidays," I said. "I could make arrangements for you to sell passenger tickets to students wanting to travel throughout the country."

He came to Cumberland on the morning that classes would end at noon for the holidays. Just before classes ended, all the students gathered in the assembly room; I stood up and said that I had a statement to make.

"We have a gentleman here who will give us special passenger service on his railway to any destination. He's sitting at a desk just outside the assembly room."

The railroad man sold forty or fifty tickets. When he finished talking with students, he looked at me and said, "This is one of the finest days I've had in a long time. You know, our passenger service during the Depression has not been so good. I'll tell you, I'm going to do more than I said I'd do for you. I'm going to give you my own personal pass that allows you to travel in my name, with a complimentary Pullman compartment, and meals — the whole works."

I got myself to Nashville where I met this gentleman. He gave me his card, we shook hands, and I got on the train.

When I got to Fort Worth, I went to TCU, and got myself a dormitory room without having to pay, and spent the holidays there. I called Gladys Simpson and told her that I had arrived in Fort Worth and would like to see her as soon as I could. She told me, without too much diplomacy, that she had another friend, Buck, whom she was seeing. So I looked up some of my old friends and spent my time with them. I caught a ride with some friends to Carthage where I spent a few days, then returned to Fort Worth and caught the train back to Nashville.

When I finished law school, I made as high a grade as you can make in law school, ninety-nine out of one hundred. I packed my cardboard suitcase and headed back to Texas where I would prepare myself to practice law in Fort Worth, my adopted home.

Chapter Four

Not Quite Home in Fort Worth

I'd always planned on practicing law in Fort Worth. I'd enjoyed myself there so much. It was where I'd gotten out of the cotton fields of East Texas and found a better way of life and wonderful friends. Somehow the people in Fort Worth and the students I knew in school never showed any indication they looked down on someone who might not have the wealth they had.

To receive a license to practice law in 1933 in Texas, you either had to study law at a university, or you could register with the Supreme Court that you were studying under lawyers who supervised your work day-to-day as you read in their office law library. The Tarrant County Bar Association decided they'd place further requirements on people to take the bar examination.

They set a time for each of us to appear before their body of lawyers for a one-hour oral examination. Prior to that, I had qualified to take the Texas State Bar examination. Judge Woolworth, president of my local Bar Association in Panola County, had written a letter of recommendation vouching for my character and qualifications to take the bar exam.

I felt rather cocky about taking the Tarrant County Bar examination, and I went with some of my classmates to take this oral exam. As I stood outside the door after they had completed the examination of one of the applicants, the door monitor said, "next." For some reason, I just walked in. They asked me to sit down.

They started asking questions. I'd answer, sometimes elaborating on the answers. Suddenly the questions stopped and they asked me to step outside. Then they called me back in and said they believed I was the only person who had come before them who had answered all the questions one hundred percent correctly. They were not only going to recommend that I be qualified, they were going to give me a special recommendation.

Then I went to Austin to take the state bar examination. The state bar written examination lasted four days, ten hours a day. It was more of an endurance contest than an examination of your knowledge of the law. I returned to Fort Worth to wait for the results of the state bar exam.

Setting up practice

I got a room at the YMCA, a room about ten-by-six-feet that had enough room for a mirror, dresser, and a small bed about half the size of a regular twin bed. The room cost me about six dollars a month. I took my meals at rooming houses in the area where, for twenty-five cents, you got all you could eat. For breakfast and lunch, I'd eat lightly, maybe a ten-cent hamburger for lunch.

During this time, I interviewed with more than ten law firms. Without exception, they stated their practice would not justify bringing in a young lawyer on even a low salary. Finally, I found a law firm with two lawyers, Arthur Lee Moore and Cal Estill, who officed in the W.T. Waggoner Building. They did not have an extra office, but said that any work I might do, or any clients I might have, could be handled in their law library instead of an office.

This firm had a great deal of criminal work, along with a heavy civil practice. A member of their firm, Jessie Martin, had been elected district attorney, which gave them an entree into the courthouse far beyond the average lawyer. There were a lot of small cases the older lawyers didn't want to fool with, such as traffic violations in the city courts.

They arranged for me to receive these calls. If employed by the client, I would collect a small fee of about five dollars to go down and plead the case and try to get the client off. If I didn't win the case in city court, I would give notice of appeal of the case to the county court in the old courthouse, some ten blocks from city hall.

If I earned a substantial fee, such as fifty dollars, I would divide the fee on a fifty-fifty basis with the firm to help defray expenses for such things as the stenographer, library upkeep and rent. At this office, they had a very fine secretary, Eva McClure, who had a license to practice law. At that time she could make more money as a secretary than she could in the practice of law. She later became one of the district judges in Tarrant County in Fort Worth. When I had problems too great for me to handle, she always helped me in any manner she could, and actually knew more law, except in procedural matters, than I did.

Outwitting the debtor

One day Cal Estill called me into his office and said he had a judgment for about four hundred dollars against a man who simply wouldn't pay. I decided I would let this law firm know just how capable I was. I first wrote the debtor a letter, telling him that if he did not pay we would get out execution to levy on some of his property to have it sold and use the proceeds to pay off the judgment. Of course, he did not reply to my letter.

I finally found a telephone number for this man and when I talked to him over the telephone he laughed at me. He asked me, why didn't I try to collect the debt because he had nothing subject to execution. As far as he was concerned, I could take all the papers and stick them "you know where," or where the sun doesn't shine.

I got out an execution, found his car parked on the street and had the deputy sheriff levy on it, regardless of whether or not it was exempt. He had to come into court and show that he was entitled to the exemptions that the state had granted. He hired a lawyer; we went into court and his lawyer proved his case immediately. I left the courtroom empty handed. In about thirty days I again levied on the car.

Instead of hiring a lawyer again, because I'm sure it was rather expensive, he came to my office with somewhat of a smile on his face. He said, "I believe you finally won after all. Here is your money. Now I don't want to be bothered any more."

I took the money into Cal Estill. He looked at it and said, "The reason I gave you that case was to test you. I didn't think you could collect it. I wanted to give you a little experience. I want to compliment you."

I told Cal that I didn't feel badly about the method I used in collecting the debt because the man owed the debt. I thought paying an honest debt would justify almost any means of effecting collection.

Secrets in the cloakroom

This law firm had a client, a bookie, who operated an illegal gambling establishment. He was Jewish, rather short, stout and wore bright-colored clothes. He had a sport hat with a feather on it, and an overcoat that must have cost him a lot of money. It could have been a vicuna overcoat.

About once a week, or once each month, the city police raided this man's establishment and placed him in jail for violating the gambling laws. Mr. Moore asked me if I would represent the man in city court, and, if he was convicted, to immediately give notice of appeal to the county court. The county court docket was so crowded that it would take more than one year for cases to reach an appeal.

After I had represented this man on two or three different occasions, to make his bond, the police began to hide him out and not tell me they had him in custody. They never had enough evidence to convict him, but they knew what he was doing.

I outsmarted them. I'd go to the cloakroom where all the inmates had hung their hats and coats. His coat and hat were readily recognizable. I would try to make his bond by confronting the city judge, saying I knew he was in jail. On one occasion, I hurriedly went to the courthouse to Judge Coley's court, and he issued a writ of habeas corpus to have the man brought before him, Judge Coley. In about twenty minutes from the time I arrived at Judge Coley's chambers, in came about four or five policemen with my client, who was smiling and knew exactly what I had done.

The policemen got into an argument among themselves calling each other vile names, saying this was an impossible situation; they knew that no one could have possibly known they had this man in custody. Judge Coley got a big kick out of this. He smiled. He told me from that time on I didn't have to hurry to the court; I could call him on the telephone and he would call the city police to have the prisoner brought before him.

This particular client liked me very much. He put me on retainer, with a fee of about five dollars a week. I thought this was so much money that I could hardly stand it. As I handled each case, he gave me another five dollars. This I could keep myself.

Where is your license?

After I had been with the firm for a short time, Cal Estill asked me to accompany him to the courthouse so that I might represent some defendants cited by publication in a civil case he was handling. As we walked, Cal Estill turned and asked me if I had received my license to practice law. I told him that I had not, but knew that I had passed the bar examination, and the license would be mailed at a later date. Cal Estill said that he didn't think I should appear in court in this manner without actually having my license to practice law.

I was so anxious to get started that I might have stretched a point in doing something short of actually violating the law. During the month of December, I received through the mail my license to practice law. That day in 1933, I did not go to the office. I unrolled the document, placed it in my view, looked at it and cried for hours.

It is hard for me to know why I cried, whether I cried because it had been such an ordeal to obtain the license in the first place, or because of pride, or whether I'm by nature a sentimental person. I no longer had any doubts that I would become a lawyer and fulfill my dream.

My only regret seemed to be that my mother had passed on during this time and could not enjoy this with me. Prior to her death she would tell her friends and neighbors that she knew that Fred would amount to something, because he was determined to get an education. I've always believed my mother became a saint at her death. I certainly know she was an angel who looked after me throughout my lifetime when I encountered ups and downs, and she always made things right. My life, in years to come, would take me on many journeys, and I always knew my mother continued to be there to make things right.

For now, I stayed on with the law firm a few more months, then all of us decided that the Depression was on and it would be almost impossible for me to establish a law practice on my own unless I was willing to wait several years. Why didn't I go back to Carthage, where I was well-known, and run for county attorney, Cal Estill asked. Maybe one day I could return and he would make me a junior partner in his law firm after I had had more experience.

Mrs. Steve Botts, a good friend, told me that after she had finished college, she had been unable to get a decent job. Finally, she and her sister had opened a hat shop in San Antonio, and their business had succeeded.

Then she told me maybe my situation was somewhat parallel to hers, and why didn't I just simply go to Carthage, open an office, and start practicing law.

Following their advice, and against my wishes, I returned to Carthage.

Chapter Five

The Underdog's Lawyer

Gene Moore of Carthage owned a drug store with offices above the store, and some of the rooms were vacant at the time. Gene advised me that he would give me free office rent until my practice would justify payment of the overhead.

I had no furniture, but had learned of a secondhand shop in Shreveport, forty miles east of Carthage, that sold secondhand furniture. I made a trip to Shreveport and found exactly what I needed: an oak desk with a chair that had arm rests, and three chairs for any clients I might have. I located a very small typewriter desk, a reworked Underwood typewriter, all for the total cost of twenty-four dollars.

I had taken with me about thirty dollars to pay for this furniture and equipment, and felt elated that I returned to Carthage with the furniture and an extra ten dollars that I'd saved to get started in my career in 1934.

I did have certain assets going for me. I had the appearance of a lawyer. People told me I was a handsome man. I dressed properly. I demanded a lot of respect because of my appearance. A man, Carey Coats, a mail carrier, said that when he saw me in Carthage, he felt so sorry for me because he knew there wasn't any way for a young lawyer to establish a practice. Experienced lawyers, such as Judge Woolworth, a well-known and well-regarded man throughout the state, had a tremendous law practice. He served as general counsel for Magnolia Oil Company. The firm of Long and Strong specialized in land title work and owned an abstract office in connection with their law firm. B. Baker was a capable lawyer, in addition to a lot of other good lawyers. Mr. Coats said he kept on watching me to see if I had a clean shirt on every morning that I came to work. He said he knew if I wore one shirt day after day without changing I was beaten. He said he knew, when he noticed I wore a clean shirt every day, I would somehow become a success.

Free legal advice

Carthage had a population of about twenty-three hundred people at the time. The older people with money wouldn't touch me, or consider hiring me as their lawyer and said, "why, that's just ole Fred Whitaker from Mitchell Community." I resented it. In time, this changed, but I had no way of knowing that would happen.

Instead of waiting in my office hour after hour for someone to come by, I simply walked around the Square, visiting with people from time to time, going to the courthouse in the center of the Square. I'd tell people that if they wanted a deed prepared, or a mortgage drawn, that I would be glad to do so without charge. People, believe it or not, took me up on this. I did my own typing and gradually, very slowly, people began to drop by. Sometime later I would charge as much as two dollars for writing a deed, or a similar type instrument.

A lawyer by the name of Sam Holt had cornered practically all of the divorce business in this county. Even though other lawyers would charge twenty-five dollars for getting a non-contested divorce, Mr. Holt, in order to get a greater portion of the work, reduced his fee to fifteen dollars.

I thought it might help me in getting new clients if I told people that if they ever wanted a divorce, I would get it for free, provided they pay the court costs. For the next three or four years, people took me up on this, and I got as many as thirty or forty divorces without accepting any remunerations. For about two or three years many people came calling in my office to obtain free legal advice. On occasion they would employ me to do work that they might have. I worked on each case as if it involved a million dollars. The unexpected results of my work for Herbert Keeling, for example, not only surprised and delighted him, he made himself a valuable asset to my law practice for years to come.

The superintendent who refused to pay

The day Herbert Keeling came into my office with some papers, he had a judgment against a school teacher for three hundred dollars with interest. The law firm of Long and Strong had charged Mr. Keeling twenty-five dollars a few years before to collect the money but had never collected a dime. The school teacher had stayed in Mr. Keeling's home for a year but had never paid him for room and board. The school teacher had done well. He had gone on to Garrison in Nacogdoches County and had become superintendent of schools there.

"Do you mean," I questioned Mr. Keeling, "Long and Strong charged you twenty-five dollars for this? They didn't give you anything. You went into the hole. You had a debt you wanted to collect and they charged you twenty-five dollars to reduce it to a judgment. That's not worth much.

"Would you give me a third of this if I collected it for you?" I asked.

"I'd be happy to."

"If I don't collect it," I assured him, "it's not going to cost you anything. That's what Jim Strong should have charged you when he took the case."

First, I wrote the school superintendent a friendly letter and asked him if he would pay this debt, that I represented Herbert Keeling. I got no response, of course. Then one day I sat there and I got mad. I said, "Well the sonovabitch ignores me but I think I can at least get his attention."

So I tried to find his telephone number. Do you know, they didn't have a telephone in this school? Garrison did have an operator who was very kind to me and said she'd help me find the number to the grocery store across the street from the school. So I said, "Give me that number."

I got that number and I called. The man on the line said, "If it's very important, I will call Mr. so and so. But I don't want to bother him unless it's important."

"This is an emergency," I said, "I need to talk with him immediately."

"Hold the phone."

In just a few minutes I had the school superintendent on the telephone. I told him what I wanted and he hung up. So the next day I called the grocery store and I got friendly with the grocery man. He said he would call the school superintendent to the telephone, after I just talked him into it. I continued making these telephone calls. Sometimes the school superintendent would come to talk with me, because he didn't know who was calling. That went on for a while. Finally, one Saturday morning, a man walked into my office and I knew immediately who he was, though I'd never seen him before. He had a big smile on his face. He said he wanted to talk with me. He sat down and he laughed. He said, "Mr. Whitaker, you've finally won. I'm going to pay you."

He counted out all that money. I'd never seen so much money in my life. I got on the telephone to tell Mr. Keeling to come by and pick up his proceeds, less my percentage.

Mr. Keeling said, "What we've needed in this town is a lawyer like you. I'm going to tell everybody in the community. Everybody who comes into my store I'm going to tell them that if they need a lawyer, hire Fred Whitaker."

I got many cases as a result of this case.

Electioneering for county attorney

Mr. Keeling lived in the Dotson community where he ran a country store and sold products to the farmers on credit. In the fall when the farmers gathered their crops, they'd pay Mr. Keeling back. As a result of this case, Mr. Keeling and I formed a very close friendship that influenced the outcome of many cases I tried.

About this time, I announced for county attorney. I met with a large number of people throughout the county on what we called "all day gatherings," and any other place that I could find to do my electioneering. Ida Ray, my former teacher at Mitchell School, volunteered to electioneer for me. I asked people to give me a chance to get started in the practice of law.

I called on people all over the county. One day I called on a family who invited me into their living room to talk with them about voting. As we sat talking, a chicken bounced into the room. The chicken's sudden appearance startled me so that I looked down and saw it had jumped up into the room from a hole in the floor. The family invited me to eat with them, which represented the greatest compliment, because I knew they would vote for me if they invited me to eat with them.

I won that election by thirteen votes and held the office for two years. I moved my offices into the courthouse where I not only took care of the state and county work, but I maintained a civil law practice on the side.

The case of the coon dogs

Right after I won the election for county attorney, a controversy arose in the Woods Post Office community, located about fifteen miles south of Carthage. Someone had killed Mr. Parker's coon dogs. These hunting dogs, colored tan and with long ears, had the ability to follow the tracks of raccoons, and sometimes humans, their sense of smell was so great.

Mr. Parker thought a lot of his dogs, but they became a nuisance to his neighbor, Mr. Kyle. One day the neighbor got his shotgun and killed the dogs. Mr. Parker filed a complaint against Mr. Kyle in the justice of the peace court in Woods Post Office. The law provided a hundred dollar fine for killing a dog, coupled with a jail sentence of thirty days. If convicted, one could receive not only the fine, but also be placed in jail.

The case was called for trial. The justice of peace in that community wanted to remain impartial. As we started trial, Sid Turner, the lawyer representing the defendant, wanted to waive a jury and try the case before the justice of the peace so that he might decide whether the defendant was guilty. The justice of the peace said, "I won't try the case. I'll disqualify myself because they are all friends of mine and I don't want to be responsible for the outcome of this lawsuit. There is so much feeling here in the community."

I thought for a minute. I knew that the law did not provide that the state could ask for a jury. The state was not entitled to a jury. Only the defendant had the right to be tried by his peers. But the case should have been tried, so I simply said, without authority, that the state would request a jury.

We selected the jury, though we could have predicted the outcome, because the Parkers were prominent members of the community, but Kyle was not so prominent. For instance, in the summer time Mr. Kyle went barefooted, wore overalls, and never dressed even for Sunday in Sunday-go-to-meeting-clothes.

We held the trial under a large oak tree. Trials were usually held in these communities in some building, such as in the back of the country store. But so many people came this time there wasn't a house in Woods Post Office large enough to hold the spectators interested in the prosecution of this case. That's why we moved out under a big oak tree that covered about five thousand square feet.

Attending court became not only a way of taking care of the business matter at hand, but court attendance served as a social gathering. People liked to come, visit, see other people. Far more than half of the people in attendance had walked to the trial. Others rode horses. At that time, in 1935, there probably weren't more than twenty automobiles —Model-T and Model-A Fords—in the county.

By placing seats provided for the members of the jury, judge and two lawyers involved in the case, we were able to stay in the shade of this tree. But, the spectators had no chairs for seating and several hundred people had come.

I looked out over the sea of people as the state gave testimony; the defendant did not introduce any evidence. The jury, in trying the case, found the defendant guilty and assessed the maximum punishment.

The defendant's lawyer, Mr. Turner, knew what his strategy was going to be all this time. He gave notice of appeal and asked that the case be transferred to the county court in Carthage. The case would be tried again regardless of what might have been done in the lower court, a trial de Nova. Judge Russell Nelson, a very close friend of Sid Turner, presided as county judge in Carthage. Every time we prepared the case for trial, Judge Nelson had to be in Austin on business for the county, or he had some other excuse to be absent.

The case stayed on the docket for about two or three years until finally we gave up on the idea of ever getting the case tried. When you have a county judge so dishonest that he will not allow you to try a case in his court, the case is finally dismissed. The effect of the case might have had some benefit in deterring crime. At least Mr. Kyle never killed any more dogs owned by Mr. Parker or anyone else. Sid Turner and I had only begun to compete in court. Neither of us could have foreseen the bittersweet end of our relationship. For the time, the community finally settled down without further controversy.

Defeat and return to Fort Worth

I served only two years as county attorney. When I ran a second time, an older lawyer, Ross Duran, beat me by only some twenty-seven votes. I thought the world had come to an end when I faced defeat. As it turned out, the defeat became the best thing that ever happened to me. I decided that politics wasn't going to be my way of life.

I went back to Fort Worth and stayed a few months. I got a position in the office of Raymond Buck, hoping to make a place for myself. However, if I won a case, Raymond Buck forgot to compliment me, and just gave me something else to work on. I felt that I was being exploited by him. When we won a lawsuit, he got credit for it. At that time, I was doing a lot of work for American Airlines. Aviation law was in its infancy so we didn't have any precedents to follow. We made our own law as we represented the airline and got court holdings in favor of the rules the airlines had promulgated for themselves.

Then a most unusual case came my way from a law firm in New York that had sent their file to our firm.

The case of the Titanic

In reviewing the file, I discovered that an insurance company had held a certain amount of money in escrow for many years. The money being held belonged to the surviving wife of a man who had died in the sinking of the Titanic. Yet, the wife refused to take the money. At one time, the New York law firm had located her in another state, but now she lived in Fort Worth and the firm instructed us to contact her again to determine if she would take the money. If not, we would file an interpleader, a suit asking the court to make disposition of the proceeds if she refused to accept the money.

Victor McCrea, a lawyer in our firm, had made contact with this woman, and he told me that she would not even talk with him about it. She had slammed the door in his face when he had gone to her place of residence in South Fort Worth.

When the insurance company had first deposited the money, or placed it in escrow for the beneficiaries — the people who had lost their lives in this tragedy — it was not a large sum. Over a period of years, with interest compounded, the money had grown so that it looked like a small fortune.

After I read the file, I immediately went out to this woman's place and talked my way into being admitted to her living room. We first had a nice conversation.

After creating somewhat of an acquaintance, I told her the purpose for which I had to see her.

When I mentioned this, she did not act as friendly and seemed to go off into some kind of a trance. Finally, she told me that she had lost her husband many, many years ago, and when he died, her life had more or less ended. She had few acquaintances, and would not under any circumstances date another man because, in her way of thinking, she would never think of marrying again. I could determine that she might be able to use this money because she lived in a very modest type of residence. But, I could in no way convince her that she should take this money. She just wanted to be left alone to try and forget that she had lost the one man she loved dearly.

As a last resort, I advised her that we would have no alternative other than to file suit and have her served with a citation to appear in court to either make claim of this money, or advise the court that she would not accept it.

Then it occurred to me that she wouldn't like any publicity at all. If I filed a suit, no doubt the newspapers would pick this up and make an interesting story for the public to read. The newspapers would take pictures of her.

This not only got her attention, she appeared to be frightened about anything that might take place in this manner. She then agreed to come to my office the following day where I would have her sign the papers. She had received a check for what appeared at that time to be a large amount of money.

On the following day, as I came to my office, she was sitting in the reception room, and had asked the receptionist if she could talk with me. I admitted her into my office where she said that she was glad now that everything had been settled. She looked rather relieved, and said that she wanted me to have at least half of the money that she had received.

I looked at her and advised that any charges my firm might make would be paid by or through the law firm in New York. But that didn't seem to satisfy her, so she remained and talked with me further about what she might do with the money.

Money could never replace the genuine pleasure I received from assisting this woman make her adjustment. Nor did the lack of money that year in Fort Worth detract from what turned into the most wonderful year I could have spent, building my confidence and experience. Some of my newly found confidence came from meeting my old adversary, Bill McLane, Jr., in court as opposing lawyer on one of my cases.

The inferiority I had felt when Bill McLane, Jr. had berated me as a newspaper carrier disappeared the day I met him in court. Mr. McLane represented a plaintiff in an insurance claim. We represented the defendant. In preparing our case for trial we filed a counterclaim, or cross action, over and against the client he represented.

Not only did Mr. McLane not prevail in making a recovery as he had expected to do when he filed suit in the first place, we actually won on the counterclaim and obtained a judgment over and against his client for the damages we had also sustained in the automobile accident. I enjoyed the victory even more since it had been such a short time — three years that he had ordered me to come to his office to collect for the newspaper that I delivered to his home.

This time I returned to Carthage full of confidence.

Chapter Six

A Case of the Doctors

I've always felt close to doctors. I believe they are, in most instances, true and dedicated professional men and women who try to do their best in treating people who suffer from diseases, injuries and ailments for which there is no known cure. In 1934, medicine existed in a primitive state in Carthage.

Carthage had no hospital. The closest, Tri-State Hospital, was located in Shreveport, forty miles east. There, Dr. Knighton operated on any woman who had difficulty with her reproductive organs or with menopause. He referred to these operations as exploratory. He paid some of the local physicians in Carthage a kickback, or a referral fee, for every woman they sent him, and he operated on, whether or not the woman needed surgery. This era introduced the practice of doctors who performed hysterectomies that served no purpose. The surgery did serve as a means of birth control.

At this time, doctors, rather than take payment for their services, took a portion of the patients' mineral rights under their homesteads. Years later I managed to get some of the rights returned by showing in court that patients had not intended to convey the mineral rights, but intended to use their mineral rights as a mortgage to guarantee payment of the doctors' bills.

Dr. Smith's troubles with narcotics

Shortly after I returned to Carthage from Fort Worth, Dr. Arthur Smith came to Carthage from the state of Arkansas. He rented a ten-room house, and opened what he called the Smith Clinic. He actually provided rooms in which some of his patients would stay overnight, or stay longer than one night, recuperating from surgery that he performed from time to time.

Dr. Smith was the most likable individual anyone could ever know. He was accommodating; he took personal interest in his cases; talked with his patients, gave them encouragement. He was far above the average doctor in knowledge and the manner in which he treated his patients.

Coincidentally, I rented an adjoining room to Dr. Smith's in Mrs. Alston's Boarding House when I returned to Carthage from Fort Worth.

Dr. Smith had one weakness: narcotics, but not for his own use. Certainly he did not use good judgment when he dispensed narcotics during this time before the use of narcotics was well-known and such a problem in this country. Federal narcotics agents bought narcotics directly from Dr. Smith. After several transactions had occurred, Federal agents arrested Dr. Smith, and placed him under bond. His case was to be tried in the Federal court of the Eastern District of Texas in Tyler, Texas.

By this time, Dr. Smith and I no longer roomed at the same boarding house, but he employed me to represent and defend him in the trial to be held in Tyler. The government made out a wonderful case. The only thing I had was a hell of a lot of character witnesses. They lined up from Carthage, people from the country whom Dr. Smith had cured of ailments which had bothered them and from which they had suffered for years.

The judge heard these people's testimony for hours and hours. I developed the truth through testimony in the trial of the case. We showed that Dr. Smith got up all hours, made trips to the edge of the county, sometimes on dirt roads when ice and sleet covered the ground. He was always there to help.

Believe it or not, we had an outright acquittal before a jury. The United States District Judge was so impressed that he complimented the jury on its decision.

I believe that in every criminal case there is always some type of defense that can help the jury in returning an honest verdict. Many times mitigating circumstances allow people charged with a crime to go free.

The doctor who killed his patient

One day the telephone rang in my law office in Carthage, and my secretary said that a Mr. H.H. Wilburn, an attorney in Henderson, Texas, was on the line. He wanted to talk with me about something very important. Mr. Wilburn related to me that a Mr. Howeth, a resident south of Henderson in Rusk County, had tried to employ him and bring suit against a doctor. Mr. Wilburn was not in a position to take the case, but he thought that I might be interested in doing so.

I told him then that I did not like taking cases against doctors because I had a lot of admiration for them, generally. He said this might be one case in which the aspects were somewhat different.

I saw Mr. Howeth the next day in my office, and he related to me his story in this manner. His wife had died a little after childbirth, and a Dr. Ross had been their doctor, with the delivery having been at their home on a farm located a few miles south and east of Henderson.

Up until this time, a woman had a lot of trouble and difficulty giving birth to a baby with either a large buttocks or a large head. A woman who gave birth to this kind of baby needed to be in the hospital so the vagina could be cut and enlarged to give more room for the baby to come forth.

Dr. Ross had failed to perform this sort of procedure on Mrs. Howeth and allowed her to have her baby without assistance. Her baby's birth caused her vagina to tear. This kind of tearing is the worse type that can occur. The birth tore her vagina to the rectum, and caused her to lose control of and empty her bladder and bowels.

With all the care that this woman received from her family and neighbors, still she should never have been left in this condition, because it caused an infection. For some two days and two nights, Mr. Howeth tried to locate Dr. Ross, but he was no place to be found.

Mr. Howeth finally persuaded a Dr. Carnathan of Henderson, who had formerly practiced medicine in Carthage, to go to Mr. Howeth's home. Dr. Carnathan immediately ordered Mrs. Howeth admitted to the hospital, but it was too late, and she died within a short time after being admitted.

Mr. Howeth later learned that Dr. Ross's brother had had an illness in Galveston, Texas and Dr. Ross had left town. He had gone to Galveston without so much as a call, or request that some other doctor take care of his patient while he sojourned.

After Mr. Howeth related these facts to me, I had no choice other than to accept employment. I took the case on a percentage basis since he had no money to pay me a fee. We would allow my fee to be collected out of a portion of the recovery, if any, he might obtain when the case came for trial.

After Mr. Howeth left my office, I began an intensive investigation as to the facts in the case and, especially, I read law cases involving negligence and responsibilities of doctors treating their patients. I schooled myself in medical terms by talking with doctors and one registered nurse in particular.

The nurse, Cynthia Young, told me, "Mr. Whitaker, I have known of lots of cases in which Dr. Ross did not perform his duties as a doctor; he allowed women in childbirth to die."

Cynthia Young spent hours helping me with this case. My petition, setting forth the cause of action, read as follows:

THE STATE OF TEXAS
IN THE SPECIAL DISTRICT COURT
COUNTY OF RUSK
OF RUSK COUNTY, TEXAS.
TO THE HONORABLE JUDGE OF SAID COURT:
Comes now S. H. Howeth and Gay Howeth, a minor who brings this suit by and through her next friend, C. S. Wood, hereinafter styled plaintiffs, complaining of Dr. Jesse E. Ross, hereinafter styled defendant and for cause of action plaintiffs would with respect represent to the court the following:
1.
That the said S. H. Howeth, Gay Howeth, and C. S. Wood are each residents of Rusk County, Texas; the defendant, Dr. Jesse E. Ross, is a resident of Henderson, Rusk County, Texas.
2.
That the said Dr. Jesse E. Ross was at all times herein mentioned a duly qualified and licensed practitioner of medicine and was a graduate of an accredited school of medicine and was authorized under the laws of the state of Texas to practice medicine; that on July 15, 1941 and for several years prior thereto the defendant held himself out as a qualified physician who practiced his

profession for hire in Henderson, Rusk County, Texas and nearby places.

3.

On or about May 20, 1941 the plaintiff, S. H. Howeth and wife, Letha Howeth, now deceased, employed the defendant herein to take charge of the maternity case of the said Letha Howeth, deceased, who was at such time in a state of pregnancy; that such contract was entered into in consideration of the sum of $25.00 to be paid the defendant for medical services, and in compliance with such agreement the plaintiff, S. H. Howeth, has paid and performed all duties and obligations required of him from such agreement.

4.

The defendant became obligated and promised in consideration of the above to make such delivery and to attend the patient during confinement including prenatal care consisting of various calls to the doctor's office that might be necessary for the care of the patient; and in addition thereto the defendant agreed to make at least two follow-up calls after the baby was delivered together with office calls after delivery for a period of two months; it was further agreed and understood that the defendant would treat and care for the patient and would closely observe her for any unusual symptoms or complications existing or developing immediately after the baby was born.

5.

On November 25, 1941 such Letha Howeth, deceased, was stricken with illness occasioned by childbirth, and, at the instance of her husband the defendant called upon and understood the treatment of the patient; and a child, Gay Howeth, was born on such date; that defendant failed to exercise ordinary care, diligence, and skill, negligently causing Letha Howeth, to become deceased on December 6, 1941 as hereafter shown.

6.

The defendant carelessly and negligently failed to perform his duties and was guilty of the following acts and omissions, bringing about her death in the following particulars:

a. The defendant failed to have and use such care, skill and diligence, as a physician, in the treatment of such deceased, as is ordinarily had and used by the member of the medical profession in good standing in the same or similar localities or under the same or similar circumstances.

b. The defendant negligently at the time failed to observe constantly so as to determine whether or not it would become necessary to do an episiotomy, thereby permitting a third-degree laceration which was torn from the vagina to the rectum.

c. The defendant was negligent in failing to examine and locate such laceration after the child was born.

d. The doctor negligently failed and refused to suture the laceration, well knowing that such omission might and likely would cause bacterial cocci or germs to be carried into the blood stream therefore causing blood poisoning.

e. The defendant negligently refused to make any follow-up visits after the child was born, well knowing that the patient was in a precarious condition needing medical care in order to survive.

f. The doctor negligently and willfully refused to keep a constant vigilance in order for him to determine if such wound or laceration had become infected whereby an immediately treatment could be administered to save this woman's life.

g. The defendant was further negligent in failing to respond to a request and plea by her husband that he return to the patient and administer treatment to her two days after the child was born, and at a time when he was informed that she was in a critical condition and would die if something was not done for her.

h. The defendant negligently and willfully abandoned the treatment of the case by leaving town within five days after the child was born, leaving town without informing the deceased or her husband as to his leaving or as to his whereabouts.

i. The defendant negligently and without warning abandoned the treatment of this patient within five days after the child was born without the knowledge or consent of the plaintiff, S.H. Howeth, or the deceased, and failed to provide or arrange for a substitute physician to treat the patient during his absence.

j. The defendant negligently and carelessly abandoned such case within five days after the child was born without proper instructions being first given as to postdelivery care.

k. The defendant was guilty of recklessness and indifference and wholly failed to exercise the degree of care, diligence and skill that he was capable in attending and treating the deceased, permitting her to die for lack of attention.

1. The defendant negligently permitted a portion of the placenta or afterbirth to be left in the uterus at such time.

7.

Plaintiffs would further show that at the time the delivery was made the doctor while acting in a careless and disinterested manner and made his departure from the bedside of this patient before he had fully removed the afterbirth permitting this woman to pass portions of same during the succeeding days and while in excruciating pain; the defendant in his haste to leave this patient failed to examine the nature and extent of the laceration in order that same might be sutured and closed preventing germs to reach her blood stream when he well knew that if same occurred the patient would likely die of streptococcus infection.

8.

The plaintiff, S. H. Howeth, avers that on the 27th day of November, 1941, he contacted such Dr. Jesse E. Ross and related to him unusual symptoms that his wife had developed and informed the doctor that she was dangerously ill and was passing dark blood clots as large as a man's fist; but the defendant with a heart regardless of social duty refused to call on this woman who was in a dying condition and informed such plaintiff that if he would listen to the doctor and ignore the advise from other people the patient would be all right; and in compliance with these instructions such S. H. Howeth returned to his wife, but when he finally concluded that she could not live without medical treatment, he returned to the office and home of Dr. Jesse E. Ross with the view of persuading him to administer and treat his wife who was in dire need of a doctor who would assume the responsibility of trust and care of such patient; the plaintiff, S. H. Howeth, at such time learned to his consternation that the doctor had departed from the city of Henderson, Texas without so much as arranging for a substitute or giving instructions as to the manner in which this woman would be attended; the plaintiff, in desperation, and without funds finally procured the aid of Dr. W. G. Carnathan, who immediately called on the patient and diagnosed her case as being critical.

9.

The patient, under Dr. Carnathan's instructions, was immediately placed in a sanitarium in Henderson, Texas, and with the belated care and medical aid administrated, she failed to respond and died on December 6, 1941 as a direct result of the said willful and malicious negligence on the defendant.

10.

Plaintiffs would further represent that the injuries and conditions above described were the proximate results of the negligent acts and omissions on the part of the defendant which caused the death of such Letha Howeth.

11.

That prior to the confinement of the deceased, Letha Howeth was a healthy young woman aged 24 years, and was capable of performing and did perform all of her household duties as a housewife; that as a direct result of the defendant's negligent acts and omissions the plaintiff, S. H. Howeth, has lost and has been denied the companionship and assistance of his wife to his serious damages in the sum of $15,000.00; that her services to him as a housewife and in the management of his home were reasonably worth $75.00 per month.

12.

The plaintiff, Gay Howeth, due to such negligence on the part of the defendant has been denied the love, care and attendance of her mother, Letha Howeth, deceased, and if she had been permitted to live she would have contributed greatly to her care, support, and education to such minor's damages in the sum of $7,500.00.

13

That the defendant in attending the deceased and in treating her after childbirth was guilty of gross and inexcusable negligence as above set out in such a manner as to cause her to die of insepticema or blood poisoning, and as a contributing cause she suffered with a uterine hemorrhage which would have been prevented had the doctor used ordinary skill and care; that the defendant knew or should have known of the various treatments, which, had they been given in time, would have successfully corrected this condition.

14.

That due to the negligence of the defendant, the plaintiff, S. H. Howeth, was required to expand an additional sum of $120.00 for medicine, doctor bills, and hospitalization, the same being the usual, customary, and reasonable prices charged for such medical treatment; that because of such unlawful death caused by the defendant, the plaintiff, S. H. Howeth, was required to expend and did spend the sum of $290.50 for burial expenses, the same being the reasonable, customary, and usual prices charged for same, and will necessarily be required to expend $125.00 for the erection of a tombstone over her grave.

15.

Plaintiffs allege that they are entitled to the sum of $10,000.00 exemplary damages due to the willful, wanton, and gross negligence on the part of the defendant in treating the deceased both at the time of childbirth and on post-delivery treatment; plaintiffs bring this suit for exemplary damages as well as for actual damages because of the criminal indifference of defendant directly causing the death of the said Letha Howeth, and that such damages are due them for the reason that her death was brought about by the heartless actions and omissions as hereinabove set out.

WHEREFORE plaintiffs pray that defendant be cited to appear and answer herein and that on final hearing the plaintiff, S. H. Howeth recover of defendant the sum of $15,317.00 actual damages; and that the plaintiff, Gay Howeth, by and through her next friend, C. S. Wood, recover of the defendant the sum of $7,500.00 as actual damages; and that plaintiffs recover jointly of and from the defendant the sum of $10,000.00 exemplary damages together with interest, cost of suit, and for such other further relief, special and general, in law or in equity, that they may show themselves justly entitled.

Attorney for Plaintiffs

Mr. Wilburn kept me advised about what was taking place in Henderson. It appeared that Dr. Ross had lots of friends in Henderson. One friend included the judge who sat on the bench, Judge Paul Brown. The doctors in Henderson held a meeting and decided they'd make some effort to have Fred Whitaker disbarred from practicing law, since he had the nerve to take a claim against such a prominent doctor as Dr. Ross was supposed to have been.

The doctors in Henderson, when they held their gathering, invited some of the lawyers to meet with them. But they made a mistake when they invited H.H. Wilburn, who put them straight. He told them that such an effort would be in vain since it was a discretionary matter for any lawyer to take a case in which the facts were in dispute as to whether this doctor was guilty of negligence, causing the death of this woman. Mrs. Howeth was very young at the time she died.

I talked with Dr. Carnathan. Rather, I tried to talk to Dr. Carnathan. He wouldn't even talk with me, saying that he would not be a witness for me, and that I would have to develop my facts in some other manner. He simply would not testify against another doctor.

I had a friend, a doctor in Henderson, who agreed to talk with me, provided I would not use his name. We devised a way to try this case, subpoenaing all the doctors in Henderson to appear in court. I planned to ask them questions, most of which would be hypothetical questions, because the actual facts would be very difficult to prove.

Then we devised a means to subpoena at least ten doctors. My doctor friend said they would answer the questions correctly, if they were under oath, whether they wanted to or not. We finally decided to place on the witness stand only certain doctors whom we knew would answer our questions correctly regardless of where their sympathies might lie.

It is not wise to use a reluctant witness, but this was the only way in which I could get my doctors to testify in the trial of this case. One of the proofs that I was required to show was whether this doctor, Dr. Ross, exercised the care that other doctors would have exercised in this locality and under like circumstances.

We asked for a setting of this case, but before we could bring it to trial, Dr. Ross volunteered and joined the Navy. This delayed us for about two or three years. I will never know whether Dr. Ross joined the Navy to avoid trial of this case or whether he was patriotic to that extent.

When Dr. Ross returned from the Navy, we soon as possible requested the case be set for trial immediately. The situation in the community had not changed. The defendant, with meager grounds, asked for a continuance. The judge immediately continued the case.

I believe Judge Paul Brown would have done anything, complied with any request made by the lawyers for the defense. It was quite obvious that the judge was prejudiced and biased in favor of the defendant.

In addition, a greater number of the lawyers at the Rusk County Bar were in sympathy with the defendant. At least half of the doctors who practiced medicine in that area were in favor of the defendant. Of course, they did not have to answer for the dastardly deed, or the lack of attention that Dr. Ross gave to his patient, allowing this woman to die.

We took the position that the doctor, by his acts or his omissions, was as guilty of murder as if he had he taken a gun and shot the deceased in cold blood without any excuse or justification. He had no excuse or reason for allowing this woman to die. He would never be able to show so much as mitigating circumstances.

We could have gone to the higher court and asked for a writ of mandamus against the trial judge, requiring that he proceed with the trial of this case. But the plaintiff had become discouraged after a wait of about four or five years, and wanted some kind of disposition of the case, whether or not it was in his favor.

We negotiated a settlement, which was far less than Mr. Howeth was entitled, because the settlement did not take into consideration the loss of his wife's companionship and the grief and worry that he had endured for a long, long time. Nor did the settlement take into consideration the loss to the surviving child who lost the love, care and companionship of her mother from infancy to adulthood.

Mr. Howeth explained to me that at nighttime he would either dream of his deceased wife, or simply stay awake, unable to sleep. This catastrophe remained on his mind throughout the long days and a greater portion of the nights.

I thoroughly believe that if we could have got to a jury we could have convinced the jury of the wrongful acts done by Dr. Ross. We could have prevailed and obtained the verdict that would have, in some manner, rectified the nightmare that had been placed on Mrs. Howeth and her loved ones.

The case did result in positive change: it appeared that every doctor in East Texas knew about this case. No doctor in East Texas ever again allowed a woman to undergo these horrible conditions, resulting in this kind of agonizing death. When the case ended, I first thought of the time Mama and I discussed my being a lawyer, whether I could do a lot of good for society. I believe I did in this case.

The doctor

Dr. Perlman was a very fine doctor. He had been a pharmacist before he obtained his license to practice medicine. He owned his own drugstore and wrote his own prescriptions and filled them. This was a very unconventional thing, as far as other drugstore owners and doctors were concerned, but Dr. Perlman did it.

A short time after Dr. Perlman moved to Carthage, he and I became very close friends. On different occasions, we spent some time together. One evening he came by the house and asked me if I'd like to drive out into the country to keep him company on a call to deliver a baby.

After we reached the log cabin, about three miles north of Carthage, we went into the cabin where kerosene lamps provided the only light. We found the woman in the bedroom in bed having labor contractions.

Dr. Perlman introduced me to the husband sitting in another room, then Dr. Perlman went into the bedroom where the woman was lying on the bed. He noted the length of time between the labor contractions and realized there would be a waiting period before the baby would come.

After I talked with the husband for a time, I took the kerosene lamp and looked into the bedroom to see if anything had happened. To my consternation, there lay Dr. Perlman in the bed, snoring, next to the woman. I did notice the woman's labor pains getting closer together. This continued for about two hours before the baby finally came.

My friend, Dr. Perlman, died in a tragic automobile accident several years later. He left a legacy of helping many patients to better health. His son, Jonathon, became a successful lawyer with the Dallas firm of Vincent and Elkins, after an outstanding career in baseball. Dr. Perlman's wife, Phoebe Sue, became a prominent civic leader in Carthage.

Chapter Seven

Judges and Their Influence

I t had never occurred to me that the judges elected to office by the people would not be fair and just to all litigants that came before the court seeking justice.

One of the first cases I handled involved a case I filed in the county court for my client's wages of less than one thousand dollars he had earned in the drilling of a shallow oil well located about one mile east of Carthage. The man had never been fully paid for the wages he had earned.

I filed the suit for the debt against the owner of the well, and citation was issued upon the defendant. Since no answer was filed, default judgment was taken for the amount of the debt after we made proof to the judge that the debt was owing, that the demand had been made, and that the defendant had failed and refused to meet his obligations.

I prepared a judgment and submitted it to the court for the judge's signature. After a number of days, execution was issued to the sheriff to collect the judgment. I pointed out that the equipment on the well would be subject to execution, and would be ample property to be advertised and sold, with money forthcoming to pay the plaintiff the money to which he was entitled.

Just prior to the date the property was to be sold under execution, the debtor's lawyer, B. Baker, filed a motion for a new trial.

Under the law, the filing of this motion came too late. Upon hearing of this motion, I pointed out to the judge that this motion could not and would not be considered by the court since it was filed late. The only remedy, if any, would be by nature of a bill of review. The lawyer, B. Baker, who was very capable, did not file a motion for bill of review since he had no facts or law to support the procedure.

The judge, and the lawyer representing the defendant, were good friends, actually had been close friends for many years prior to this time. The judge, when the hearing was completed, simply noted on his docket that a new trial would be granted, and asked Mr. Baker to prepare an order to be entered.

We may have had a remedy by simply perfecting an appeal to the Court of Civil Appeals in Texarkana, Texas. But the plaintiff had no funds even to the extent of paying the cost of court. In discussion, he advised me as his lawyer not to prosecute the case further.

This dwelled on my mind for many years. The case made me fully aware of the obstacles that a lawyer must necessarily face in attempting to get justice for his clients in a court of law.

I felt we had avenged ourselves to a certain extent when a story appeared in *The Panola Watchman* in Carthage about five years after that time. The story reported that Russell Nelson, the county judge who had tried this case, had been convicted of embezzlement of public funds while working for a youth program, supported by federal funds, in Beaumont, Texas. Nelson had controlled the program's funds, which he made subject to his disbursement, and saw fit to divert money to his own benefit. After federal authorities charged him with embezzlement, a grand jury indicted him. He was tried in U.S. District Court where the jury assessed a term in the federal penitentiary.

The case of estate fraud

There are many temptations for lawyers actively practicing law to obtain money or other remunerations through unlawful or unethical means.

On one such occasion, in 1961, District Judge Fred Erisman, of Gregg County in Longview, came to my office in Carthage and said that he had a case he wanted to pass on to me.

"You can make a great deal of money," he assured me. "The Sellers estate is being administered by the executor in Gladewater, and the terms of the will provide certain distribution of the property, provided that the First National Bank in Dallas trust department be in charge of the estate. The man in the trust department is a friend of mine and you will work with him in getting the money out of this estate by simply filing a motion to set aside the will that has been offered for probate."

When I asked how, he said it had been predetermined that the trust department would participate and pay out one million dollars to settle the claim without the case ever having been tried or determined if there were merits to the challenge.

"In fact," Judge Erisman said, "there are no merits, but I wanted the contest to be filed. An elected official of Gladewater is involved and I want him to be paid well out of the million dollars."

The public official of Gladewater, Judge Erisman said, had the contact with the bank in Dallas, and it was a fixed deal. The lawyer would challenge the will in court for parties not named as beneficiaries in the will, and say it was not a valid will; Judge Erisman would approve the settlement, and the bank trust officer would deliver the money. The million dollars would be divided with one-third going to Fred Erisman, in whose court the contest would be held to approve the settlement. One-third would go to the official in Gladewater, and one-third would go to me, the lawyer who would represent the contestants of the will.

Looking back now, it seems strange to see how we could have split the money three ways without someone, who was contesting the will, being involved. I have no way of knowing, but maybe the official in Gladewater was the interested party.

We discussed the matter at length and after I told Judge Erisman I wouldn't be interested because it wasn't right, I asked, "How can this lawyer, like I myself would be, get this money but then give it to you and the man in Gladewater without the record showing that the lawyer received all the money?"

"You know," I cautioned him, "the collector of the Internal Revenue Service has a way of snooping around and uncovering these large transactions. The deal might come off appearing that the lawyer received more than he actually received. He might get into trouble with the IRS."

I refused to take the case. A short time after that, I saw Fred Erisman and he said, "I sure hate to see you pass up making a lot of money. I have finally gotten a former Land Commissioner for Texas. Few people know it, but he has a license to practice law. He took the case. He's going to make a lot of money."

"Fred," I said, "you just let him have the case. I don't want any part of it."

Several months later, I read a newspaper story that the former Land Commissioner was being tried in a federal court in Fort Worth for income tax evasion of funds received from the Sellers estate. I was not surprised.

The temptations I had in the practice of law, from time to time, did not bother me too much. If you have in your possession ill-gotten gains, you will usually pay for them. Judge Erisman remained as district judge in Gregg County for many years and it was well-known that he got involved in such cases in some instances. However, no one ever called him in to account for his actions. He eventually died of cancer.

Dangers in running off with the marbles

District Judge Spot Sanders probably gave me the best advice I've received from anyone pertaining to my profession. He caused me to realize that the practice of law sometimes contains hazards for the lawyer who actively engages in the practice of law.

The first three or four years I practiced law in Carthage, I did not do anything spectacular. I did do everything possible to establish myself as a lawyer without violating any of the rules of evidence such as advertising or soliciting cases.

When I reached about twenty-seven years old, I tried four or five jury cases, all civil cases, in the District Court in Panola County where Judge Spot Sanders presided as district judge. The lawyers opposing me on the other side of the cases were Long and Strong, well-establish lawyers in Carthage.

When I prevailed in each of these civil trials, it not only gave me confidence, but I could tell that people began circulating information in the community that I could successfully try cases, whether I represented the plaintiff or defendant. Most of the cases involved disputes between citizens of Carthage, such as property line disputes, but some cases involved insurance companies.

A short time after I won all these cases, Judge Spot Sanders called me from the courthouse and asked me if I would come by and discuss a private matter with him. Of course, I hurriedly went to his office.

Judge Sanders was a large man with a head so large he had a difficult time buying a hat. He wore glasses with thick lenses. He made up for his physical appearance by having a lot of common sense. He was a self-made lawyer who had gotten his license to practice law after studying and reading law, but without a formal education. He knew human nature. The greatest portion of my practice took place in his court, and he enjoyed watching me progress as a young lawyer.

As I sat on a chair in his office, he said, "Fred, it looks like you're going to run off with all the marbles. You're doing pretty well. You're winning these cases. These older lawyers are not going to take it. Don't be surprised if you have some trouble."

"I have one thing I want to be sure to tell you. You not only do the right thing in all the cases you handle, you lean over backwards and be damn sure you do the right thing. Don't even do anything that looks near to something that allows someone to take advantage of you."

"Why don't you do this? Take notes of all you see that goes on in the offices of Judge J. G. Strong. We all know he bends the law sometimes and he does things that a lot of people think are not exactly right. At least you'll have something on him if he ever comes at you."

Everyone called J. G. Strong Judge Strong because he, at one time, had been county judge, but now he had a private law practice. I went back to my office and set up an entire notebook on things I knew about Judge Strong. I kept a record and added to it from time-to-time.

I took Judge Sanders' advice to be very careful. I knew from that time on that as my practice grew and I became as well-known as other lawyers, a great jealousy would arise among the lawyers, just as it does in most small towns such as Carthage. Sometimes clients become disgruntled, whether or not it's justified, and these people may attempt to frame you, make up stories that cannot be proved.

On some occasions, Judge Sanders, during a recess, would point out some of the weaknesses in my case and the tactics he thought I should dwell upon. I remember one case in which I was suing a party who had been involved in the deaths of two small children who had been run down on the highway.

I represented their parents to obtain damages. There wasn't much we could do to show loss of money the children might have earned over a lifetime for the benefit of their parents. About the only thing we could do was show the love and affection the parents would have enjoyed throughout their children's lifetimes.

Judge Sanders said, "Why don't you just dwell on proving what alert, beautiful children these were? At least get the sympathy of the jury, whether or not you're able to prove other facts to the jury's satisfaction."

After Judge Sanders told me that, I went back into the courtroom and put emphasis on the beautiful children— of how they'd learned to sing and sometimes sang duets together to the amusement and enjoyment of their neighbors.

Even though one child had not gone to school, the other had started and was doing well. I dwelled on that so much that the sympathy from the jury resulted in a victory. We prevailed in the case primarily due to the strategy that Judge Sanders had suggested.

He helped me learn how to try a case. If I had a case that was weak in some ways and strong in others, I avoided the weak points as much as I could and stressed the strong, then left it at that. As I argued the case to the jury, if I couldn't explain away a point or a fact situation, sometimes I'd pass over it and dwell intensely on the part I thought worked to our benefit.

Chapter Eight

Death and Violence

Judge Spot Sanders' advice to study and make notes of every event that transpired in the courtroom helped me sharpen my skills at becoming a student of human nature. Not long after I began to make notes of courtroom events, a judge who didn't like me tried to cast doubt on my skills by assigning me as lead counsel in a case the judge knew would probably end with a death penalty.

In 1940, while stil lrather young, I tried one of my first murder cases. It was a murder so gruesome that it affected me so profoundly and I continue to think of it today. I believed my reputation as a lawyer hung on the outcome of this case.

Luther and Nellie Mae Hill lived in the servants' quarters, a small house, on the farming property of a well-established couple, George Furrh and his wife, in Panola County. Each morning, Luther Hill would see his wife stop at the barn on her way to George Furrh's home to cook the Furrh's breakfast. One morning Mr. Hill hid himself in the barn rafters and saw his wife making love with George Furrh.

Luther Hill watched this many times. He'd secret himself, sometimes getting up into the barn rafters, or the second floor of the barn. This finally drove Luther Hill crazy. He couldn't tolerate it anymore.

One day Mr. Hill got a large bottle of kerosene, saturated Nellie Mae's body with this fuel, and set her on fire. He burned ninety percent of her body with second and third degree burns. She lived exactly ninety-one days after that.

The white and black people in the community tried to treat Mrs. Hill the best they could. Her body hurt so badly that she couldn't wear clothes, so they built a tent over the top of her and tried to keep enough warmth in the room so that she would be comfortable. The dead cells continually rotted off her body. When people came in the front gate they could smell the obnoxious odor that her body gave off. The neighbors, both whit e and black, came to her rescue, brought food, and did the best they knew how.

This continued until she died. I remember the exact number of days she lived because the Hills had an insurance policy that provided insurance if Mrs. Hill died before ninety days. If she lived more than ninety days, then the insurance didn't pay anything.

The case went before the grand jury after Luther Hill burned his wife and on January 11, 1940 the grand jury indicted Mr. Hill for assault with intent to murder. When Nellie Mae Hill died, the grand jury indicted Mr. Hill for murder.

Judge T. 0. Davis and I had had some words previous to this case, and he didn't like me at that time. Judge Davis knew, within reason, that there would be a death penalty, because Mrs. Hill's death was the most horrifying murder that had happened in Panola County or in any of the adjoining counties. Judge Davis appointed me to represent the defendant, and we worked without pay. To make the legal representation appointment look like a natural thing, Judge Davis appointed a young lawyer who had just gotten his license to practice, and another young lawyer with only one year's experience to assist on the case. Of course, they couldn't do much except act as water boys for me.

I feared that my reputation was at stake. After I looked into the case, I felt like Mr. Hill should have to serve time in the penitentiary because nothing could justify what he had done. But there were mitigating circumstances, and George Furrh should have been tried with Luther Hill because George Furrh brought about the murder. At that time, many white people treated black people as if they were slaves and white men felt they could do anything they wanted with black women. White people treated black people like objects.

We tried the case and it went before the jury where all except one man voted for the death penalty. The court declared a mistrial. Mr. Hill stayed in jail all this time and I would take him magazines to read. We tried the case again in the next term of court in about three or four months. The second time we tried the case, the jury gave him the death penalty. The law wouldn't allow me to make his bond while his case was on appeal. I perfected an appeal and went to the Court of Criminal Appeals and there I argued the case.

I had one good sound reason for reversing this case. During the trial of the case, Wardlow Lane, the district attorney, kept pushing Nellie Mae Hill's clothes around on the table where he was sitting so the jury could see the clothes. I noticed an obnoxious odor coming from these clothes, and it kind of made me sick, but I didn't think to do anything about it. All of a sudden, Sam Holt, the county attorney assisting the district attorney trying the case, got up and stated to the judge, "Judge Davis, the odor from these clothes is making me sick. I can't stand it any longer."

I stressed District Attorney Lane's tactic to the Court of Criminal Appeals. In the law at that time, I found cases saying that if any evidence was introduced for prejudicial purposes that does not shed any light on the facts or issues of the case, it was cause for reversible error. The law considered displaying Mrs. Hill's clothes as extraneous matter. The Court of Criminal Appeals reversed the case and sent it back to Carthage for a new trial.

I'd worked on the case for months without pay. I was tired.

I should not have gotten tired. I should have worked as hard three years after we first tried the case as when I had originally defended Mr. Hill. For some reason, I decided I couldn't go to another jury and take a chance on getting the death penalty again. Maybe, I thought, I'd bring out the true facts. I decided I'd let Luther Hill testify how he'd seen his wife underneath George Furrh. At first Luther Hill didn't want to say that. He told me, "They'll kill me if I say that."

"You'll die anyway if you don't say it," I told him. When it became known that we were going to introduce this as evidence, a man, Sly Osborne, who had married George Furrh's daughter, came to me and said, "Fred, if you plan to bring that out on the witness stand, you better not do it. We're not going to allow it."

To me that represented a threat on my life and on the defendant's life. I thought about it for a long time, and then decided I'd let the defendant tell it all. In the next trial Luther Hill told all the details. He told how many times he'd seen George Furrh make love to his, Mr. Hill's, wife. I thought that would be enough to cause the jury to give him a life sentence. They gave Luther Hill the death penalty again.

I did have another option in trying this case; I could have pled temporary insanity. Luther Hill did, literally, become temporarily insane when he committed his act in the sudden heat of passion. I lay awake at night thinking about this type of defense, I finally thought, it won't work in defending a black man against an act instigated by a white man. It won't work.

I did take the case up on appeal but I didn't have any points of error to help me reverse the case. The Court of Criminal Appeals affirmed the lower court's death penalty.

I kept Mr. Hill alive three years which, in a way, was a victory, but it was not enough. I have always felt like I should have gone to the Governor of Texas and had a private talk to see if the Governor might have some compassion for Luther Hill. The Governor had the authority to commute Mr. Hill's sentence to ninety-nine years in the penitentiary. I didn't go to the Governor. I've always regretted I didn't.

This case caused such an uproar in our community for the black and white people that the case, instead of hurting my reputation, helped my reputation as a trial lawyer because I kept Mr. Hill alive for so long. *The Panola Watchman* reported on April 30, 1942, after the final Court of Criminal Appeals ruling: "Hill was ably represented by Fred Whitaker, attorney of this city, who was appointed by the court to defend him. Mr. Whitaker made a hard and sincere effort without money or price but the higher court finally says that the defendant must pay the price for his crime." I did learn good trial work and the effective elements for appeal working for Luther Hill.

Luther Hill died in the electric chair on July 5, 1942. In July, Panola County's district clerk received a bill for twenty-five dollars from the Texas Prison System Warden for the execution of Luther Hill. The warden had attached the following official death execution to Panola County's bill. This read:

THE STATE OF TEXAS
IN THE DISTRICT COURT
VS.
LUTHER HILLOF PANOLA COUNTY, TEXAS
<u>WARDEN'S RETURN AFTER EXECUTION</u>

RECEIVED: The Death Warrant, together with the body of the above named, LUTHER HILL, from the Sheriff of Panola County, Texas, May 4, 1942. Said Death Warrant ordering the execution of the above named, LUTHER HILL, on June 5, 1942. A.D.
FURTHER: In accordance with the judgment of the District Court of Panola County, the said LUTHER HILL, was duly executed on the 5th day of July, 1942 A.D., at the hour of 12:03 A.M. by Warden A.C. Turner; by causing to pass through his body a current of electricity with sufficient intensity to cause his death. The said LUTHER HILL, was pronounced dead by Dr. M.D. Hanson; Medical Supervisor of the Texas Prison System, eight minutes after application of the electric current.
FURTHER: The body of the said LUTHER HILL was buried in the Prison Cemetery in Huntsville with full Christian rites and the grave is suitably marked.
Signed: A.C. Turner, Warden

During the next election, I helped the people defeat T. 0. Davis for judge. It still seems a crime to me that two people died horrible deaths all caused by George Furrh. He has never been held accountable in this life, but surely he will be held accountable in the after-life.

The case of the woman no one could resist

During the uproar of the Hill case in 1941, another murder case came to me. A husband and wife arrived at my office in Carthage to discuss with me their daughter who was in trouble. She had gotten in trouble in Borger, Texas, an oil town a few miles north of Amarillo in the Texas panhandle.

The young woman had been charged with murder. The facts had shown that she had left Carthage several months prior to that time, about one year before, with a man with whom she was living without the benefit of clergy. It was rather unusual at that time for people to live together as husband and wife without being married. As most of us know, it is quite common today. It happens in the best of families and not just among poor people, as it happened in 1941.

The facts, as they developed, showed that there were no eye witnesses to the crime, but that the daughter had signed a voluntary confession, admitting that she had killed her common law husband. This would be sufficient to make out a case for the state.

At that time, I had tried several murder cases, both for the prosecution and the defense, and I was still anxious to build a reputation as a trial lawyer. After discussing the facts in the case, I felt that I would be able to help the parents, and maybe get an outright acquittal for the daughter. I could at least keep the sentence down to a short term in the penitentiary.

We agreed upon the fee that would be paid; the case had already been set for trial and we had only a short time in which to prepare for this trial. We had quite a bit of traveling to do, too, because about five hundred miles separated Carthage from Stinnett, Texas, the county seat of the county in which this case was to be tried. It behooved us now to try to find witnesses, but the only thing we were able to do was to arrange for character witnesses to travel from Carthage. My client was able to pay the expenses of these witnesses, but could not and was not in a position to pay them for their time.

The sheriff in Carthage, Corbett Akins, a very colorful sheriff, knew these people quite well. County Judge Bill Crawford knew them slightly, but well enough to act as a character witness. These two men devoted a big part of a week accommodating us in providing testimony that we desperately needed.

It is the customary practice for lawyers in trying a case out of the county to engage local counsel to assist in the county where most of the lawyers' legal work will be done. We engaged a lawyer in Borger, Texas to assist us mainly in selecting a jury.

The lawyer and I got well acquainted by telephone. We arranged that I would drive into Borger on a Sunday afternoon, late, spend the night in his guest room, and proceed on to court early the next morning, some fifteen miles north of Borger.

Borger, a thriving oil town of about seven thousand people, straddled the main highway going north from Amarillo. Nothing about Borger struck me as unusual because it looked like any other busy small Texas town.

We started the day early on the morning in which this case was to be tried by first having a very nice breakfast prepared by this lawyer and his wife. As I recall, we ate homemade biscuits, with syrup, bacon and eggs. After breakfast, we proceeded on to Stinnett where the courthouse was located.

Stinnett looked unlike any town I'd seen. The highway passed within three hundred feet of the courthouse. The two-story light-colored brick structure stood alone in the surrounding prairie with the exception of an occasional cow I could see in the distance, and a tin shack about one hundred feet from the courthouse. The tin shack represented downtown Stinnett: its one and only country store.

It occurred to me that I first should see my client, who had been confined in jail for several months prior to this time. I had the jailman bring her out of the confined part of the jail, and she met me in a kind of living room area of this jail, because the jail had facilities for people to spend the night, and contained two or three bedrooms, baths, and a reception room, which acted as a living room.

As a matter of fact, I noticed that she had the freedom to come and go as she wished, and wore a white dress usually worn by nurses or maids in the homes of the wealthy people who were able to provide help in this manner. It astounded me to see such a beautiful, attractive young lady of about twenty years of age. It first appeared to me that someone of that type would be unable to commit murder. Then I realized a woman this sexy might have to commit additional murder at any time to prevent men with ulterior motives from forcibly ripping off all her clothes to commit acts to perpetuate the human race.

In talking with her, it appeared that she and her husband had been fighting, as they did regularly when she took beatings from him. Finally, one day she had had enough, and she simply shot and killed him. Of course, this was not a defense for murder, but it goes a long way in mitigating the circumstances bringing about this situation that might end in tragedy, such as had occurred in this instance.

That day the judge ascended the bench and called out the cases that would be tried during the week in which he was holding court. It appeared that a damage suit would be the first case to be tried and that our case would then be called a little later in the week after the first case was completed. This gave us a great deal of time to further look into the facts and circumstances surrounding all of this matter.

I went back to the jail to discuss the facts and circumstances surrounding my client's situation. She had been in the courthouse for several months prior to this date. The more I noticed how attractive the defendant was, the more concerned I became about what she had been doing, living in jail for several months. I asked her if she knew the judge, and she told me she knew him very well, that he was a very friendly, kind man. She cooked for him in the little apartment-type suite in the jail; she did his laundry, ironed his shirts. I had an idea there might be more intimacy than that, but at that time these sorts of things were difficult to discuss.

I finally asked her if she would tell me how close she was to the judge. She hesitated, but finally admitted that she'd had a very close relationship and was sleeping with him each night. I knew then that the judge would be at least fair, maybe a little biased in our favor.

Wouldn't it be a wonderful thing it suddenly popped into my mind, if we could waive a jury and try this case before the Judge? But I had known, and every lawyer in Texas knows, that you cannot do this. After visiting with the district attorney for hours and hours, about what we might do, I asked what if the State waived and did not ask for the death penalty.

The district attorney had had a few drinks when he agreed with me. He said, however, he knew the judge would not allow this to be done, but if I could talk the court into waiving a jury, it would be agreeable with him to try the case before the court without jury intervention in deciding the facts.

This county had provided a very complete library just off to the side of the reception area. There, I immediately started working to see if I could find a case wherein the jury could be waived and all the facts submitted to the court for its decision. I finally, after hours and hours of research, found an old, old case that had held that we could do so provided the district attorney, or the State, waived its right of asking for the death penalty. I felt somewhat relieved when this appeared to be possible.

During the recess of the trial of the other case, I mentioned to the judge that the district attorney and I had worked out an agreement so that this case could be heard within a short time, eliminating the long drawn out proceedings that would be necessarily done in the selection and impaneling of a jury.

He told me he didn't think I could do it, but if I did find some authority, he would allow the case to be tried before the judge without the intervention of a jury. On Wednesday evening, after we had waited around the courthouse for hours and days, we learned the case then was to be heard at about four o'clock in the afternoon.

Just prior to this case's coming before the court, I had had Corbett Akins, who liked to take a few drinks, to visit and talk with the district attorney, who liked to drink a lot. When the case was called and we announced we were ready, the district attorney stood up and wavered a little bit because he was slightly inebriated. The district attorney and I had worked out an agreement that allowed my client to be given a five-year suspended sentence; if she did not commit other crimes during the five years, she would never have to serve any time.

We announced ready for trial. The State announced ready for trial, and we announced ready for trial subject only to the first case being disposed of prior to the time in which this case would be tried.

Then something unusual occurred in the courtroom. It had been so quiet, with only the bailiff, the judge, and the parties to this matter present in court. Suddenly up in the balcony appeared a school teacher with about fifty students, about the ages of thirteen to fifteen years. We later learned that it was a civics class in Borger, Texas that had decided to visit the courthouse and learn what they could about the functioning of our government, especially the judicial system.

To my surprise and consternation, the proceedings did not go in the quiet way that it usually does when an agreement has been reached. Instead, the district attorney kept looking up in the balcony. Then he decided that he would make a speech, which lasted about thirty or forty minutes, all for the benefit of the spectators who had come to hear the case to be tried.

The event did not affect the agreement we had entered into. When the argument was completed by the State, the defendant would waive argument, and the judge would promptly ask the defendant to stand and approach the bench so that he could pronounce sentence. The judge thanked the State's attorney, the parties to the action, and the defendant's attorney for reaching an agreement, eliminating the expense and cost to the State in prosecuting this case further.

He reviewed the facts showing that the defendant had been abused by her husband, and the good reputation that she had had in the community where she lived and was best known by the sheriff of our county and by the county judge.

Finally, he stated that he would find the defendant guilty and assess her punishment at five years in the state penitentiary. But, because she had never before been convicted of a felony in this state or any other, that she enjoyed an excellent reputation, the sentence would be suspended.

What a relief I felt at that time because it had been a very difficult case. Finally, I believe that justice was served, and that this woman should not have served time in the penitentiary.

Just remember this: my experience had taught me that usually the injured party is a son-of-a-bitch and asks for this sort of thing. I sincerely believe that the injured party in this case had brought about his own end in this instance. After we had arrived back in Carthage, the parents of this young lady came to see me. Then all of a sudden other people heard about the case. It got in the newspapers. So the mother and father told people all through that community that if they wanted a lawyer who would really work hard on their behalf, then just hire Fred Whitaker.

This continued the reputation that I had built up through the years by working darned hard on any case in which anyone employed me.

The prayerful approach

As I developed my reputation as a successful trial lawyer in murder cases, all varieties of people came into my office looking for help. That's how I met the prayerful minister.

In the 1950s, a murder occurred about six miles north of Carthage on the Marshall Highway. Immediately after the murder took place, the constable arrested the man who had committed the wrongful act and brought him into Carthage where he was incarcerated in jail to be tried later if the grand jury indicted him for the offense.

A lay preacher appeared on the scene, got into the act, and started going to the jail to talk to the accused. Then the preacher came to me about representing the man in jail. I told the minister that before I'd accept employment I'd like to talk with the man charged with this offense.

In some manner, the preacher was allowed to bring the accused to my office accompanied, of course, by one of the deputy sheriffs. The group arrived in my office for the accused to talk with me about what had actually happened.

While we were discussing the case, the minister suddenly wanted to pray. He asked us all if we would kneel. The defendant kneeled, of course, because he was in a prayerful mood and needed help wherever he could get it. I hesitated, but I knelt, too. The minister gave a beautiful prayer, though I kept looking around to see if I could find anyone watching. When we got to our feet, I again looked around carefully to make sure no one was watching.

I felt a little embarrassed to be kneeling in a situation such as this: a lawyer in his own office kneeling with a prospective client. This experience stayed with me a long time. I did not take the case simply because the man didn't have a fee to pay me. Eventually, the court appointed a lawyer for him.

Witnessing violence

During my career as a trial lawyer, I tried more than fifty murder cases either for the prosecution or the defense. I do not take death lightly, particularly violent death. To this day the violent death I witnessed as a young county attorney remains a vivid memory.

It was the duty of the State's attorney to go to the scene of accidents and crimes. One night, as I worked in my office, I had a telephone call saying there had been a terrible accident at the Santa Fe depot in Carthage. I rushed out to the place, and became one of the first people to arrive on the scene. I found that a man, named Browning, had attempted to board a freight train as it was leaving Carthage, and had been thrown under the train. His body had been cut exactly in half. The lower half of his body, which included his legs and belt, lay beside the tracks. His upper torso lay about fifty feet north of his lower body.

This did not bother me too much, but as I walked about fifty feet and saw the upper portion of his body, something occurred that almost put me in shock. The expressions on his face continued to move. His face showed him attempting to talk, and the contortion of his entire face showed that he might still be in a great deal of pain.

A doctor appeared on the scene a short time later and made out the death certificate. The justice of the peace appeared on the scene to do his duty, showing the cause of the death. I slowly went back home but did not sleep one minute for the remainder of the night.

I often wonder how men in time of battle, when they see their friends die in conditions that could be as graphic as the one I had witnessed, survive the memory. This experience has come to my mind many times. I have tried to avoid the sight of this type of violence as much as possible because I'm simply not a person who can witness this without being very much affected.

"I just killed a man."

I have never known a man charged with a crime when there were not mitigating circumstances.

I had one such case as a young county attorney.

One evening after dark as I worked in the courthouse, I heard footsteps. The sound indicated that a man had only one leg, that one of his legs was a peg leg. I could only hear the peg leg as he used it every other step. At the time this sound occurred, I had a weird feeling that something terrible had taken place.

The door opened and a black man by the name of Peter Johnson walked into my office and said, "Mr. Whitaker, I just killed a man."

I asked him to sit down, took his statement by typing it myself since I did not have a secretary to help me. Here is the story Peter Johnson told me.

He said that he had often been embarrassed throughout his lifetime because he had only one leg. A bully in the community took great delight in making fun of him and reminding him of his physical defect. On this evening, Mr. Johnson had just taken it as long as he could.

He said he shot the man and didn't have any regrets, but wanted to tell me exactly what happened, that I could put him in the penitentiary or do whatever the law directed.

I believe it is the duty of the State's attorney to handle cases like this in a humane way. The suffering and humiliation that the dead man had caused this person, leading him to a point of committing an act like this was, in my opinion, much greater than the act of taking another man's life. The antagonizer had threatened to take Mr. Johnson's peg leg and throw it into the bonfire that a group of men had gathered around to warm themselves, tell jokes, and generally have a good time.

The bully, to embarrass and humiliate Peter Johnson further, repeated he would burn Mr. Johnson's peg leg and just maybe throw him into the fire. Peter Johnson was a man of small stature which enabled the bully to take advantage, making Mr. Johnson's life hell by tormenting and harassing him.

We presented the matter to the grand jury. The grand jury heard all the testimony. One of the men on the grand jury asked me, as he looked at me, "Mr. Whitaker, what would you do if you were on the grand jury?"

"I'd no bill him," I promptly answered.

The grand jury no billed Mr. Johnson and he was never tried for murder. I have no regrets in taking this position, of perhaps influencing the jury to a certain extent.

Justified murder

I know of one other case where a justification of murder was shown in which the defendant did not make any physical defense, such as the defendant's trying to protect his own life when he believed that he was going to be severely injured or murdered.

A man had married a young wife known around the community as being a little loose with her favors. After the man married, another man, who had dated the woman before, took great delight in poking fun of the gentleman, and taunting him with stories of the loving that he had enjoyed, wanting to know "if it was still that good." The man made that statement one too many times, and the husband pulled his gun and shot the man one time exactly through the heart.

In law school, we had been taught that we should be very careful in cross-examining women (who often appeared to be like saints), little children, and talking about the dead. In this instance, in defending this man for murder, I decided that I would use tactics that I had been taught not to do. I didn't have to cross-examine a woman, and I didn't have to question children, but I did want to talk about a man who had died, had been killed, and had a bad reputation.

In the argument to the jury, I said, "We might be trying the wrong person. The defendant should be not only acquitted, and not found guilty of murder, but he should be given a crown and a medal for eliminating a very low, undesirable character living among decent people in our society."

I shook in my boots, not knowing whether this would help or ruin any chance that I had of getting this man out of the trouble in which he was charged, or even getting him a light sentence. My approach must have been right, because the jury acquitted him.

The intent to murder

In another case tried in Carthage, I defended a man for assault with intent to murder. The trouble began over a woman. The woman, who each of these men cared for and fought over, was so attractive and so sexy that I had her appear before the court and jury as often as possible throughout the trial of the case. I wanted the members of the jury to see that every part of her body had the exact right curve and the right attraction that so many women are endowed with.

It developed during the trial of the case that one man had chased the other with a shotgun over this woman and, as I related and developed the story to the jury, the story became comical. The jury started laughing; the judge disappeared as he knelt down behind the bench to laugh himself because he didn't want people to see that he was laughing. When he came up he was wiping tears from his eyes because it had been the most comical story he had heard in the courtroom.

The judge declared a recess, and the man who had paid me the fee to defend his employee, chewed my ass out, and told me he didn't pay me to conduct a comedy in the courtroom. I looked at him and said, "Look, you bastard, a jury will never convict anybody as long as they're laughing."

We received a not guilty verdict. To this day, I believe that the main testimony we produced in the trial happened in a spontaneous and comical way that we hadn't anticipated. We simply took advantage of it and won the case.

The public forgets that most men who are really guilty of wrongful acts are just plain mean as hell, horrible persons whom society would be better off if they did not live among decent people.

Murder case sets precedent in law

There are exceptions, however. One of the most important cases that I took, and one which became the most interesting, involved a murder case in which L.T. Prince was charged with the murder of his wife in 1948.

The facts, as they developed, showed that Mr. Prince's wife sat on her front porch facing Highway 59, the highway that ran from Carthage to

Houston, and allowed her dress to come up above her knees to attract attention. On some occasions, some of the men would drive on down the highway, then return and pay her a visit, since she made it very obvious that she was inviting friends with whom she might have relations.

This occurred for some time. Even though all the neighbors knew about it, it finally came to the attention of her husband, who didn't accept his wife's behavior. Finally, in desperation, he shot her with a single barrel shotgun, and blew the greater part of her head completely off.

It was a gruesome murder. Within two or three days after the crime was committed, an uncle of L.T. Prince, a mail carrier of Joaquin, Texas, came to my office and paid me a fee to represent his nephew. The uncle wanted me to do what I could in getting Mr. Prince out of the trouble that he had placed himself in.

The sheriff allowed me to go into the jail and confer with my client. L. T. Prince was very anxious to tell me all about what had happened, but his story did not jive with what I had been told. Even though he told me what his wife had been doing with other men, he wanted to let me know that he had a perfect alibi because he was in Marshall at the time it happened.

He told me that when he left that morning to go to Marshall, some thirty miles north of Carthage, his wife seemed to be happy and in a good mood, but that when he returned, he found her lying on the floor with a gun lying by her side. He knew in his own mind that he had a perfect alibi and defense. All that we'd have to do was to show that she had committed suicide by using this gun to blow her own head off.

I talked with the sheriff about the possibility of her having committed suicide, and he told me that he had anticipated that suicide might be used as a defense. Because of the length of the gun barrel and the position of the wound, it would have been impossible for her to have arranged to use the gun in this manner to end her own life.

The wife's suicide theory we eliminated entirely from the defense, and we then went into the question of an alibi. That is, we discussed his contention that he was at some other place when the infliction of the wound brought his wife's instant death.

L.T. Prince had gone to Marshall that morning. We established that. The question was, did he shoot his wife before he left for Marshall, and would the state be able to show that in going to Marshall, he had gone with the idea of establishing an alibi to deceive the prosecution?

I wasn't sure that we could keep him from volunteering information about his wife's committing adultery with all the men whom she could seduce. Her behavior lay on his mind so heavily that he could not refrain from telling me about it every time we discussed the defense of his case. I felt quite sure that he would be the same on the witness stand.

The question of alibi, and the misconduct of his wife remained completely in conflict; the conflict supplied the motive that the state needed in making out its case. It was simply, in order to defend this man properly, a question of pleading or proving one or the other — his alibi of being in Marshall or that he killed his wife because of her misconduct. The two just would not jive.

As soon as the uncle employed me in the case, other things developed. A Texas Ranger began to appear at the jail to see Mr. Prince, about three or four times a week, for more than a month. When I would see my client, he had evidence of beatings, torture. At times, his eyes would be black and his face swollen. All up and down his back I found swollen ridges with slight bruises, showing that he had been hit by a rubber hose by the Texas Ranger in his effort to bring about a confession.

Even though my client had agreed with me not to ever, ever sign a confession, the torture became so great that he finally signed a confession, admitting that he had killed his wife, as the state had contended.

I then began to read case law involved with the question of obtaining confessions by force and coercion. The Texas cases on this very question had always held that if the jury was submitted an issue and held that the confession was voluntary, then we had to rely on their decision, which was final and there was nothing to review on appeal.

But in examining the cases that went before the Supreme Court of the United States, I did find that cases had been reversed and remanded for a new trial when this issue had been before the court. The jury only decided if the confession was voluntary or not.

Before our case was called for trial, I prepared a motion to eliminate the introduction of the so-called confession because it was not a voluntary confession, but a confession obtained by force, and only signed because the accused could not withstand the torture and the pain that he had to endure unless he did sign this instrument.

This was urged before the court, but the judge advised that this very question of whether the confession had been voluntary would be submitted to the jury, and the jury just might find that it was not volunteer.

I explained then and there that that wasn't enough. A jury oftentimes would become so prejudiced and so unmindful of how the volunteer confession was obtained; the jury oftentimes became more interested in what the content of the case showed and the other evidence introduced by the state in obtaining a confession.

The case was tried before a jury. During the trial, while the defendant testified — he could hardly speak above a whisper — he would look to his right and left before he made any effort to answer the question propounded to him by his own counsel.

Then something occurred to me. I might test the old law. I made an objection to the court and asked the court to have the various officers of the law remove themselves from the courtroom or at least find a chair that was not within close proximity of the witness.

Actually, whether you believe it or not, three officers, including the Texas Ranger who had obtained the confession in the beginning, sat within five feet of the defendant while he testified.

The trial judge, Judge Spot Sanders, said that the objection I made was correct and ordered the officers to change their position, even though Judge Sanders did not ask them to remove themselves completely from the courtroom.

When the officers moved, I purposely waited about five minutes before resuming the questions that I had arranged to ask the defendant in the defense of his case.

He then, without too much hesitation, told me about the various beatings that he had had, the torture that he had endured, and why he signed the confession, and that he signed the confession only because he could not do otherwise.

I do know that we got the attention of the jury, who knew it was quite wrong to obtain a confession in this manner, but did hold in its answer to an interrogatory propounded to them that the confession was volunteer.

After about two days and two nights of deliberations, the jury came in and found the defendant guilty, and assessed punishment at fifteen years in the state penitentiary.

I promptly filed a motion for a new trial, and set out to show the court erred in holding that the confession was volunteer. We deemed it necessary for the Court of Criminal Appeals to review in order to determine if the defendant had a fair and a just trial in the court in which this case was tried. In Texas, the Court of Criminal Appeals acts as the Supreme Court for all criminal cases. A lawyer must request permission to argue the case orally, or else the case is submitted on written argument.

In our submission, we emphasized from the beginning that the volunteer statement was not a volunteer statement or confession at all.

Then in due process, an appeal was perfected, and it was filed with the Court of Criminal Appeals in Austin, Texas for its review. During the argument before the Court of Criminal Appeals, I argued about the officers being in close proximity to the witness, asking that this be a basis of reversal. Judge Beecham asked: How did I ever think of making an objection because of the close proximity of the officers with their big guns to their sides.?

I replied that I could see that the witness was intimidated and still under their influence, and that he would not be able to testify freely if this continued while the case was being tried.

To this day, I believe the case would have been reversed on this point, had they not used a point of law that should have been reckoned with, and changed prior to the time in which the L.T. Prince case was heard on appeal.

We elected to argue this case before the Court of Criminal Appeals. In my argument, I defied them to hold that this confession was volunteer, with all the facts and circumstances. I assured them that the case would go to the Supreme Court of the United States if they held otherwise.

I was not defiant in all of my argument. In the closing part of it, I lowered my voice and pled with the court to make it the law of this state that a so-called "volunteer confession" obtained in this manner could not, as a matter of law, be held otherwise because twelve thinking people could not differ in this respect.

The Court of Criminal Appeals did exactly what I urged them to do, and reversed and remanded this case on the grounds that L.T. Prince's confession had been obtained by coercion.

The leading newspapers in Texas carried articles of this case that changed the law. I was overwhelmed within a short time with telephone calls and letters from other lawyers congratulating me in having the court make this decision. I'm sure a lot of the lawyers had been trying to do so for many, many years, but had been unable to do so.

It had been simply that if the jury found it was a volunteer confession, then it was in truth and in fact a volunteer confession. Now, if the facts warranted that the confession had been obtained by coercion, as had happened in this case, the confession would not then be a volunteer confession, and no one could be convicted with this type of testimony.

As you know, when a case is reversed and remanded for a new trial, more often than not the case will be called again by the State for a new trial. On the court's own motion, the case was transferred to Marshall, Texas in Harrison County, since it had more publicity than any murder case that had ever been tried in Carthage. When the case was called for trial again in Harrison County, Dudley Davis of Center, Texas served as prosecuting attorney, with the district attorney in Harrison County assisting him in the trial. We did not have the question of volunteer confession to contend with because it had already been ruled on by the higher court.

We stressed our defense of establishing the alibi and relying, to a large extent, on the weakness of the State's testimony. The State, at the second trial, was forbidden from offering the volunteer confession that had been used and relied on so heavily at the first trial. The jury then retired to its jury room to deliberate the case. A juror by the name of Pate, originally from Carthage, made a statement to the other jurors that: "We ought to be just as good as they were in Panola County when the case was tried there and give him a fifteen-year sentence."

This comment must have influenced this jury because the jury, after deliberation in Harrison County, brought in a verdict of guilty and assessed Mr. Prince's punishment at fifteen years in the penitentiary, just as the jury had in Panola County.

The case was then appealed. We had what we thought was a sure chance of reversing the case because the jury heard testimony not admitted in the trial of the case, but from one of the jurors who told them about what had happened in the case in Panola County. This was a flagrant error. I was so confident that the case would be reversed on this ground that this became the only point which we raised on appeal for review before the higher court.

Judge Lloyd Davidson, one of the three judges on the Court of Appeals, wrote the court's opinion. The Court immediately reversed the case on the point of hearing outside evidence not introduced as evidence in the trial of the case.

We were notified of the reversal. However, District Attorney Dudley Davis, suddenly filed a motion for rehearing without saying why or in what manner the case should be heard a second time in the higher court.

After this second motion was filed, two members of the court, Judge Morrison and Judge Davidson, got into a cussing fight. Judge Morrison picked up the files in this case and wrote a second opinion confirming the lower court. I was left speechless and dumbfounded. This had occurred about three years after the alleged commission of this offense.

At that time, the State Bar of Texas had its annual bar convention over the Fourth of July holiday. The convention convened in Dallas, with headquarters in the old Baker Hotel. One of the first people I encountered at the meeting was Judge Morrison. We greeted each other, and I noticed that tears had formed in his eyes. He told me that he was especially glad that he could see me at this convention because he had something on his conscience he wanted to talk with me about.

He first told me that he had not done anything while on the appellate bench that he had any regrets about except one thing. He had done something wrong. One of the first persons he wanted to talk to about it was with me to see if anything could be done to rectify a wrong that he had committed.

He told me that he had deliberately written an opinion, a second opinion, on the L.T. Prince case because of the anger and animosity he had for his colleague, Lloyd Davidson. While we were standing on the stairway discussing this matter, I told him that as far as the appellate procedure was concerned, there wouldn't be anything that the court could do or that he could do. But, I just wondered if we might obtain a pardon from the Governor of the State of Texas.

The procedure then was to go before the Board of Pardons and Paroles Committee first, get its recommendation, and then go on to the governor for a final pardon, if the Governor saw fit to grant the pardon.

I looked at Judge Morrison and knew of his concern, and I asked him if he would go before the Board of Pardons and Paroles and relate to them what he had just told me.

When I got back to my office in Carthage, I determined that this approach might be available to be used to obtain what we had been entitled. I would ask for an immediate hearing before the Board of Pardons and Paroles.

The Board informed me that my client would have to serve one year before he would be entitled to a hearing. More often than not, he would have to serve a large part of his sentence before the committee would look upon this sort of thing favorably. I convinced the Board that this was an unusual case, and that as it would be developed, they would know that it was unusual. After much persuasion, the case was set immediately for hearing.

Judge Morrison, in an effort to do the right thing, did go before the committee, and within thirty days L.T. Prince was pardoned and paroled, and released from prison.

There never has been a lawyer as elated as myself when this man was finally pardoned of any offense he might or might not have committed. I know within my own mind and heart that I had done something for society, because it is so utterly wrong to convict anyone on testimony obtained by force. The Gestapo in Nazi Germany was no more guilty than we were in the state of Texas when this kind of coercion was allowed. I feel today that I have contributed to society, that the many people who might have had to serve time in prison, will not have to do so because the court reinterpreted the law. A new precedent had been established.

As I recall, I was paid only five thousand dollars for representing L. T. Prince on the charge for which he had been incarcerated. The pleasure I obtained in doing a good job was incalculable. If I looked at my success in monetary terms alone, the many, many cases that came to me after this case was successfully handled probably caused my income to more than double through other cases. Justice finally prevailed.

For months and years thereafter I received letters and telephone calls from other lawyers asking me how I managed to obtain this decision from the higher court. The practice of criminal law, where the emotions run high, is one of the most thrilling experiences a lawyer can have. The lawyer has the thrill and satisfaction of defending people in criminal cases, preventing them from having their lives and the lives of their families wrecked by charges against them when the people are either not guilty in the first place, or are being tried unjustly.

Death by strychnine poisoning

In 1956, I saved a woman, whose life had been punctuated with tragedy and unjust treatment, from the death penalty. Vera Mae Jeter worked as a clothes presser for a dry cleaners located in the Carthage Whitaker building. Many days when I walked to work, I'd see her through the window pressing clothes. Never did I think that someday I'd be representing her to defend her from a charge of murder.

The first time I heard of her murder charge, I received a call from members of her family to arrange for bail to be made so she could get out of jail, and go back to her job to await the grand jury action. We made her bond, and the next day I saw her working at the cleaners pressing clothes. A little later, the grand jury indicted her for murder, and she was charged with murdering her husband, Homer, by poisoning him with strychnine. Her bail bond served as her bond for her appearance.

The alleged offense was to have taken place on May 21, 1956. When I first talked with her, she did not admit committing the offense, but the district attorney had had her at the courthouse questioning her before I got to talk with her. The district attorney had fabricated a volunteer confession but made the mistake of using terms that this woman would never have used. You cannot make a black woman use vulgar, four-letter words. She just won't use them. The district attorney used these terms in the volunteer confession, and set them out continually in the confession.

On a Sunday night, the day before the case went to trial, I went to my office to read law and brief the case, learn all I could about the amount of strychnine it would take to cause a lethal dose in the stomach. I got to thinking that maybe something else could be used in defending this woman. Then I happened to remember that Vera Mae's husband had been under treatment with Dr. Perlman for heart trouble. I called Dr. Perlman and he said, "Yes, Homer Jeter had a very bad heart condition. He could have passed on at any minute."

"You know," I said, "the State's going to contend that he died of strychnine poisoning. I want you to review a little with me so I can handle this situation. I contemplate that the pathologist didn't examine Jeter's other organs other than the stomach. But I'm not sure. In case this happened, I want to know from you, Doctor, would there be any humanly way for him to know if Homer Jeter died from heart trouble or strychnine poisoning?"

"No," Dr. Perlman answered, "he would not be able to know."

I didn't know if the pathologist would tell the truth because he got paid the same whether testifying for the State or the defense. When I got him on the witness stand, I talked with him several minutes. Then I suddenly brought in Dr. Perlman's treatment and asked him point blank if he could truthfully say that Homer Jeter died of poisoning.

"Did you examine the heart?" I asked the doctor.

"No," he said, "I wasn't instructed to examine the heart.

They told me to examine only the contents of the stomach. The stomach showed that it contained enough strychnine to be a lethal dose."

I brought out that Dr. Perlman, a doctor in Carthage, had been treating Mr. Jeter for heart trouble for many years. Then I asked a hypothetical question. "Can you truthfully say, Doctor, whether this man actually died from heart trouble or from strychnine poisoning?"

"It would be impossible to do so," he said.

This weakened the district attorney's case.

The district attorney brought out that Vera Mae Jeter had bought some strychnine from the drugstore in Carthage and told the druggist she was going to kill some old crows. Sometimes, black people called other black people *crows*, and the jury found this funny.

I turned to the jury and asked, "If she had wanted to kill someone, she wouldn't have done that, now would she?"

In the argument to the jury, I reminded them that this woman would not have used the vulgar terms found in the so-called volunteer confession. I told the jury, "This was not her volunteer confession; it's the statement of the district attorney, thinking that if he put all these vulgar terms in there you'd become prejudiced against this woman." I looked at the district attorney and said, "Shame on you. Doing this sort of thing makes you almost as guilty as what you're claiming this woman has done."

We then brought out a lot that we hear constantly of now but never heard of then. Homer Jeter molested his two small daughters. He had fondled them. The defendant brought this out herself, that he'd smell their undergarments. He acted like an animal instead of a human being. This might have kept the sentence low because he was a no-good bastard and society would have been a lot better without him. We don't need people like that in our society.

I got so worked up over this case that I believed she was innocent. I thought that if I couldn't get her acquitted, I could get a reduced sentence. However, the evidence was so overwhelming that the jury couldn't do anything but find her guilty. But the jury gave her only fifteen years, a very low sentence. They could have given her the death penalty or life in the penitentiary.

Vera Mae Jeter only served one year in the penitentiary. I've never known anyone in the community, white or black, to feel like she should have been in the penitentiary. People would come to my office and ask me if I couldn't do something about getting Vera Mae out of the penitentiary. I knew I had nothing to take on appeal. Then I thought we might get a petition signed by people in the community, recommending to the Board of Pardons and Paroles and Governor of Texas that she be paroled. Over half of the people living in Panola County signed that petition. I took the petition to apply for parole. On one delay of about six months, the parole board set a hearing of the case. I went personally and brought in all the facts showing that there were a lot of mitigating circumstances in favor of this woman.

The Board of Pardons and Paroles recommended that the Governor grant a pardon. I took that recommendation to the Governor and related to him the facts of the case and he promptly granted a parole that would become a pardon as Vera Mae Jeter made her place in society taking care of her family and becoming a law abiding citizen.

Then there was the question of how this woman would pay me. She only made about fifteen dollars a week pressing clothes. She used this entirely to support herself and her daughters. Her husband, even though he had worked occasionally, did not make enough money to support himself or his family. Vera Mae Jeter supported the family. She didn't have any money to pay me.

However, she had worked hard through the years and bought a six-acre tract of land on the river hill, on Highway 71 leading from Carthage to Shreveport, Louisiana. There she had a small house where she kept her family sheltered, fed and clothed.

It is not lawful for a person to mortgage their homestead for any purpose. We arranged for her to give me her land as though she had sold it to me. But we fixed the price, and we agreed that when she had the money to pay me that she'd get back her deed to her house.

After she got back from the penitentiary, she lived in the house for four or five years. Then one day I decided she should pay me my attorney's fee. If it hadn't been for me, she'd still be in the penitentiary working at hard labor. I called her in and told her to pay me or I would have her vacate her property, and I'd take the property and sell it to pay me the fee.

At this time, Vera Mae Jeter worked at housework for my sister, Sue Morgan. I got a call one day after this from Sue, saying she wanted to talk with her little brother. "You're not about to take this poor woman's house," she said.

I explained to Sue that this was how I made my living, that I'd more than earned my fee. This did not satisfy Sue. However, within a few days, Sue had taken my client to the First National Bank in Carthage and arranged for a loan for the amount of my fee. Vera Mae Jeter got the money and brought it to my office and paid me in full.

Vera Mae's daughters eventually attended college and were awarded degrees. They loved my sister, Sue, and I felt so proud of them.

So often the difference between a lawyer's success or failure hinges on the use of common sense.

The famous courthouse on the square in Carthage. Built in 1885

Early Carthage Square, about 1909, when cotton was king.

John and Elizabeth Whitaker, grandparents of Fred came to Texas in a covered wagon when Fred's father was 2 years old.

The 4 Whitaker brothers. From left are, Fred's father, Joseph Calvin, Wesley, John E. and Ed.

Fred standing in front of the old corn crib where he and his mother worked "picking off peanuts" to pay a $2 lab fee.

Fred, age 9, right, with his brother, Travis and their dog, Shep.

Carthage High School football team, about 1927. Fred is kneeling on second row, third from left.

Methodist Church in Rockhill community as it looks today. Fred's mother and father attended an All Day-To-Do resulting in getting drenched during a thunderstorm.

Fred's mother, Annie Lucy English Whitaker, holding daughter, Sue.

W. Henry Matthews, Panola County
Sheriff, 1920-1924.

Fred with Gladys Simpson while
attending Texas Christian University in Fort Worth in 1931.

Fred Whitaker and Gladys Simpson
with friends while attending Texas
Christian University.

Corbett Akins, Panola County
Sheriff, 1942-1952.

Panola County Sheiff Corbett Akins, known throughout Texas. Shown with deputies.

Panola County's colorful sheriff, Corbett Akins, with deputies, 1940s.

Panola County Sheriff Corbett Akins, pictured on right, with his famous bloodhounds. Left is Deputy Cush Reeves.

Fred and friend in front of President Andrew Jackson's Hermitage while attending Cumberland University.

Fred graduating from Cumberland University, Lebanon, Tennessee, with law degree.

Fred looking out his office window during Rodeo parade in Carthage.

Fred at age 30.

Fred at age 35.

Newly elected County Attorney in old Carthage Courthouse, age 25.

Fred visiting with friend, Mr. Todd, in drugstore.

Dr. John Whitaker and sister, Suzanne, taken in early childhood.

Mary Elizabeth (Dixie) Simpson. The reason Fred returned to Chicago.

Dixie with Melinda.

Refurbished County Jail where Jakeleg Hudson and other clients of Fred's were held.

Dixie and Fred holding Melinda, age 3, and Jennifer, age 2 mo., at home in Carthage, 1944.

Fred Whitaker
Of Carthage
For
Congress
3rd District
NEWS

A man of proven ability—check the qualifications of the candidates for this post and elect the ablest.

Fred Whitaker of Carthage ran for Congress in 1948 for the 3rd Congressional District.

Fred and Dixie honeymooning in Mexico in 1941.

Fred and Dixie, first place winners at a costume party at the Cherokee Club in Longview. Fred, an English gentleman dressed for the races, and Dixie, dressed as a Gibson girl.

Fred and Dixie Whitaker attending Steeple Chase Ball in Ft. Worth. 1944

Fred's handsome brother, Tony Whitaker at age 25.

First National Bank in Carthage where Fred had upstairs law office.

Fred, as a young lawyer, sitting at poolside at the Shamrock Hotel in Houston.

Whitaker building under construction about 1948.

Fred, Panola County Attorney, with son, John, about 1935.

From left to right, Jake and Ed Durham, from Lufkin, one of the most outstanding families; Earl Mayfield, son of U. S. Senator Earl Mayfield of Tyler; Weldon Bradley, later State District Judge in Fort Worth; Fred Whitaker and Jim Ferguson, nephew of former Texas Governor Jim Ferguson.

Mark Whitaker, age 5.

Fred with son, Mark.

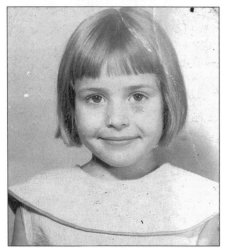

Debbie Whitaker, age 5.

Debbie "playing lawyer" in her father's law office, 1955

Jennifer Whitaker, sophomore at Stephen F. Austin University.

Melinda Whitaker.

Fred with 4-H Club member and her prize-winning steer in Center.

Fred with registered Hereford bull purchased from David and "Tex" Ritter, country entertainer.

First National Bank in Center. Purchased by Fred in 1964.

Fred traveling by train to the Kentucky Derby with fellow passenger.

Fred "playing cowboy" with prize-winning bull, "Sunrise." Jack Turner in middle, former owner. Son, Mark, standing on left.

Fred and Dixie shown with the No. I prize winning Hereford at the Louisiana State Fair in Shreveport. Her name was Peaches.

First meeting after purchasing First National Bank of Center, Texas. From left to right, Prentice Sanders, Mrs. Michael Sanders (daughter of Bill Nettles of Dallas), Michael Sanders, Ambassador Ed Clark (chairman of board) and wife, Dahlia Sanders, Dixie and Fred Whitaker, president of bank.

Oil well being drilled by Fred Whitaker in the 1960s.

David G. Baird of New York. One of Fred's friends and investors who gave more money to charity than any other man in the U. S. at the time.

Dallas Theater Center Board of Directors meeting on February 3, 1977. Back row: Paul Baker, Robert W. Davis, Carl L. Yeckel, Alan M. May, Sidney Stahl, Waldo E. Stewart, Dr. Jere Mitchell, David George, Dr. Charles Hunter and Mrs. Brooke Blake. Center row: William C. Edwards, Jr., William Smellage, Charles J. Wyly, Jr., Richard C. Marcus, Roosevelt Johnson, Jr., Edwin R. Daniels, Robert Henry Middleton, Donald J. Malouf, Mrs. Peter Paddock, Fred Whitaker, Mrs. Robert M. Meltzer, Mrs. James Hart, Mrs. J. T. Lontos, Mrs. Robert Zech, Christopher Simpson, Joel T. Williams III and Mrs. Frank Nick. Seated on front row: Mrs. Leon Rabin, Mrs. Dale Cunningham, Dr. Robert I. Kramer, Mrs. Milton P. Levy, Mrs. Robert D. Stecker, Mrs. W. J. Hilseweck, Mrs. Henry Hawley, Jr., Mrs. Mary Louise Sweatt and Mrs. William Plack Carr.

Texas Christian University homecoming. Fred standing behind woman on second row (far right).

Fred in his home on Swiss Avenue in Dallas about 1975.

Fred with Grace Stemmons about 1973.

Recent photo of Fred in his office and residence at 3525 Turtlecreek in Dallas.

Present home of Fred Whitaker, located on land purchased by his grandfather upon arriving in Texas aftrer Civil War. 2 miles north of Carthage.

Beautiful home in Carthage where Whitaker family lived. Landscaped by Lamberts' (famous landscaping architect).

Chapter Nine

Common Sense and the Law

The best lawyers are those who have the most common sense. Common sense tells a lawyer that first he or she should, before taking a case, meet with the client and advise the client whether a lawsuit should be filed. Lawyers should not encourage litigation in many cases.

When I first started practicing law, neither the law nor lawyers were perfect, but we came close enough that almost everyone had his day in court. Common sense, used judiciously, encouraged the court and jury to render a just verdict.

The case of the missing body

Four or five years after I started practicing law, a group of black men came to my office and said they wanted to obtain some advise from me. One of their brethren had died without leaving enough money for a decent burial, and his body, or remains, had been left with the funeral home in Marshall.

They were not able to collect donations enough to pay for the expenses: over five hundred dollars, far more than the usual and customary prices charged at that time for a simple burial without any fancy additions connected with it.

The gentlemen in my office felt saddened and in no mood for any witticism or joking at the time. I saw a great deal of humor in a situation such as this, though I did not let them know what I was thinking. I thought for a few minutes and told them that I could give them some advice that would surely work. Simply go back to the funeral director and tell him that they were not able to get enough money to pay him, and that he would just have to keep the body.

They did as I instructed and it worked just as I had anticipated. When the owner of the funeral parlor became convinced that he could not collect the exhorbitant amount he was charging, and had no earthly way of disposing of the body without additional cost, all to be born by himself, he then got down to business and reduced the amount of his charges so that the friends and relatives of the deceased could make payment of about one-third to one-fourth of the amount he originally wanted to charge.

I believe everyone was satisfied except the owner of the funeral parlor, whose business got set back somewhat because he was not able to gouge or swindle the public for the services he had rendered.

The brothers who shot up Tatum

My use of common sense influenced the outcome of another case that involved family members prominent in Henderson and Tatum. If you're a small town lawyer, it is not unusual to receive a call on Sunday about a criminal matter. One Sunday afternoon, I received a telephone call from the president of one of the banks in Henderson, Texas.

"Fred," he began, "I have a very difficult situation. My two brothers-in-law became infuriated over the fact that one had found his wife trifling on him. To let off some steam, the brothers got drunk in Tatum. It's a small town, you know, with a population of about six hundred people."

"They went all over Tatum shooting up the town. They shot holes in the roofs of houses, but never shot in any direction to injure anyone. They caused all hell to break loose in Tatum. Everyone ran for cover. People got under beds, on the floor as if war had started. It's the most frightening thing to happen in Tatum."

The bank president, a very dignified man who felt seriously about his family, said, "I don't think there's any defense in a case like this. If anyone can get them out of this, it's you."

I immediately left for Henderson where the sheriff had put the two men in jail. I visited with them, made their bond, and got them out of jail.

I thought and thought. I didn't know of anything on our statutes that made their actions a violation of the law. Maybe Tatum had a city ordinance that forbade anyone to discharge a firearm in city limits. But I knew of no law and I began to realize I had an easier case than what they thought.

They arranged to pay me a very nice fee, knowing at the time that I might not have to do too much work because I'd already sensed that Texas had no statutes saying it was unlawful to discharge firearms as long as you didn't intend to kill, which they certainly didn't intend to do, nor injure anyone.

As we arranged for a defense in the case, I decided to go this route. I'd try to beat this case before the grand jury met. I knew the president of the bank had a lot of influence, and we could talk to members of the grand jury, but we sure didn't want to offer them anything because, if we did, we violated the law. We could, however, tell them our side of the story.

We decided that we'd talk with members of the grand jury. The brothers were popular and well-liked by everyone. We began to talk to some of the grand jurors who would be impaneled shortly to investigate this case, and we did a good job of politicking. The case was brought before the grand jury and the brothers were no billed.

The brothers made restitution for any damages in Tatum. Later, the people of Tatum thought about the humor in what had happened and began to laugh. The people of Tatum did like the brothers and they knew the men had to let off some steam.

I had no qualms about the fee I charged. I knew I'd done an excellent job. If we'd gone another route, we might have helped the State make some kind of case against the brothers.

The case of the altered ballots

I used a different approach in a case in which the district attorney falsely accused a woman of vote fraud.

When I had attended the eighth or ninth grade in Carthage, around 1926, a teacher by the name of Ray Davidson served as principal and taught classes in civics, government, math, and other subjects we studied.

Ray Davidson was a fine man. He encouraged, cajoled and admonished all of us to get a good basic education. He taught us to say "Please" when we asked for something. He spent a considerable amount of time with me, telling me that I could obtain a good education, and maybe even become a lawyer if I worked hard enough. "It can be done," he would say, and I felt encouraged and deeply influenced by his help and counseling. I knew he cared about the future of his charges.

He told us how he had worked hard to make his way through school, and had received a degree from one of the state teacher colleges in Texas. This enabled him to finally leave the worn out old farmstead that had been his early home in the nearby Rockhill community.

He later moved from Carthage to Port Arthur, located in the southeastern Gulf Coast of Texas. He prospered in Port Arthur and ultimately became mayor and developed a popular following for his efforts. He thoroughly enjoyed the office he held.

During this period, Ray met and married the sister of an attorney in Orange, Texas, a town about twenty miles from Port Arthur. His new bride's father and brother were partners practicing law in their own firm, Stephenson and Stephenson. They were capable men and their firm was well-known throughout the state.

In about 1955, Ray Davidson and his family returned to Carthage and he established a hardware business. Naturally, he remained active in politics, both locally and statewide, and became a close friend of then-Governor Alan Shivers.

Ray was very interested in a local county commissioner's race, and his sister, Ruby Davidson Barber, served as an election judge at one of the precinct polling places where this particular race became a highly contested and heated race. After the polls closed, and the votes had been counted, one of the candidates became disgruntled and was far from satisfied at the number of votes he'd received. He immediately filed suit seeking a recount.

In the process of this recount, it came to light that, indeed, some ballots had been altered or changed, especially in the Governor's race, and as well in the local commissioner's race.

Fred Hudson, the Panola County district attorney, and a Harvard graduate trying to make a name for himself, accused Ruby Barber of altering the ballots. Under his direction, the grand jury indicted her. In some cases, sadly, Fred Hudson looked downright silly or maybe stupid in the course of his work as the state's local attorney. Fred knew well that

Ruby did not actually change those ballots. However, through some subterfuge, he tricked her into going to Dallas with him and undergoing a lie detector test.

As most people know, such test results merely determine the guilt or innocence of a subject in about ninety-nine cases out of one hundred. In this case, the test brought in certain "side effects," so to speak. The test indicated, for the first time, that poor Ruby Barber had allowed her brother, Ray Davidson, to deliver the ballots from her precinct to the courthouse for counting and certification. This revelation indicated that the ballots were actually in his possession for a certain period of time, and that situation may well have violated the Sanctity of the Ballot.

The district attorney, Fred Hudson, aware of this fact, knew the defendant, Ruby Barber, was not actually guilty of the crime in which she was charged, and that in all probability her brother, Ray, was the culprit. In a strange sort of way, District Attorney Hudson advised the defendant he would dismiss the case against her if she would turn state's evidence and aid him in the conviction of her own brother. Naturally, she refused to do that and the case was called for trial.

For the several months before the trial, it seemed as though everyone in the county was only interested in Ruby Barber's being exonerated. People would often come to my office to talk about the case with me since they knew I had been retained as local counsel to represent her. People noted that Ray Davidson often accepted contributions from various county residents interested one way or another in the outcome of this stellar case. It came to my attention on several occasions that people told me that they had contributed money toward my fee. For some odd reason or unexplained reason, I never saw any of that money. But I did receive a very small retainer fee of about a thousand dollars.

Ruby's brother, Ray, knew he would have to use his family members to handle his sister's case since they were prominent and very competent lawyers.

Now, Ruby Barber was a very attractive young woman and, when she was about nineteen, had obtained her teaching certificate. She had become an instructor in one of the lower grades of the Mitchell School which I had attended as a boy. Ruby's family was one of the finest in East Texas and her husband was the brother of the famous golfer, Miller Barber, whose prowess on the golf tours was legendary. I had read of him in the newspapers for many years.

I had always admired her as did anyone who knew her, and I was certain that she was virtually incapable of committing that crime or any other wrongdoing. Someone with her sweet nature and kind heart could never, ever allow her brother to be tried. She would rather stand trial herself, embarrassing as it was to do so.

Ray Davidson's in-laws, Stephenson and Stephenson of Orange County, Texas, acted as lead counsel. I worked on the pretrial details of this case as though I were leading counsel. As local counsel I planned to assist the lead counsel primarily in selecting the jury and assisting them through the trial. I prepared motions to quash the indictment, knowing well that without doubt it was defective. If the court did not sustain that motion, we would then stand on good ground to reverse the case on appeal in the event we needed to carry the case that far.

When a case such as this is called for trial in a courtroom, there is a noted solemnity throughout the court. A certain quietness falls over the parties and the interested spectators, officers of the court and attorneys and, indeed, the defendant. All combine in affording one of the tense occurrences to be found in our society. In this type of case, the very structure and the sanctity of our government are being challenged, just as is the individual being tried before his or her peers.

When the State announced as ready, we had eliminated the motions that had been filed earlier and urged to the court; the case came to trial. The State, through their illustrious Harvard Law School graduate, Fred Hudson, proceeded to made out the State's case, introducing into evidence the ballots that had been altered. Additionally, the civil case had been filed, showing that the remarkable changes in the results of the entire election, both locally and statewide, were fraudulent.

Fred Hudson made a short, but adequate, case for the State of Texas. Mr. Stephenson, Ruby's chief attorney, asked if I would take the witness, who was none other than Fred Hudson, on crossexamination.

The lie detector test given Ruby Barber brought out that the custody of the ballots was not kept in Ruby Barber's possession at all times, but were handed to her brother, Ray Davidson, who in fact took the ballots to the courthouse in Carthage to the election authorities. This, of course, led the district attorney to the information that if Ruby Barber did not commit the crime, then Ray Davidson was in a position to have altered the ballots.

After Fred Hudson determined that the guilty party was likely Ray Davidson and not Ruby Barber, he stated to her that in order for her not to be prosecuted for this crime it would be necessary that she give state's evidence against her brother so that Ray Davidson could be indicted and prosecuted for the offense. Ruby Barber refused to give evidence against her brother. She stood on her honor and, in a way, defied the district attorney to proceed with the case against her. She knew she had not committed a crime and surely the state could not prove she had altered the ballots.

After that cross-examination, instead of the wonderful case Fred Hudson thought he had, he looked like, as Charles Dickens said of the law, "an ass, an idiot."

During a court recess, we attorneys for the defense went into the jury room to further discuss the case and current situation. We were now ready to proceed with our defense witnesses. During this time, something happened that gave me one of the greatest compliments and most satisfaction I've ever enjoyed. Mr. Stephenson turned to his brother-in-law, Ray Davidson, and said, "I've heard about the abilities of that Fred Whitaker as a trial lawyer. It already shows in this case, and I can tell you now Ray, I will absolutely not interrogate any more witnesses in this case. If I argue this case before the jury, I'm going to take up very little time so that Fred Whitaker will have the opportunity to fully discuss and argue the defense of this case."

Testimony was then introduced by the defense, a great portion of which was character witnesses. Then the defendant herself, Ruby Davidson Barber, took the stand. She denied she had done anything wrong. Though the results of the lie detector test were available to me, I didn't want to use that even though it could work in our favor. I felt it might backfire in some manner, and it was my gut feeling that we did not actually need this vital and very valuable testimony.

Fortunately, the case was tried before an attentive and highly interested jury. As the state opened its argument, and made its plea to convict, Hudson never, at any time, told the jury they had to convict the defendant because of the "Sanctity of the Ballot!"

How he managed to not make use of that term, I will probably never know, because it had given me great concern for all these strenuous months and, truthfully, I had no answer to that type of argument. It came as a great relief when he did not use any common sense when he overlooked, or simply did not make use of such a valuable tool, in spite of his straight "A" average in both his prelaw and law school studies.

When the time arrived for me to take the principal argument to the jury, as I recall, the court allowed me but one hour to do so. I had much to talk about because I knew I was on the right side of this case. Near the end of the argument, for some reason, I turned around and looked at the defendant. She was still radiantly beautiful, and suddenly it seemed as though all my previous life on the farm and that country school rushed back at me.

I wouldn't have been human if tears hadn't come into my eyes as I described her in days past and, as I so well remembered her as a young woman teaching in that rural school in Mitchell community. I described her sensitivities and deep feeling for good in everything which would alone prevent her from committing a crime such as was before the court.

Lowering my voice at the conclusion, I asked the jury to do one thing, a thing I had never before asked a jury to do in my entire career in the practice of law. I asked that they go into the jury room, but not sit down as they normally do, remain standing, elect a foreman, take one vote and come back to the courtroom within a very short time with an acquittal for the defendant.

I told the jury Ruby Barber had been tormented long enough and her every moment seemed an eternity to her. We'd like her acquittal in short time. She simply was NOT guilty.

Later, spectators told me all twelve jurors from time to time used their handkerchiefs to wipe away their tears. The jury then retired, and I had scarcely had time to sit down before they returned. Just as I had asked, they then in short formality acquitted my client.

The courtroom had been packed so that there was standing room only, packed in like olives squeezed into a jar, throughout the trial. When the jury gave its verdict, a mighty rush of people moved to reach the front of the courtroom and even behind the bar. Scores of people, it seemed to me, kept coming up to me with words of congratulations and thanks. It was embarrassing. Almost.

One, Carey Coats, a long-time Carthage resident, put his arms around me and whispered, "That was the best sermon I've ever heard."

I don't know why he likened that appeal to the jury to a sermon, but I'm told he had the credentials. Others regarded him as very religious, and he attended church regularly. I later noticed the pad on my left shoulder was damp. He hadn't embraced me for more than twenty or so seconds, but he certainly shed enough tears of joy.

District Attorney Fred Hudson didn't pursue the case against Ray Davidson because the State had no evidence that Ray Davidson had violated the law. It is certain to me that Ray Davidson knew that I was a most capable attorney, but somehow or another he could never quite grasp the gravity of this important case. He still envisioned me as that little country boy going to school and being taught by him, or simply it might have been that he was loyal to his family, who were my co-counsels, whom I recognized as very capable attorneys. Although I started as a mere local counsel, in the end I became the leading trial lawyer in this highly important case.

A good criminal lawyer serves a very good purpose in the society in cases like this when the State attempts to prosecute people who are not guilty of the crime with which the State has charged them.

The Case of Chicken Massey

The same year of the successful out come of the Ruby Barber case, I got into another case pushed by an overzealous district attorney which began by a telephone call from my distant cousin, Charlie English of Houston.

"Can you come to Houston immediately?" he asked. "I'm involved in a civil lawsuit and I may be in more serious trouble than I realized."

"Look," I said, "you should have hired me months ago so I could have prepared the case for trial. I've never gone into a case after it's already being tried by some other lawyer."

"You've got to do it this time because I'm in trouble. They're making a much stronger case against me."

I reluctantly got into my car and drove to Houston. When I got there I found this case against Mr. Massey and Charlie English. The two had made so many telephone calls to each other that it appeared that they might have conspired to steal loads and loads of broiler chickens out of Shelby County and ship them to Houston where the chickens were sold.

Chicken Massey didn't have any money and didn't intend to pay for the loads of chickens he'd contracted for and yet received money when he resold the chickens. Charlie English didn't get any of the money, which made him think he wasn't involved.

In Houston, I found the case being tried in Judge Sterling's court, in Federal Court, if you please. An opposing lawyer, from a large law firm involved in the case and I got to making jabbing remarks at each other, matching wits. The remarks entertained the judge so he allowed us to continue. Soon it developed that all parties involved had come from one little rural neck in an East Texas county. I stopped suddenly and turned to this very intelligent corporate lawyer, the short man I'd been matching wits with and said, "Isn't it a fact that you're also from Timpson, Texas, only fifteen miles from where all this is supposed to have occurred?"

He got up on his feet and he started talking and talking. There wasn't any defense, and he made an ass out of himself. We didn't settle down the court for thirty minutes because this struck everyone as being so funny.

We got English out, but we didn't get Massey out. However, he didn't care because he was what you call judgment proof. That is, he didn't have any property on which they could levy to collect the judgment.

The case didn't end, however, and I got so interested in the case, and had had so much fun that I pursued the case because I thought I could defend Massey successfully. A prominent man in Shelby County, Mr. Parker, who owned the Ford agency and the Coca Cola bottling company, in Shelby County decided to press criminal charges against Massey and had the grand jury indict Chicken Massey for theft of the chickens which had never been paid for. I didn't think the State could prove its case against Massey. The seller, Mr. Parker, had no market for his chickens and he had to sell them because the chickens would have become too old to sell. In addition, all the transactions took place at night.

Shelby County had been an economically depressed area and had decided to copy the chicken raising business in Arkansas. Big companies came to Shelby County, the bank financed them, then built hundreds of chicken houses where they raised broilers and laying hens. They had a brooder that hatched a million chickens a day. Sometimes the market fell out of the chicken business, and no buyer would take the broilers. So the producers would find a buyer who would pay below market prices and ship the live chickens. If they could get a price in Houston, they would ship the chickens to Houston. It was a kind of bootleg business.

Massey thought this could be easy money. He'd just buy some of these chickens and sell them below price. However, Massey didn't pay for the chickens when he picked up the trucks loaded with chickens. Mr. Parker was glad to move the chickens to get them off the costly feed. Massey took several truck loads of chickens to Houston, sold them and got the money in Houston. Massey didn't pay Mr. Parker. Mr. Parker wasn't out a lot because he had chickens that had very little value.

Massey was a very handsome man. He had dark eyes and hair, and an olive skin. He had only one leg which gave him further distinction.

Even though he could only pay me a small fee, I defended Chicken Massey against the charge of theft in a criminal case in Shelby County. The sheriff put Massey in jail, then switched him from jail to jail when I came to town so I couldn't talk with him.

Judge Sanders, who had been my good friend, acted as judge but in this case he sided with the people in the community because he had originally come from there. Wardlow Lane served as special prosecutor, and Dudley Davis served as district attorney and prosecutor. When the case came to trial, the courthouse filled with spectators.

Every day, the same women sat on the front row. One day when I left the courtroom, they called me over and said they'd always wanted to see some lawyer who could try a case better than Wardlow Lane, and they were seeing it. Wardlow Lane had just tried a case against the Attorney General's office in Washington, D.C. and the Washington lawyers said Lane was the best trial lawyer they'd ever gone up against.

We were having a lot of fun at this trial. Then I got bold.

Suddenly Lane put a man on the witness stand who wore two guns strapped to his belt that hung under his big belly that pooched way out in front of him. He was a big fat man, and a game warden who wasn't supposed to be a deputy sheriff enforcing the laws except in his only field of game laws. However, the sheriff had allowed this man to go with him to investigate the case because the law allowed the game warden to carry a gun. This man testified to some of the facts that were not very material to the case.

When he finished testifying, I asked, "Will you stand up, please?" He stood up. "Will you face the jury?" He turned toward the jury. Then I said, "Have a seat." You could see that he realized he looked ridiculous. He didn't like it at all. Sometimes you can make a witness look ridiculous and discount his testimony just because of his appearance.

Dudley Davis tried to condemn my client as an outright thief and he was doing a pretty good job of it. When I argued the case to the jury, I tried to overcome that. "Mr. Massey is a poor businessman trying to make a living," I argued. Then I looked around at Dudley Davis, the district attorney, and said, "Let's compare them. My client must be an angel compared to your district attorney. He'd do anything for a conviction. He moved my client so I couldn't see him." Everyone clapped. The people didn't like their district attorney either.

That evening when court adjourned, we walked across the street to a restaurant and here sat the game warden with as much hatred and contempt on his face as is possible. I realized then that I'd gone into a very hostile territory. I wondered how I could get out alive. There wasn't any way to fight a man that big.

After I finished my meal, which I hadn't especially enjoyed, I got up and walked out the front door, and sure enough, there stood the game warden waiting for me. He took a haymaker swing at me and he swung so hard I could hear the wind pass over my head when I ducked. About that time, Mr. Adams, a former sheriff of Shelby County who didn't like this game warden, came up from the side and hit him so hard that it staggered the game warden. He fell to the ground where he and Mr. Adams rolled around for a while. Mr. Adams beat the hell out of the game warden.

We went back to the courthouse waiting for the jury verdict to come. When Judge Sanders heard what had happened, I approached the bench and asked, "Judge Sanders, are you going to be judge in this court and hold this man in contempt or are you going to be a weak judge and lose all your dignity as a fair and impartial judge carrying out your duties?"

"Fred, what you say is true, but there is so much feeling in this community," Judge Sanders responded. "I'm not in a position to do what you ask."

The jury knew that Massey was not guilty but they still thought they had to come in with a guilty verdict. They were so convinced that they had to convict him that they gave him a short term in the penitentiary for two years and assessed a fine against Chicken Massey, but he didn't have any money. Even so, the community became very hostile to the jurors because the people thought members of the jury hadn't done the right thing. We won the case, as far as the feelings of the community were concerned.

Shortly after Massey's conviction, I obtained his parole, brought him to Carthage, and put him in business as a leather craftsman making boots, belts and other leather goods for western wear.

It has long been my personal credo to recognize that every citizen in need of legal defense deserves the help of a knowledgeable, caring attorney. I have observed in recent years, and my observation has been noted by many others in the legal profession, that lawyers who actually care about their clients, in the practice of law today, have dwindled in percentage from the time I began my practice so many years ago.

An innocent's seduction to drugs

Alton Stanford, Sr. got elected tax assessor-collector of Panola County during the year of 1943. He lived in the little town of Gary, located about ten miles south and west of Carthage. He had a very fine family, an attractive wife and two sons. His wife, it developed, had health problems. In order to ease her pain, the doctors in Carthage prescribed for her narcotics that might or might not become habit forming.

Within a very few years after this treatment got started, she became addicted to the medication that she was taking. Then, her addiction seemed to become the greatest of all her health problems.

Their oldest son, Alton Stanford, Jr., opened up a radio and television shop in Carthage where he sold radios and television sets and repaired them. It got to be a very fine business, but to everyone's consternation and surprise, he had for the past several years been taking some of the medication that had been prescribed for his mother. Then he became addicted.

He had a post office box next to a box used and rented by one of our high school teachers in Carthage. At times the postal clerk mixed up the mail and got it in the wrong box. This teacher's mail was accidently placed in Alton Stanford's box. By that time, the income he made from his business wasn't enough to support the drugs he was buying, which sometimes became very expensive.

When the teacher's bank statement got into Alton's box by mistake, he began to practice forging this teacher's name. He withdrew several hundred dollars from her bank account before he was caught and apprehended for violating the law in this respect. As a matter of fact, he had forged her name on three or four occasions. When the grand jury investigated the case, they indicted him on not one case, but on two or three cases of forgery to obtain money in this manner.

At that time, his family hired me to represent him. Luckily enough, when the case was first set for trial, we obtained a continuance. However, even though I might have successfully defended one case against him, such as getting a suspended sentence, the State would have called the next case for trial. It was hardly possible that I could save him doing time in the penitentiary for violation of the law in this respect.

The people in the community had very little sympathy for people who took dope at that time, even though Alton came from a good family and enjoyed a good reputation himself until all of this occurred. While he was out on bail and awaiting trial, he forged doctors' prescriptions, and went to Shreveport, or out of town, to have them filled, thereby obtaining the pain killers or narcotics of which he was in dire need.

Then one day I received a telephone call from Alton. He first said, "Would you like to know where I am?"

"No," I said, "but it could be very interesting."

"Well," he said, "I'm in jail in Shreveport, Louisiana, and I've been charged with possession of narcotics. The district attorney says that because of the other trouble I've been in, he is going to prosecute this case to the fullest."

Then he told me that he wanted out of jail. "Please, please, by all means, make my bond so that I can come home."

Can you imagine a person being placed in jail in the first place, and wanting to be released with the effects of narcotics dwindling. This situation is nothing less than hell on earth. "I'm not sure I want you home," I told Alton. "Just stay there until I can get there."

I immediately left the office, drove to Shreveport, some forty miles east of Carthage, and arranged to see Alton Stanford. I told him that this case might be the best thing that ever happened to him because in federal court they had a program whereby they would treat people by placing them in the hospital for a period of time, and that I wanted to talk with the district attorney to see if Alton could come under that type of program.

The district attorney was amenable. He was sympathetic, and told me that he would agree for my client to go to the hospital in Leavenworth, Kansas. Within a few days, Alton Stanford was on his way to the hospital under the care of a United States marshal.

In Carthage, in the state court, Stanford's cases were again called for trial. I felt pretty confident at that time, because my client was already in custody, the bonds would not be forfeited, and I would have a little more time in which to prepare my case for trial. As a matter of fact, if you can give a defense lawyer enough time, it is much easier to get an acquittal than it is if the case is tried immediately after the crime is committed.

The district attorney, Emmitt Wilburn of Carthage, knew this defendant and his family, and privately told me, "If there's any hope of rehabilitating Alton Stanford, I do believe that the best interest of society will be served; and not if he must actually serve time in the penitentiary."

I asked the district attorney in Carthage if he would let the cases remain on docket without being called for trial so long as the defendant behaved himself and was not guilty of any other violations of the law.

Alton Stanford did straighten up and violated no other laws. In the next several years, the cases against him were dismissed and he actually served no time in the penitentiary, other than the confinement and incarceration in the hospital in Kansas. The hospitalization, of course, benefitted him, and really saved his life. When he left to go there, we saw no end to what might have taken place when he was so heavily sedated with drugs. He often did not know what he was doing and acted as if he were totally out of touch with reality.

I was paid a small retainer's fee when I first accepted employment, but during the next few years, Alton had no cash money which he might use to pay his attorney's fees. We then mutually decided that he would convey to me his electric shop, and that had a sort of comical ending. What would a lawyer do with an electric shop that had very little property or inventory by way of liquidation?

We finally agreed that I would convey back to him this shop, which he ran and maintained for many years thereafter.

This case reminds me of the type of lawyers we often had at that time, who are unlike the lawyers of the present day. It never occurred to me that I might have been working without remuneration for many years, but I did do something for a human being who finally rehabilitated himself to the extent that he lived more or less a normal life. He was not a detriment to society after he was cured and gained control of himself and his actions.

Jake Leg Hudson

Jake Leg Hudson had a problem similar to Alton's, but Jake Leg's life took a completely different turn.

In the late 1930s, Carthage was in what we called a "dry" territory. It was unlawful to sell, consume, or be found with any form of intoxicating liquor on your person. It was a misdemeanor to violate the law in this respect.

Jake Leg Hudson, for some reason during Prohibition days, drank a certain kind of alcohol manufactured for medicinal purposes. The use of this alcohol caused the user to develop a certain type of paralysis. When he walked, his body jerked at each step and, eventually, this paralysis disabled him. This is how he got his name: Jake Leg Hudson.

In order to make a living, he engaged in selling liquor to his friends and to those in the community. He became a bootlegger. On occasion, the sheriff would catch him violating the law in this respect. Then Jake Leg would hire me to represent him. On all occasions, we were able to get an acquittal.

Finally, the sheriff's office gave up trying to convict Jake Leg. Instead, they had the Liquor Control Board out of Austin come in and handle this sort of case. The Board accepted the challenge. They came to Carthage and finally managed to buy liquor about seventy-five times from Jake Leg.

The ambitious county attorney filed the complaints and information and set aside one whole term of court to try this man on the many offenses he had been charged. It occurred to me that I might be able to get an outright acquittal or maybe persuade the jury to give him a very short term. But there were so many cases that Jake Leg Hudson and I decided that we might plead guilty on each charge provided we only received a ten-day jail sentence, without any money being assessed for punishment, for each conviction.

There were so many cases the amount of time he would have to spend in jail totaled almost one year. We made this trade-out with the county attorney and, with reluctance, we agreed to the terms. Jake Leg Hudson was incarcerated in jail to serve his term as punishment for the unlawful sale of liquor.

This came as a shock to the community when Jake Leg Hudson got taken off the streets of Carthage. Jake Leg's punishment would not have been so severe except that it prevented him from having available whiskey for his own use. When he was first placed in jail, some of his friends, without too much difficulty, brought him small bottles of liquor. They brought it as an act of friendship and compassion.

Finally, the sheriff and his deputies decided they would not tolerate this kind of conduct. They isolated Jake Leg in jail and forbade anyone to talk with him. I was allowed, as his lawyer, to see him. On one occasion, after this rule had been invoked, he said he had to have some liquor and would I please provide him with something he could use.

I happened to think that I had a small bottle of Cascade in my office at the time. Jake Leg said, "Necessity is the science of invention. I will take a heavy string and lower it down the side of the jailhouse. If you will tie on the bottle, I will ease it back up."

I decided, in a playful sort of way, that this would be fun. I did as he instructed. About two or three hours later, I happened to be in the courthouse in the sheriff's office. I heard loud voices coming from the sheriff and his deputy. They stopped using profanity long enough to say, "We know damn well it was impossible for him to have this liquor. No one has been in here."

They knew he was drinking liquor because he had a little left in the bottle and was just as drunk as Cooter Brown. I stopped for a minute and thought, how little I realized that what I had done, in a joking way, would cause such repercussions. I found it difficult not to break out in laughter. I decided this would not be a good time to take up any business in the sheriff's office. I retreated to my office and had a big laugh about what had taken place.

I didn't take Jake Leg any more liquor. He served the rest of his term without the use of intoxicants. But as soon as he got out of jail, he resumed his old way of life: selling whiskey and drinking his own profits.

Drinking the evidence

During the latter part of the 1930s, in the days of prohibition when I served as county attorney, we continuously tried to obtain convictions for people who had intoxicating liquor in their possession.

As a young lawyer during one trial, I was introducing evidence showing that the defendant had intoxicating liquor in his possession for the purposes of sale. During the lunch hour, we adjourned court from twelve to about one-thirty and when we returned to the courtroom the evidence, a quart of white lightening liquor, had disappeared.

We looked on the other side of the courtroom where we found Mr. Soape, who had found the liquor and drunk our evidence. When we found him, he lay in a state of intoxication. We found this so amusing that the court and jury got into the act with a big laugh. The judge dismissed the case and exonerated the defendant and Mr. Soape, who had enjoyed the benefit of the evidence.

These sorts of episodes kept us enjoying life while practicing law in a small community. Too frequently today, lawyers do not receive pleasure from serving their clients. The contemporary lawyer seems to work hardest at extracting money, in the way of fees, from his client.

Chapter Ten

Divorce East Texas Style

Lawyers involved in divorce cases today can strip a client of most of his life's savings. Too many times a man involved in divorce has three enemies: his own lawyer who may try to charge him $250 an hour whether or not the lawyer works; the judge who expects the lawyer to donate to the judge's political campaign with part of the proceeds the lawyer gets out of the case; and the opposing lawyer who has not so much interest in his client as he does in trying to prolong the case and run up his attorney's fees.

The practice of law, in the beginning of my career, I found so exciting that I looked forward to Monday morning so that I might become a part of the activities taking place in and out of the courtroom located in the center of the square in Carthage. It thrilled me even to get employed in a divorce case where the fee would not be more than twenty-five dollars.

In one such case, a gentleman by the name of Coleman, a black man who had many friends in Carthage, employed me to obtain a divorce from his wife. We filed suit for divorce by depositing five dollars court cost. After the case had been on file thirty days, we went before Judge T.O. Davis to obtain the noncontested divorce.

We had the defendant testify, give the date of the marriage, the date of separation and the grounds for divorce. We had alleged infidelity as grounds for divorce in the petition,and we were able to prove this by the witness testifying that he had left town early one morning to be gone for the balance of the day. For whatever reason, he didn't leave town, but returned to his residence where he found his wife in bed with another man.

This part of the testimony was rather quiet and solemn. I then asked Mr. Coleman to name the man who was wrecking his home. He thought for a minute, and said in a very low, base-tone voice, "It was our p-a-s-t-o-r," dragging the word across the courtroom.

T.O. Davis, a dignified judge, reminded me of Judge Attwell of Dallas who behaved so stiffly and sternly that he neither looked right nor left when he came into the courtroom. Judge Attwell always took his seat, and admonished and corrected all lawyers for their misconduct whether or not they had been guilty of misconduct.

When Judge T.O. Davis heard Mr. Coleman make the statement that the adulterer had been his *p-a-s-t-o-r*, Judge Davis lost all the dignity that he had been able to maintain and muster throughout his term of office. He broke down laughing. Mr. Coleman remained very quiet and solemn. He found nothing amusing about his situation. Judge Davis did grant the divorce.

The incompatible wife

Some thirty years later, in 1964, a gentleman came into my office to employ me as his lawyer to get a divorce from his wife to whom he had been married for more than fifteen years. I've eliminated the names of this couple since they are now happily married.

The parties to this marriage contract accumulated about sixty-five acres of land, a 1962 GMAC pickup, a 1964 Oldsmobile, a large amount of welding equipment situated on a Ford tractor, seventy head of cattle, and a savings account of five thousand dollars which was in the wife's possession.

This gentleman worked about twelve hours a day looking after his farm and holding down a forty-hour a week job he had in Longview in a trailer factory.

At that time you were unable to get a divorce based only on incompatibility, but had to show grounds for divorce. The grounds of cruel treatment covered a multitude of things.

We decided that the grounds for the divorce would be based on cruelty, and cruelty it was. The gentleman said that for many years prior to that date, his wife was engrossed in looking at television each evening before she retired for the night. She never came to his chambers prior to the time he had gone to sleep and that she had ceased being his wife. He no longer had any desire to live with her further as husband and wife.

We thought perhaps this could be a friendly case. As I filed suit for divorce, I mailed to the wife a waiver of citation for her to sign, eliminating the necessity of the sheriff's serving her with citation.

The next day after this waiver and letter were mailed to this lady, she came rushing into my office without allowing my secretary to announce her and advise me that I had someone whom I should see.

The lady's general appearance showed that she was in a wretched state of mind. She asked me immediately if there wasn't some way that she could save her marriage. I thought for a few minutes, and then slowly and carefully advised her what her good husband had told me two days prior thereto, when I was engaged to represent him in the divorce suit.

She listened very carefully, thanked me for my time, and made her departure just about as fast as she had when she entered the office some thirty minutes prior.

Early the next morning the husband came to my office and, without mincing many words, asked me if I would kindly drop the divorce proceedings. I knew then that the discussion I had had with his wife had taken effect.

At a cocktail party in my home a few nights later, I related to my friends what had taken place in one of my divorce cases. As I told the story, I omitted names of the persons involved. I ended the story by telling my friends that the woman had gone home and had literally screwed me out of my divorce fee.

Other rewards of saving a man's marriage

Immediately after World War II, Pat Patterson of Carthage increased the size of his insurance agency considerably. He probably wrote as much as one half of all the insurance that the different agencies in Carthage provided for their customers. He placed most of his insurance business with Traveler's Insurance Company.

A great many of my lawsuits, as they sometimes developed, were against Traveler's Insurance Company because Traveler's had an agent in Carthage who sold the most insurance. Actually, at one time, I had more than fifty insurance cases in my office, and far more than fifty percent of the cases were against Traveler's.

An insurance adjustor out of Longview would come to my office two, three, and sometimes four times each month to discuss settlement of the claims that I handled for my clients. A greater part of the time the personal injury cases were settled because the adjustor was able to evaluate his cases as far as the insurance company was concerned, and I certainly was capable of evaluating the claims I represented for clients. The evaluations were based on medical reports, the facts surrounding the accidents, or automobile collisions, and the extent or duration of injuries the person may have sustained.

With a concerted effort on each side, we settled more than ninety percent of the claims, either before suit was filed, or after the suit was filed. We reached out of court settlements approved by the trial judge with whom the cases were pending.

I give you this background information to try to relate a very important divorce case I handled for the adjustor out of Longview whom I had known for many years.

In the 1960s, this gentleman, the claims adjustor out of Longview, called me one evening and said that he had something very, very difficult to talk about with me. It appeared that he had domestic trouble and didn't want to tell me about it over the telephone, but would like to see me as soon as possible.

We set up an appointment early the following day. At the time he walked into my office, I hardly recognized him. He had lost sleep the night before, and his mind was in turmoil over the infidelity of his wife who had caused him to almost lose his mind and reasoning.

He told me that at first he had thought seriously about killing the man involved, but after thinking it over, he decided that I would be the lawyer whom he would select to represent him in filing suit for divorce. We discussed the case at length, and I had him to agree with me that he would not take any violent action toward anyone unless and until he had notified my office in order that I might reason with him and cause him not to do something that he would later regret.

I accepted employment to represent him in filing suit for divorce, but purposely delayed the filing of the suit so that I could more or less win his confidence and have him to consider the matter further before he decided definitely to end his marriage.

This case happened after the Kinsey Report had been published, when we came to realize and learn the percentage of people, both men and women, who had outside marital relations. I believe the Report showed at that time that almost thirty percent of the women had had extramarital relations.

Finally, after several consultations and discussions of the matter with him, he finally agreed with me that it might be to the benefit of his family, and of himself, if he could forgive and forget, and try to save his marriage. We discussed the fee he expected to pay me for the work that I had done. If I had charged by the hour, as lawyers do at this time, the total fee he would have owed me would have been far in excess of five thousand dollars.

I explained to him that the benefit that I had derived in working with and helping him would be my fee. I refused to accept any payment for the time that I had spent working to solve the many difficulties that he had to overcome and settle in his own mind.

About ten years after I had worked with this insurance adjustor, I was walking on the street in another Texas city when I saw the same gentleman walking toward me. A great smile came on his face. I believe that we spent two or three minutes shaking hands, because we each were very, very glad to see the other. He thanked me over and over for what I had done, and said it was by far the best thing that he could have done. He was rearing his family and he was very happy. He was a very happily married man.

I don't believe that every man can forgive and forget and resolve matters like this man did. If it is possible, as it is in so many instances, it is the best policy to follow.

At one time he asked me if there was anything that he could do for me. Of course, any request I made of him would not have caused him to be in conflict with the work that I was doing with his company. I thought of one thing that I would like to know: the number of cases, and the amount of money collected each year by each lawyer for their clients in lawsuits against insurance companies in the east Texas area, which comprised about forty counties going north as far as Texarkana, Texas.

He thought about this for a little while, and said that he could not think of anything that would be detrimental to his company if he gave me this information. The company, along with other companies, had completed a survey recently concerning the very question that I had asked.

He first asked me if I thought that I would be number one, the lawyer who had collected the greatest dollar amounts for clients. I told him that would be impossible because I had to compete with law firms, but that I would like to think that I would be maybe about ten from the top, or within the top ten.

When he told me that I ranked better than that, I said, "Then, would it be ninth?"

"No," he said, "it's better."

"Then, would it be eighth?"

Then we went on and on until I said, "One."

"By far you collected the greateds amount that insurance companies paid lawyers or law firms that represented people in insurance cases. You not only are number one, but you have collected three times as much as the lawyer next to you in settlements and litigations."

On different occasions, other lawyers and people asked me why I was able to make a great deal more money than other lawyers in the same vicinity of that part of East Texas. In replying, I tried to explain that I had gained the respect of insurance companies by taking them to court from time to time and blistering their asses, tearing them apart. This caused the companies to settle more often than they would have done if I'd have been the usual type of lawyer.

I had, at that time, two well-qualified secretaries who could take dictation about as fast as I talked. This fact enhanced my ability to handle a large number of cases.

It further occurred to me that my income was rather high because in almost every instance I represented clients on a contingency basis. I got paid out of the proceeds of the settlement, or judgment recovered, which averaged about one-third of the amount that they finally got out of their claim or lawsuit.

This may appear to be rather high to people who are not familiar with this type of practice. Remember, though, clients paid me knowing that if they did not recover any money, neither did I. I do not recall that I've ever had anyone whom I've represented complain about the fee that I received when I took the case on a contingency basis.

Many times my greatest victories occurred in criminal cases that never went to trial. In certain instances, I could show the county attorney that my client, who had never before this one-time violation broken the law, would never again commit a violation. I could save that client's reputation by persuading the county attorney to drop the case. In other instances, I won so many cases against insurance companies that they soon learned that they could save money simply by settling out of court in favor of my client. These victories demanded my greatest skills as a lawyer.

A lawyer's hidden worth

Even my relatives did not understand the skills I'd developed to assist my clients. A cousin of mine, Billy Whitaker, had appeared in a feature story published in the *Panola Watchman.* The article described him as one of the fine men of the area, that he had obtained his degree in agriculture at Texas A & M University, and had studied one year in England. He was an outstanding person.

However, the night before this article appeared, he had had a feud with his girlfriend, had picked up a fifth of vodka, and had drunk it all. Then he had gotten into his car, and proceeded to drive to Longview. On the way to Longview, two highway patrolmen noticed his car weaving from side to side. They stopped his car.

When he got out of the car, he wasn't about to be arrested. So he beat up these two highway patrolmen. Thankfully, they did not use their guns. They were finally able to subdue him, brought him into the courthouse and placed him in a cell to sleep off his drunk. At first, they placed him in a cell that had only a mattress for his own safety. They must have given him a match to light a cigarette, because the mattress caught on fire. The jail attendants put out the flame before Billy injured himself.

The article in the *Panola Watchman* announced that Billy had just received a job to work with the farmers in Upshire County. A short time after Billy's arrest occurred, he and his father, John Edward Whitaker, came into my office to retain me to represent Billy. The situation for Billy looked pretty bad. I knew that he could not retain his job if he were convicted of a felony or any other serious violation of the law.

At that time I had many friends. I talked with Fred Erisman, my old TCU classmate and now the district judge in Longview. I talked with Noble Crawford, sheriff of Longview. I preferred not to talk with the highway patrolmen because I felt sure they would not be very receptive. I explained to these officers of the court that this man's career would be wrecked completely. Billy had never violated the law before this time. He probably would not violate the law again.

I told them that it might be in the best interests of society if he were not prosecuted. I asked them to let the case stay on the docket for a while, not set it for trial, and to observe the conduct of this man. If they did agree with me, the case would not be continued. Billy Whitaker never again violated the law.

I charged John Edward Whitaker a fee of fifteen hundred dollars. About six months later, John Edward Whitaker came into my office. He suggested that my fee was excessive since the case was never tried. I found it difficult to get him to understand that the disposition of the case in this way was a far greater achievement on my part than to have tried the case, especially since there likely would have been a conviction of some kind.

It always made me sad when a client did not understand the hard work that a lawyer does. However, lawyers, like those professionals in the field of medicine, must at times set aside their personal feelings and focus on serving their clients.

Chapter Eleven

Rough Times Demand Tough Tactics

When I grew up in the Carthage area, people thought of me as a shy person. However, when I became a lawyer in Carthage and represented my clients in such a forceful manner, some thought of me as arrogant. One woman's response showed me this.

The woman from Carthage became involved in a railway crossing accident and received very severe injuries when a train hit the automobile in which she was traveling. After she had been in the Marshall hospital for several days, her husband decided he should contact me in Carthage to determine if I would take the case against the railroad company to collect damages for the injuries his wife had sustained.

When I finally went to see her in the hospital, about two or three weeks after she had been injured, she informed me about why she had hesitated in the first place to have her husband come see me to be employed as her attorney. She told me that, as a young girl, she had been in a civics class in Carthage when the teacher arranged for them to go to court. The children ranged in age from about twelve or fifteen years. They went to the courthouse and sat down in the back of the courtroom to hear a trial being conducted at that time. There she saw me as a lawyer for the first time. She mentioned that when she heard me on cross-examination she saw me as a forceful lawyer. Then, lo and behold, she heard the argument that I made to the jury and she decided that I must be a mean man to tromp on witnesses and conduct the trial as I did. She decided that this was the picture she had of me as a lawyer and she did not want me to represent her in this case, because I was a mean person.

Of course, she didn't realized that a lot of times we lawyers fought fire with fire. The other side in the litigation behaved in the same way, possibly not as forcefully as I did. However, my forcefulness resulted in my many successful outcomes.

The successes I had in these cases resulted so often that the insurance companies and railroad companies worked out settlements because they knew the results I had in other cases. Most of the cases I became involved with, from the time I gained this reputation, were settled out of court. This was better for the litigants and everyone concerned. In fact, I settled her case favorably out of court without the necessity of the case being tried.

Cleaning up my act

Another client, though, profoundly influenced my behavior. About thirty years ago, I represented a black man who was somewhat of a lay preacher. He had had an accident, a car accident between Carthage and Gary. Even though he was able to escape and get out of the car, all of his efforts prevented him from being able to pull his wife to safety because the car went up in flames almost immediately after the impact of his car with a truck going in the opposite direction.

I felt so touched by this gentleman, and tried to help him get through the grief that he suffered from this catastrophe. I do not recall the outcome of the civil matter, or the claim that I handled for him, but I do remember him so very often because of how much he influenced my life.

Prior to this time, I had gotten into the habit of using profanity to more or less reinforce a point in my ordinary conversation. One day he said something to me in a very quiet and tactful manner, and spoke to me as if I were a child who must approach his elders. He told me that he had noticed that I used a great deal of profanity, and that he wanted me to abstain from using the profanity.

I listened to him and I realized that even though I took the Lord's name in vain, I hadn't really meant to do so in my own heart. I had developed such an awful habit in my life, and in my speech, that my use of profanity had gotten to be a natural way of speaking.

I told him that from that day forward, I would stop using profanity. A few slips continue to occur from time to time, but I still try to control and abstain from such a habit.

I feel so indebted to this gentleman for calling my attention to this habit, and influencing me to make a very important decision in my life.

Lawyers face tough situations

Perhaps I fell into using profanity because I continually faced the many tough situations that most lawyers, particularly trial lawyers, must deal with every day. One case caused me to face the possibility of my own death.

Kelly Carter had married into the Williams family prior to World War II. On the death of Mr. Williams, in about 1945, his son employed me to probate the last will and testament made by Mr. Williams prior to his death.

The son, named executor in the will and duly qualified, took the oath of office, filed an inventory and appraisement, and took charge of the properties left by his deceased father. However, Mr. Williams' brother-in-law, Mr. Kelly Carter, did not recognize the fact that by provision of law, he and his wife, Mr. Williams' daughter, were not entitled to any of the properties until proper distribution was made at or before the closing of the estate.

The executor of the will, Mr. Williams' son, came to my office and related to me a very strange thing that had happened the night before when he observed Kelly Carter taking a large number of cattle, loading them on trucks and taking them to Fort Worth to be sold at auction.

We took necessary steps to correct this violation. I believe a criminal complaint may have been filed with the district attorney. The matter was then to go before the grand jury for investigation, for action to be taken by the grand jury, if they saw fit to indict for the theft of cattle. The theft of cattle is always considered a very serious offense, even today. In the early settlement of Texas, sometimes the death penalty was meted out by hanging even before the thief was placed on trial for the offense he may have committed.

Kelly Carter, for some reason, decided I was the sole cause of the trouble to which he had been subjected, and started from the very beginning making threats toward me as to what he might do if I continued to mistreat him, as he claimed I was doing.

This led up to an occasion that, as I worked in the trial of a case on the second floor of the old courthouse, a man by the name of Ocie Ross came to me and whispered that Kelly Carter was in the sheriff's office talking with a deputy sheriff named George. Mr. Ross had heard Kelly Carter say that when Fred Whitaker came out of the courthouse, he was going to shoot him and kill him there on the spot.

I began to take this a little more seriously than I had in the past, and asked a young assistant of mine if he would go to my office across the street and bring me my .38 Smith and Wesson.

When I left the courthouse, I placed this gun underneath my small attache case, so it would not be seen by anyone, even though I could hold the case in my left hand and the gun in my right hand underneath the case.

Sure enough, as I walked by the sheriff's office, Mr. George and Mr. Kelly stood close together waiting for me to make my exit from the courthouse. I walked on by, but stopped about thirty feet from the front door of the courthouse to see if they had nerve enough to carry out their threat.

I remained standing there for a couple of minutes, and the two men walked out slowly, and came toward me. Mr. George had his .44 caliber in a holster on his left side, hanging near his hipline. Mr. Kelly walked to his left where he could take the gun to do his dirty work.

When I stood and did not back up or say anything, they remained silent. For some reason, unknown to me to this day, I wanted them to make the first move. I even walked a few feet forward so that any move they made, I would kill them both immediately. They never made a move, and eventually turned around and walked back into the courthouse.

In all my life, I do not recall when, if ever, I started an offense, but I certainly thought that to run or to back away was an act of cowardice. The many times that I have thought about this ruckus, I have thanked the good Lord that nothing happened. I'm sure there would not have been any action taken against me if something had occurred, since there were a lot of witnesses who knew that I was simply acting in defense of my life. However, there is a difference in being brave and being a fool.

I do recall that I did not suffer any fear, but only felt apprehensive about what might occur. At the time, it did not occur to me that I might have prevented this confrontation, but I am glad that I didn't tuck my tail and run. I would have had deep regrets all the rest of my life if I had not done exactly as I did, facing what I know now could have been sudden death.

We finally won the case involved in the Williams' estate. Later distribution of the properties was delivered to the people named in the will, according to the terms stated in the last will and testament of Mr. Williams.

I certainly had the skills to protect myself, though. Robert Carswell of Carthage, a very dear and close friend of mine, had joined the Federal Bureau of Investigation in Washington. When he came back to Carthage on a visit from time to time, we would go to my farm two miles north of Carthage and practice target shooting.

Bob admitted to me that he had developed great skill in his profession in handling weapons. He seemed to be astounded that I could shoot as well, and, in most instances, a little better than he could after he had received the training and practice necessary for him and in his duties as a professional agent for the F.B.I.

At the time this case occurred, no doubt neither the deputy sheriff, nor Kelly Carter, knew about any skill that I had developed along the lines of defending myself. If they'd known, they might have reconsidered carrying out their threat.

In many ways, I came by my use of profanity and shooting skills honestly. Life in Carthage and in East Texas did not attract the faint of heart.

Little P.O.'s vocabulary

Even though law prevailed in East Texas before and during the oil boom days of the 1930s, people still carried guns and consumed life as if only the present day mattered. Little P. 0. Rowland, Jr.'s favorite word, "sonovabitch," probably said more about life in East Texa during these times than any other explanation.

Little P. 0. Rowland, Jr.'s father, P.O. Rowland, owned and operated the Hilltop Restaurant. The Hilltop Restaurant acted as a decoy, more or less, for P.O. Rowland, Sr. to use for a place to provide illegal intoxicants for a large number of people. At this time, Panola County was dry and the only source of whiskey came from the Hilltop Restaurant where they hid it underground. Little P.O. provided the most interesting asset in this restaurant and the P.O. Rowland family. Around the age of about three or four years old, he hung around the restaurant where people picked on him, and taught him to use four-letter words. Even though he hardly knew the meanings of the words they taught him, he could use them fluently.

Late one evening, a gentleman with a Louisiana license plate hurriedly drove into the parking area in front of the restaurant on Highway 79 going from Carthage to Shreveport, Louisiana. As the man walked into the restaurant, he sat beside little P.O. and, for some reason, he started picking on him, making little cute remarks. Little P.O. suddenly had all he wanted. He turned around and, in the most fluent curse words you have ever heard, called the gentleman everything in the world from a sonovabitch to a ....

The gentleman from Louisiana had just taken a few sips of coffee when little P.O. started with his onslaught. Of course the man couldn't fight this small kid sitting on a stool, so he took it for just a few seconds, then got off the stool, and ran to his car. You could hear the shrieking of tires on gravel for blocks as he made his departure back into the state of Louisiana.

Little P.O. was likable and had the mind of a more fully developed child twice his age. At Christmas, his parents arranged for him to receive a lot of gifts. They bought him a billy goat and a billy goat wagon, and many other attractive toys that any child would have been happy to receive.

When they called him downstairs to see the array of toys that had been laid out for him on Christmas morning, he came down half asleep, stood for a few minutes looking over the many attractive gifts that they had arranged, and suddenly said, "Is this all the sonovabitch brought me?"

He turned around and ascended the stairs to the consternation and surprise of his parents and members of his family.

No one ever knew whether little P.O. realized how funny and comical some of his actions appeared to others, but he always interested everyone who knew about him.

On one occasion, Johnny Brodie called the fire department to say that he had lost his little son, known also as Johnny Brodie.

Pretty soon, not only the fire department came to their residence, but people in Carthage arranged for a group of people on horses and in cars to go and look the countryside over, and find little Johnny Brodie.

P.O. Rowland and little P.O. Rowland joined the group ready to scour the countryside to find Johnny Brodie. Little P.O., squatting on the ground beside the house, raised his hand and said, "Look, fellows, I see the little sonovabitch under the house."

P.O. Rowland, Jr. finally grew up and became a very attractive man, respected by everyone, and one of the most outstanding businessmen in Carthage.

The man who loved to fight

Another Carthage character, Jack McDaniel, had been born and reared in Carthage. There would not be anything unusual about this person except that he loved to fight. He not only enjoyed defending himself in case of an altercation, but if someone else didn't start a fight, he would just simply start one himself. The fight always ended with him beating the hell out of the person with whom he had these fights.

I had an occasion to run into him in a service station just after I had served one term as county attorney. We talked about the peculiar trait that Jack had, and I told him that if I were ever in a gang fight, I would surely want him on my side because he could beat everyone up even if there were more than one or two people he was required to engage in the fight.

I decided at that time to try to advise with Jack McDaniel not to engage in this type of conduct. I reminded him of the fact that regardless of how tough, mean and capable anyone would be, there just always was someone a little bit tougher and meaner whom he might have to contend with at some time in the future.

Jack married a sweet young girl, and it appeared that he was going to reform, settle down and stop doing this sort of thing. A short time after his marriage, sure enough, he had another fight. This time he fought a man named Downing who lived in the small town of Gary, Texas, just ten miles south of Carthage.

Downing went to the sheriff's office in Carthage and talked with Sheriff Lorenzo Hunt, but Lorenzo Hunt advised the Downing fellow that what he should do is just kill Jack McDaniel because he always seemed to make trouble wherever he went.

Mr. Hunt gave Downing enough money to buy a box of shotgun shells, and Downing went back to the small town of Gary, seeking out Jack McDaniel so he could kill him with the gun that he had, a double barreled shotgun with both barrels loaded. When he located Jack, Downing walked up in front of him and killed him without any further warning or conversation.

A grand jury convened a short time afterward, and the district judge appointed Curtis Keeling, Herbert Keeling's brother who advised me on jury selections, as foreman of the grand jury. While the grand jury met in session, Mrs. McDaniel, wife of the deceased, came to my office and advised me that it was her understanding that Mr. Hunt had gone before the grand jury and had used his influence in getting Downing no-billed.

Mrs. McDaniel arranged to employ me as a private prosecutor in the case. During the lunch hour of that day, I contacted Curtis Keeling, foreman of the grand jury, and advised him of my employment, and that I certainly thought that the facts in the case warranted an indictment.

Keeling advised me that they had already voted on it and had, in fact, no-billed Downing. I told him that their vote should not be final, and they could vote again to see what might be done. Since I knew many of the men on the grand jury, I talked with other people privately and asked them to reconsider, which they did, and finally indicted Downing for the crime he had committed.

Then the case was set for trial. The defendant's attorney used as one of the defenses the reason for the defendant having had his gun with him at the time: he had been on the way to go squirrel hunting.
We then put on evidence to the effect that Downing, because of a very serious defect — he was blind in one eye — could see very little out of the other eye. We contended that his defense was absurd. It in no way explained the fact that he had the gun with him in the first place.

The defense had imposed the law of self-defense. They said that McDaniel was again attempting to start a fight, and that Downing shot him to save his own life, or prevent serious bodily harm.

The jury did not go for this defense, and the jury found Downing guilty of murder. They assessed the sentence, or punishment, at fifteen years in the penitentiary.

About ten years later, Downing came walking into my office. At first, it occurred to me he was coming to see me for the purpose of getting revenge for the vigorous prosecution that I had done. I actually had caused him to go to the penitentiary in the first place.

But first he smiled, and we shook hands. He said he was looking for a good lawyer to represent him in a workman's compensation case, and that he had seen my work and knew that I could do this job for him as well as or better than anyone else.

Oftentimes people hold a grudge against a lawyer who represents the adverse side of a controversy. In many instances, such as this, however, the parties seem to forgive and forget, and only have an interest in employing a lawyer whom they feel will do a good job in representing them, whether in criminal or civil matters.

Few people in East Texas knew how hard I worked to win cases for my clients. I cultivated every relationship available to me. For example, that effort allowed me to approach Curtis Keeling at the beginning of the McDaniel case and ask him to persuade the grand jury to indict Mr. Downing.

Tailoring my jury selections

Curtis and Herbert Keeling lived in the Jumbo, or Dotson, community where Herbert, as you remember from Chapter Five, ran a country store, sold goods to the farmers on credit and then in the fall, when they sold their crops, they repaid him. He extended credit to most of his customers. The Keeling brothers and I formed a very close friendship after I recovered Herbert Keeling's three hundred dollars owed by the school teacher who left town and refused to pay his overdue rent.

One time Herbert Keeling offered his opinion about a certain potential juror in a case I was trying. His advice proved helpful and so it began that when I had to select a jury, especially in a murder case, I would call him and ask him to review the jury list with me. He would come by my office even though he had to make a fifteen mile ride in an old model Ford.

I'd review the jury list with him and ask him questions about the people in his community. He'd say, "Don't take this man, but you can take this man." After two or three years of doing this, he finally said, "I can't tell you about this man until I talk to him."

"You'd better be careful when you talk to him," I cautioned Herbert. "You might disqualify him. You sure don't want to offer him anything because you will violate the law and get in trouble. I'd be terribly embarrassed. Promise me you won't ever do that."

But I discovered he would talk with the person, even talk about the case. There is no law that will prevent a person from doing this, but it's not a good practice. From the information he gave me, I'd select my jury. When I saw how effective this was, I got myself a key man in Deadwood, then in all the various communities. When I had a very important case, I'd work this method well. My best man, Sam LaGrone, told me one day, "To get friendly with these people and get them to commit to me what they'll do, I need to entertain them."

"You can entertain them," I said, "but I'm not going to entertain them. I'm not going to have anything to do with that. You'll do that without my knowledge or consent."

Sam LaGrone would buy a case of beer and put the beer on ice the Saturday before the case was to be tried on Monday, and he'd give persons on the jury list a drink and talk with them. Then he would let me know who to select and who to cut. Soon I had such a following as a successful lawyer in the community, I could hardly do anything wrong. I won almost all my cases. The other lawyers seemed too lazy, or at least not enterprising enough, to go to the trouble to learn what potential jurors might or might not do, if selected on a jury.

I established my legal reputation in Carthage by the time I reached my late twenties.

A friend, Sydney Roe, said, "Fred, by the time you're forty years old and gray around the temple you're going to have a good law practice. You're going to be very capable with all that experience."

I looked at him, and I said, "Sydney, how about right now? I'm not going to wait that long. I'm going to work hard, build up my practice and not wait until I've got one foot in the grave before I'm a success in life."

The success and accomplishment I achieved resulted in a tremendous enjoyment and self-satisfaction. One day I jokingly said to a Carthage friend, Herman Soape, that people sometimes referred to successful lawyers as sonsovbitches because these lawyers stepped on a lot of toes and made lots of enemies, and created controversies in small communities where only litigants opposed each other. A large numbrer of the citizens took sides in these controversies since everyone knew everyone else's business.

I told Herman that since I was going to be called a sonovabitch, I just as well be called a rich sonovabitch. Herman Soape never let me forget this story even though I said it in a joking way. Little did I know that I had foretold my own future.

Chapter Twelve

Honky-Tonk Oil Boom Days

The East Texas oil boom, which started in about 1930 when Dad Joiner discovered the tremendous East Texas Field about ten miles west of Henderson in Rusk County, Texas, added to our rough and tumble way of life. Within a very short time after the oil field discovery, large numbers of people in all walks of life came to East Texas to reap the benefit of the newly discovered black gold.

This oil field produced more oil than people could sell or dispose of. As a matter of fact, at one time the lack of market shut down the entire field. When the Texas Railroad Commission, that regulates the oil industry, limited production, the producers would not always comply with the regulations ordered by the Railroad Commission.

Producers would do anything to get as much as ten cents per barrel for oil. Producers used one method, hiring oil trucks to load in the field during the night, to get around the oil regulations. Trucks would start traveling east to an oil refinery in Shreveport, Louisiana that would pay as much as ten cents per barrel.

It was not difficult for these trucks to get out of Rusk County because none of the law enforcement officers had any desire to enforce the law.

But as they came into our county, I thought we should try to prevent this sort of thing from happening. A member of the Railroad Commission, Mr. Stanley, and myself, with one of the deputy sheriffs in the county, would proceed by automobile, stop the trucks, make an arrest, and prepare the case for trial at a later date. When we started stopping the trucks from going through our county on their way to Louisiana, a gentleman by the name of Jesse Rains approached me and said that he thought I would have a golden opportunity to make a lot of money, so much that I'd never have to work again in my life.

He suggested that I come over to the oil field near Kilgore where I would receive cash as long as I agreed to desist from enforcing the law as the trucks proceeded on through Panola County. I could just imagine how I would have felt if I had taken part in this scheme. Great wealth is always attractive. But if you have to get it by devious means, it becomes worthless. I could have charged Jesse Rains with attempted bribery, but I had known him for many years, and thought he didn't realize that he might be violating the law by attempting to influence me in this manner.

The trucks kept coming through Panola County. At that time we had few paved highways, and the trucks traveled on dirt roads trying to avoid the officers. It is hard to describe how more or less one hundred trucks, traveling at a rapid rate of speed, could raise so much sand and dust that layers of dirt settled on houses and clothes throughout the county. This continued for months because we could only arrest a few truckers each night.

Angus Wynne, one of the most prominent lawyers in Texas, lived in Longview at that time. He advised me later about the main reason he had moved his offices to Longview: he had been placed on retainer fees by a lot of the hot oil runners. Any illegal oil was called "hot oil," whether or not it was taken during the night or day.

It might be interesting to note that the term *spot market* used today had its origin at this time. The term *spot market* derived from oil truckers who would drive by wells producing illegal oil, and buy oil "on the spot," or at the wellhead. Then the truckers would proceed to make the delivery.

Few people knew the economics and business of oil production; the producers, the truck lines, and the men who worked on the oil rigs and built the pipelines. Their glorified social life interested everyone.

The highway leading from Henderson to Kilgore and on to Longview had been built overnight. Temporary shacks and houses appeared over-night along the highway and operated as honky-tonks. The buildings had sheet iron tops, sides covered with black tar paper, very little if any foundation, and dirt floors unless the owner found some sawdust to cover the floor. A solid mass of these buildings, hundreds and hundreds of them, lined the roads. These illicit businesses sold beer, wine and other intoxicants. They always had the girls present to entertain the men looking for a good time. People would go from place to place, watching the floor shows of women who danced topless or completely nude.

Sometimes these places had card tables set up where the men played cards and played poker. At other times men placed a board on the floor where they played dice games. Most of the players drank too much and would become belligerent before the evening ended. Then a fist fight would break out and everyone in the place would get into the fight.

A man from Longbranch, Texas approached the lawyer, B. Baker, and myself to come to a place he had discovered about six or eight miles west of Henderson on the highway between Henderson and Tyler. Out of curiosity, we accepted his invitation, and met him at this particular honky-tonk, a tar paper sided building with a tin roof. He was sitting at the table waiting for us when we came in.

"Just you wait," he said, "I'm going to show you the most beautiful girl you've ever seen."

This particular honky-tonk had a small section in the same room set aside as a kitchen where they prepared hot dogs and short orders. A couple of good carpenters could have built this building in one or two days.

A short time later, the woman came out on the dirt floor and did a slow-type dance without music. She stood on her head; and she didn't have on any clothes. We had to admit one thing to this friend from Longbranch: she was very beautiful. We could tell that he was sweet on this girl. We stayed around and, after we had a couple of beers, we departed. We had come in the middle of the afternoon, but the activities continued into the night when two men usually played the guitar and fiddle.

Later, we learned that this man, who had invited us to this high class place of entertainment, had lost his mind over this particular woman. It seems strange to me a person could actually lose his mind over such a relationship, but he actually did. Reputedly, this man later took his own life over this woman.

One particular honky-tonk located near Henderson, Mattie's Ballroom, had an outstanding reputation. People of all walks of life came to this place each evening for entertainment. Even though the county was dry, law enforcement officers allowed Mattie's people to sell beer and other intoxicants.

The fifteen or more beautiful girls whom Mattie arranged to entertain the men who came to her place for an evening on the town provided the most appealing attraction about this place. For ten cents, a man could chose one of the girls to dance with him. As the evening grew warmer and more cheerful, the man could arrange to pay three dollars to Mattie and then choose one of the dancing girls, and go out to one of the cottages in the back of the main building. There they could enjoy the lovely intimacies of the girls with whom the man had been privileged to dance, paying ten cents each time they took the dance floor.

This kind of activity became such common practice that it was accepted by all the people in the vicinity, although it might not have been approved by the people of the Baptist faith.

A friend I'll call J.D. told me of one experience he had one evening. After having several drinks, he found an attractive girl to accompany him to his automobile for a little chat and smooching, as it was called in those days. For some reason, they climbed into the back seat of J.D.'s automobile. J.D. had learned previously that the man who had brought this girl to the place in the early part of the evening was rather jealous.

So as J.D. made love to his newly found friend, he would, from time to time, raise his head to look out the window to see if this man was making an approach. He did raise his head, but before he could notice if the man was there, the man drew back his right fist, and poked J.D. in the left eye. J.D. said that the passion that he had was subdued in one-half second. The party ended.

As the East Texas Oil Field developed, the people became settled, and Mattie's Ballroom moved from Henderson to Longview. Mattie changed the name of her club to the Palm Isle Club, with a lot of support from people searching for high class entertainment.

Mattie booked the big time bands out of New York, such as Jan Garber, Tommy Dorsey, Glen Miller. They all came under protest, but since their agents required them to go where they were booked, they had no choice.

The Palm Isle Club looked like an old barn, a very large old barn, where people of all walks of life danced to the tunes of the big bands. It couldn't have happened anywhere in the world except the East Texas Oil Fields.

This place operates even today. On Wednesday afternoon each week the wonderful people from all over this area of Texas come to the Palm Isle Club for a bottle of beer and to get acquainted with the nurses, school teachers, and others of all walks of life. The hotels and tourist courts throughout the area remain well-booked, and it is impossible for a stranger to come into this area and get a room for the late afternoon or night on Wednesday of each week. People use the terms, nurses and school teachers, with respect and in an attractive way. As Will Rogers said, "Nurses and school teachers are good dates the world over."

The BOOM that shook Carthage

Three or four years later, Norman Kinsey assembled a large block of oil and gas leases in and around Carthage and later drilled a well known as the Jordan No. 1 well, located on Highway 79 going to Henderson, some one or two miles west of Carthage.

They drilled into a section of about sixty-three hundred feet, known as the Petit Formation.

Oil well workers, or crew, cemented, or set, the production pipe and waited about thirty or forty hours for the cement to set. They then perforated the well; that is, they shot holes in the pipe to allow hydrocarbons to come to the surface and empty into the slush pit. They connected a two-and-a-half-inch pipe to the well head and extended it about seventy-five feet into the slush pit. A valve was opened which allowed the high pressure gas to flow into the pit where it was ignited. The gas explosion reverberated for miles around, breaking windows and lights in Carthage. All hell broke loose.

The slow, sleepy town of Carthage changed overnight. Lease hounds with maps in one hand and cash in the other rushed from place to place trying to locate landowners who had not previously leased their land. Everyone wanted to get into the act of enjoying tremendous wealth in the oil and gas boom that shook Carthage.

Before I knew anything about the oil business, I leased to Union Producing Company, now Pennzoil of Houston, a one hundred-acre lease for five dollars an acre. Little did I know at the time that I had leased this land in the Petit Formation and in the Cotton Valley Formation which would produce future income of about ten million dollars..

We simply did not know what we were doing, but the oil companies knew what they were doing. The different oil companies leased a large portion of the county at a price of five to ten dollars per acre. The oil companies had met and agreed no company would pay more than ten dollars an acre. Farmers and landowners had no way of bargaining. Land owners signed leases on the usual 88 Form Lease, a simplified lease with no provision for pooling acreage with other acreage.

In 1942, the cost of drilling and completing a well averaged about $75,000 for one well. A great deal of controversy arose between the lessee and the lessor, the lessor being the operator of the properties. A well-known Carthage law firm, Long and Strong, had an abstract office connected to their own law offices and did about ninety percent of the title work for all of the oil companies operating in the Carthage gas field.

Landsmen working for the oil companies contacted hundreds and hundreds of landowners and prevailed upon them to sign a pooling agreement supplementing the old lease agreement they had entered into when the land had been leased many months prior to this. Oil companies placed the law firm Long and Strong on retainer's fee to represent all the oil companies and to help them advise and prevail upon the landowners to sign pooling agreements without any consideration whatsoever. Oil companies had prevailed upon the Railroad Commission to pass an order that one well would drain the entire acreage of six hundred and forty acres. This allowed the oil operator to tie up a landowner's property for years and drill only one well on six hundred forty acres of land. The landowner who had pooled his land received less or a reduced royalty income from a producing well in the pooled acreage.

Even though I was not a prominent and well-known lawyer at the time, a number of oil companies contacted me and offered me a small retainer's fee to back them in letting the landowners know that it would be to their advantage to sign this pooling agreement. It became quite obvious to me that it would not be to the advantage of the landowner, but would enable the oil companies to work a tremendous fraud on the mineral owners in a large part of Panola County.

At this time I decided not to take employment from any oil company and, instead, would represent the underdog, the landowners throughout the county. This was probably the best decision I ever made in the practice of law.

Even though I could not have prevented most of the landowners from coming under the influence of oil producers who encouraged them to sign pooling agreements that worked to their detriment, a few landowners did confer with me about whether they should supplement their original lease agreement.

I simply told them that I would never sign a new lease form, or any agreement to change it, from the terms and conditions of the lease form that I had signed previously unless the oil producer paid me a reasonable amount for doing so. In my opinion, signing a pooling agreement was tantamount to leasing your land all over again because the operators of leases would not drill more than one well on a total of six hundred and forty acres. Union Producing Company, now Pennzoil, held a large percentage of the leases.

As time went on, I began to understand the values of oil properties, such as the royalty left to the landowner, a royalty which usually amounted to one-eighth of all the oil and gas produced. I had not built up a large law practice at this time and people looked upon me as being rather young, and sometimes thought I did not know what I was doing. However, I got my friends and relatives who owned land surrounding my land two miles north of Carthage to hold out with me and not sign new lease agreements, or pooling agreements without reasonable remunerations.

My effort to persuade others took place over a period of more than one year and I had to visit about fifteen people to reassure them that we were doing the right thing since Long and Strong, as well as others, were putting the fear of God into them, saying if landowners did not sign these agreements they would never get a well drilled on their property.

One of the active landsmen, Mr. Fitzgerald, worked out of Shreveport where Union Producing Company kept their home office. He said that he wanted to talk with me personally and suggested that I come to Shreveport for a discussion on this matter with his people. He said he felt sure they would make me a proposition that I could not refuse. I refused to go and talk with him privately.

For the next several years different landowners and people who had lost their land or mineral rights to other people, retained me to represent them. I accepted employment on a percentage of the land or minerals which I recovered for my clients.

In this way I amassed a great deal of royalty, or minerals rights. Then, too, I occasionally made small royalty, or lease, purchases. It never occurred to me that I might borrow money and make large purchases, so I only invested as my resources enabled me to do so. To this day I receive a check each month from more than one hundred and seventy-five wells in Panola County for royalty. A large number of the checks are very small, but the total amounts to a far greater income than the average income lawyers realize in their law practices.

In about 1950, I became acquainted with J.C. Trahan of Shreveport, Louisiana. At the time we became acquainted, he worked as a salesman for Mid-Continent Supply Company, owned by the Davis family of Fort Worth, selling oil supplies to local oil and gas operators. Mid-Continent headquartered in Fort Worth and manufactured and distributed oil and gas supplies.

Mr. Trahan, a very ambitious man, told me that he planned to get into the oil business and make a lot of money. Without any money at all, he had rented a drilling rig and drilled one well at a time to a depth of about fifteen hundred feet near Oil City, Louisiana. His drilling and completion costs totaled about fifteen thousand dollars.

He got into the flush production too, and, in only sixty days, sold enough oil to pay almost half the amount it had cost him to drill and produce these wells. Then the production would settle down to about two barrels of oil per day at a price of about three dollars and fifty cents per barrel. It took a long period of time to pay the balance of the initial cost before he realized any profits. This, of course, was not good economics, but it did enable him to make certain contacts and to learn something about the oil business.

He called me on a Sunday morning and asked me if I would come to Shreveport and to the location about fifteen miles from Shreveport to see this wonderful well he had flowing. I met him and I liked what I saw. The oil flowed into a tank and as it flowed it took on a dark green color. Mr. Trahan turned to me and said, "Somehow it catches your attention, doesn't it?"

I decided then and there that I would put up my part of the money and take one-half interest in the next few wells that he drilled in this manner. I then had the money to do this on income I received from my law practice. I learned a hell of a lot about the oil business. I did not make money on this endeavor, but I did break even.

By this time J.C. Trahan had bought two or three drilling rigs on credit and had started drilling Petit Wells in Panola County at a depth of about sixty-five hundred feet. At that time I did his title work and later put together deals for him to drill.

When he billed me for my part of the cost, he often times billed me for "lease cost," though I knew that the lease had cost nothing because we had received it on a farm-out agreement. The bills I received had been padded to the high heavens but, again, I learned a lot about the oil business even though I paid dearly for the experience.

By this time J.C. Trahan, now known as Trahan Drilling Company, began promoting a lot of money out of New York and began drilling a large number of wells both in the Carthage field and in various places in Louisiana. It occurred to me that I might also get investors, and might drill in my name some of the inside locations in the Carthage Gas Field.

I went to New York with this in mind and visited some of the bankers and anyone who would talk with me. I came back emptyhanded; no one showed the slightest interest in making investments with me. It is not easy to promote money, even though people with large incomes pay a greater portion of their incomes in income tax. The oil business, at that time, allowed them to invest mainly at the cost of the government or as a means of reducing the investor's tax liability.

The cost of drilling and completion of a well for income tax purposes would show a loss of about seventy percent of the amount invested. If the well should be dry, or a failure, the investor deducted one hundred percent from the total liabilities; that is, the total amount of taxes that he might pay. This provided a real incentive for investors. To find investors, though, I had to make contact with people of tremendous wealth and income.

The case of the stolen truck

While I searched for oil investors, I continued my law practice to earn income I might invest myself.

On a Saturday morning in about 1954, a young gentleman came into my office and, before I saw him sitting in my reception room, I heard him weeping. When we met, he could hardly talk, and then he began to relate to me his trouble.

He had bought a pickup truck from Panola Motor Company in

Carthage about two months prior to that time. He had taken it back for a checkup before his second payment was due and, when he had gone to retrieve it, it was gone. The dealer told him that the truck had been foreclosed. This he simply could not believe. I found it difficult to believe that anything so dastardly could happen.

Ross Hopkins, who owned the automobile agency, served as mayor of Carthage, and he had also gone into the finance business so that he could finance most of the automobiles that he sold. I'm sure that from time to time some customers had delinquent payments, but Mr. Hopkins decided that this would not become one of his problems. He went to Port Arthur, Texas and found a tough character, a man of Italian descent, whom I shall call Alfredo Guiscardi. He had a reputation for keeping past-due payments to a minimum. The appearance of this man reminded me of the mafia, and he behaved just as tough in his business dealings.

Mr. Guiscardi told me by telephone that he had, as a matter of fact, foreclosed on my client's truck because he had found out that the truck owner was being transferred to Illinois to follow a pipeline contractor. This surprised me, so I made every effort to adjust this matter by saying that we would make the last five payments in advance, showing our good intentions to pay for this truck. He said he did not want to go to the trouble of maybe, just maybe, having to foreclose on this truck at a far distance, then having to recover it and return it to his principal place of business in Carthage.

I couldn't believe what he was telling me; I asked him to repeat it and he did several times. He said, "If you don't believe what I'm telling you and what I can do, why don't you just sue me?"

After he told me about the third time to sue him, I asked him how long he would be in the office. He said he would be there until about five o'clock.

I called the district clerk's office, which opened on Saturdays at that time, and they said they would wait long enough for me to file my petition and get out service. I hurriedly dictated my petition, showing that the property had not been foreclosed at all, but had actually been stolen from my client. We asked for punitive damages. It occurred to me that this dealership carried on this type of business without the knowledge of Ford Motor Company.

I made Ford Motor Company a party-defendant, and instructed the sheriff in Michigan to serve the president of Ford Motor Company, with this citation. So we had three corporations and two individuals as defendants: Panola Motor Company, Carthage Finance Company, and Ford Motor Company, Ross Hopkins, and Alfredo Guiscardi.

As we started fighting in court, my client felt somewhat relieved, went on with his work and depended on his lawyer to rectify a great injustice that had been done to him. I interviewed his fellow workers and they said that during work breaks, the truck owner would go out to his truck, take a cloth and wipe off the dust. He was only nineteen years old and loved this truck as though it were a new toy.

The entire community of Carthage and Panola County became interested in this case. When we read the pleadings to the court and the jury, the courtroom filled to capacity because people found it difficult to believe that the most prominent man in Carthage could be sued in any event no matter what he might have done.

The entire Panola County Bar Association turned against me and against us. They provided a lawyer, Neil Powers, Jr., to show during the trial of the case that no wrongful acts had been committed and to make sure we walked away from the courtroom bowing our heads in shame and defeat.

A great deal of property was not involved in this lawsuit, but the moral principle involved overwhelmed me. My fee, of course, was very small, but I have never wanted to win a lawsuit as much as I wanted to win this one case, even though the amount of only ten thousand dollars was involved. This included the exemplary damages.

The judge trying this case had difficulty maintaining decorum. Feelings ran high. We provided testimony by placing the defendants on the witness stand under the adverse witness rule to make our case. Here we learned that Mr. Guiscardi had not only taken the truck, but had sold it to a man named Gulley, who became an innocent purchaser in another part of the county. Guiscardi and Hopkins were not in a position to deliver this truck back to my client, something they had not made known to us from the beginning of our negotiations.

We placed the bookkeeper, or accountant, in the office of the finance company on the witness stand to testify as to the amount of the indebtedness represented by a note and mortgage. The records showed the entire transaction from the time my client bought the truck until a few months before the trial began. The bookkeeper testified that the finance company required payments every twenty-one days instead of the usually thirty days, but she had no evidence to support this contention.

Mr. Guiscardi claimed that the finance company had other contracts and other installment notes that required payment every twenty-one days instead of the usual thirty days. In order for the jury to have benefit of other contracts, the court instructed Mr. Guiscardi to locate some of these contracts during lunch hour and have them in court so that he could testify to the names of the makers of each note, showing that it wasn't unusual to have payments due every twenty-one days instead of thirty days apart.

After lunch when Mr. Guiscardi took the witness stand, we asked him if he had searched his records and if he would give us the names of the people who had this type of contract. As we suspected, he had no such agreements in his office. I next asked one question: whether he wanted the jury to believe his first testimony or the testimony he was giving now: that he had no contracts that required payments every twenty-one days.

In courtroom strategy, we oftentimes paused for two or three minutes after asking this type of question. Without exception, the witness always broke out in a sweat. Beads of perspiration came to his forehead, to his face, and his eyes focused down toward the floor. These hardened people, who had falsified all their lives, could not hold face on such cross-examination.

My client had the appearance that could have almost won his lawsuit without his having to testify. He looked like a typical American boy with clean, wholesome habits, and an ambition to live a good life as our country makes available.

Mr. Hopkins, though, could not stand the heat of my interrogation. Oftentimes he would rise from the witness stand with his fist clinched and start toward me. Through my training, I met this in such a way that he appeared to make an ass of himself.

"Why don't you come on and do what you're threatening to do," I challenged him. "Or are you yellow, just as yellow as when you stole this man's truck?"

He would relax, get back to the witness chair, and then I would pound him again with other questions that he did not want to face.

Mr. Hopkins wasn't the only person making threats to me. Their strongarm man rose and took steps in my direction. I turned on him and suggested, "Why don't you come on and carry out your threats? Are you yellow? A coward?"

In my summation to the jury, I told them that I found it difficult to argue this case before them because nothing of this sort had ever happened in this land. I tried to think of one event that could be similar to this. What if they invited a neighbor to come to their home to break bread but, after the bread had been served, the thanks given before the meal began, the hostess or host arose from his chair, took a few steps toward his guest, and drove a dagger in his back, killing him in cold blood.

I told the jury that if they allowed this sort of theft to happen, they would let the defendants get by with what amounted to cold blooded murder. I said that I had read stories describing such wrongful acts; I had seen television stories that set forth such plots, but no one imagined that such dastardly things occurred in our home town, our little town of Carthage, Texas. It couldn't happen, but it did.

This trial lasted more than two days. In the evening, on the second day of the trial, Carthage High School played a football game. I went to the game and, while there, a friend, Chick Pipes, came to me and told me that I had better be careful. One of the defendants in this case had told him that he hoped that I came to the game because when the game ended, he planned to whip my ass.

"Fred, I don't think you should dirty your hands fighting this man," Chick said. "Let me do the fighting for you."

"Stay out of the fight," I urged Chick. "If the man has a knife, you can intervene. Otherwise, I plan to meet him head-on and see if he can do what he threatens to do."

As this defendant came down the ramp, I met him. He took one swing at me and knocked off my hat when I ducked. I hit him one time but this didn't stop him. He reached into his pocket, took out a knife and, as he pulled the knife, I stepped back. Chick Pipes hit him and knocked him to the concrete floor and beat his head against the concrete.

Everyone tried to stop this fight, including myself because we did not want anyone to get killed or severely injured. The man did get hurt and someone took him to the hospital. The hospital soon released him, after the doctors examined him to make sure no severe or permanent injuries had occurred.

As the case resumed trial the following day, our tough man didn't look so tough. He had a few bandages and scratches, and a very black eye. I did not feel proud of myself. I had no ill feelings and had won the battle without doing anything to take credit for the results of the fight. It had to have affected the jury because they now saw what kind of people we dealt with.

The jury returned its verdict, giving us the cost of the truck. Of course, the truck could not be delivered to us because the dealership could not give us title. We asked ten thousand dollars punitive damages, but a gentleman on the jury, Mr. Tiller, told me that he cut down the amount somewhat because he thought the case might be reversed if I got a large amount of money for exemplary or punitive damages.

The end of the trial did not end the sequence of events instigated by the controversy, or trial. Herman Jacobs, president of the First National Bank in Carthage, refused to discount the paper for Carthage Finance Company. Mr. Jacobs told Ross Hopkins that he didn't want to do business with any man who would let Fred Whitaker make such an ass of him at a public tribunal in Panola County.

Ford Motor Company took the franchise from the owner of the agency in Carthage. Our victory almost, but not quite, compensated us for the wrongful act that had been perpetrated against us. During this time, I felt almost as much emotional distress as that of my client.

About five years after the trial, I got a call one day from Panola General Hospital saying that Ross Hopkins, the main defendant in this case, wanted to see me. I went to the hospital, got permission to go to his room, and found him dying. He told me he wanted to clarify one thing that had been on his conscience for the last several years. He had at one time hated me, and now he did not have any ill feelings for me. I had been right in representing my client.

He explained to me that before the case had been called for trial, he had been worth one million dollars. Now he lay dying with very little money because of his own wrongful acts. He said he had been influenced by the community to a certain extent; he had been advised by all the other lawyers who disliked Fred Whitaker to show me up. That had been impossible.

He shook my hand in a very weak way and told me that he had forgiven me, that he wished me well, and that he could die in peace. Mr. Hopkins, a diabetic, lost both his legs to amputation when the doctors tried to prolong his life.

Alfredo Guiscardi lost his job, of course, because the finance company had been ruined as a result of the lawsuit. He remained in Carthage for several months without a job. I announced my candidacy for Congress and none other than Mr. Guiscardi contributed to my campaign. He said he had such admiration for me; more admiration than for any man on earth. He hoped and prayed I would get elected to Congress, and then to President of the United States. I felt so complimented and happy that he felt this way.

Crime doesn't pay. I sincerely believe that a person such as Ross Hopkins, actually a good man, suffered so greatly that his immune system failed to function properly. Oftentimes early death occurs when the person suffers, worries a great deal, or develops a guilty conscience that stays until the person passes to the world beyond.

I lost my bid for Congress, but I didn't lose my quest to become an oil and gas operator.

Chapter Thirteen

The Search for Oil
and Visions of Wealth

Needless to say, I had a lot to learn when I first started drilling wells in East Texas. Even though I carried a heavy, or extensive, law practice, I found time to purchase oil and gas leases either at night or on weekends when my law practice didn't consume all my time.

I would drill a well, complete it and, before selling the oil, obtain a tender from the Railroad Commission to sell the oil. With one or two secretaries, I managed to continue my law practice and pursue my oil business.

During this time, around 1955, I met Eddy Scurlock. He had been born and reared in the small town of Tenaha, in East Texas near Carthage, where he had lived in a shotgun house in simple circumstances. When, in his twenties, a storm blew away his home, he told me that this seemed to be a good time for him to make a move. He moved to Houston where he formed, or organized, a truckline to move oil for others or oil he had purchased himself for resale. You could see his truckline signs on public roads and highways, Scurlock Oil Company, throughout the oil belt.

The first oil I produced as an operator I sold to Scurlock Oil Company.

We had to prepare the division order, that is, what each investor or royalty owner would be paid and in what amount; the royalty owners usually held a one-eighth interest. It was customary for the purchaser of oil to receive a title opinion, but Eddy Scurlock dispensed, or waived, that requirement and allowed me to write him a letter setting forth the manner and amount in which each owner would be paid.

I first called Eddy Scurlock by telephone to determine what his requirement might be, and he told me that I would not be required to do anything other than write him a letter directing the payments to be made according to the interest owned by the different owners in each well to be produced.

This saved a hell of a lot of trouble and expense. But I've often wondered why Eddy Scurlock had so much confidence in me as an individual to make payments under my direction in this manner. If he had not made appropriate payments under my direction, he could have been personally liable for any wrongful disbursement.

Several years after I begin selling oil to Eddy Scurlock, I visited with him in his palatial home in River Oaks, Houston. We discussed our backgrounds in East Texas, and I asked him how he felt living in such luxury, having come from such a humble and simple background. He could only reply with a great deal of humility that it was wonderful, but the wealth had never changed him as an individual. He had always been a religious person and continued throughout his lifetime to actively work in the church to which he belonged, paying, I'm sure, ten percent of all his vast earnings to the church, his tithe. Eddy was elected to the board of directors of the Texas Commerce Bank, then the largest bank in Houston. He belonged to the Houston Club.

When I would arrive in Houston, to either attend to legal matters or on oil and gas work, Eddy had me to lunch at the Houston Club as his guest. In all my dealings, both in law and in the oil and gas business, I have never known anyone whom I admired more than Eddy Scurlock. He always remained such a wonderful person with a continuous smile on his face, enjoying life.

On one occasion, after we had worked together for a few years, he introduced me to his son-in-law, Jack Blanton, president of Scurlock Oil Company. My acquaintance and association with Jack Blanton has been as agreeable and enjoyable as it has been with Eddy Scurlock. There have never been gentlemen more entitled to the term, gentlemen, than Jack Blanton and Eddy Scurlock. They were capable, lovable, and successful. Their word was their bond. Friends and acquaintances greatly admired them.

A number of people in the northern and eastern parts of the United States developed a prejudice against Texas oil men, viewing them as braggadocios, loud and vociferous. I only wish that people who have been prejudiced against oil and gas operators could have known that only a few men caused this image to exist. The vast number of oil and gas operators remain great and admirable people. Eddy Scurlock and those of his company, Scurlock Oil Company, remain people with whom you would like to do business.

Washington discovers Carthage

As an oil and gas operator, I always made sure our dealings stayed within the laws as set by the federal and state governments. During the Roosevelt Administration, congress enacted laws to protect people from having fraud perpetrated upon them when they bought stocks, bonds and other securities through stockbrokers. During this time, the government created the Securities and Exchange Commission, located in Washington, D.C., to enforce any violations that might occur.

The sale of investments, or securities, included the sale of an interest in oil and gas properties to be drilled and developed. An oil and gas operator who promoted money had to either obtain authority to sell interest in an oil and gas property, or to be exempt so that he did not have to comply strictly with this provision of the law.

Mr. Tell White headed the Securities and Exchange Commission at the time I first drilled wells in East Texas and when various investors took an interest in this oil and gas operation. Strictly speaking, we might have been guilty of violating the Securities and Exchange requirements of selling securities without a permit to do so. We were all aware of this, of this law, and were at times apprehensive of the fact that we might be violating some of the rules and regulations that had been promulgated.

I felt somewhat relieved in reading various cases wherein it was shown without exception that persons prosecuted under this law usually committed not only the technical part of the law, but their actions, coupled with fraud, injured people protected under the law. We were certainly not committing acts of fraud, and so we felt somewhat relieved that we would never be accountable for any technical violations that we might have committed.

Even though I had corresponded with Tell White, I had never actually met him. On a quiet day in Carthage, my secretary announced that a Mr. Tell White was in my office to see me. At first, I thought my secretary had to be joking. Then it came as somewhat of a shock to have such a distinguished man out of Washington to be at my office in Carthage.

As he came in and introduced himself, with a big smile on his face, I realized that it was Mr. White in my office, but I wondered, just wondered, why he might be calling on me in Carthage. It was a relief and a surprise when he told me that he was from near Texarkana, Arkansas, which is about one hundred miles north of Carthage. Each year, he said, he spent his vacation on his peach farm in Arkansas. Since he had heard about and knew of my extensive oil and gas operations, he decided that he would drive to Carthage and visit with me.

He said the first thing he wanted to know was how I could get as many distinguished people to invest with me in oil and gas operations in the East Texas, or Arkla-gas area. At that time, our list of investors looked like Who's Who in America.

Tell White and I had lunch at Joe's Cafe in Carthage. Through the lunch hour and the visit we had in the office, which lasted three hours, I became so well acquainted with him that I told him that I had been fearful through the years that I might have violated laws that he might enforce.

When he left, he laughingly told me that he might have to protect me from being taken advantage of by some of the outstanding investors, such as Allen Kirby of New York who had invested with me. At that time, Kirby paid more income tax than any other individual in the United States. He owned control of the Allegheny Corporation, the largest holding company in the United States, whose holdings included the New York Central Railroad Company, banks and other properties. Tell White jokingly tried to tell me Kirby might be a shrewd person in the oil business, and I might need to be protected from Mr. Kirby under the laws that had been passed to protect the widows and the innocent people who might be buying securities.

Rewards found in Europe

My involvement with oil and gas investors of substantial worth had begun with a bar association meeting. One day, while reading the *Texas Law Journal,* I noticed that the American Bar Association had worked out an arrangement for members, after attending the annual meeting in New York, to go to London for a joint meeting of the American Bar Association and the lawyers, or solicitors and barristers, in London.

I thought to myself: this not only would be a wonderful trip, meeting the outstanding lawyers and judges throughout the nation and England, but might enable me to make contact with people interested in joining me in the drilling and development of oil and gas properties in my part of the world.

It appeared to me that it would be a hell of a good idea if I could spend two months in Europe making contacts and seeing a part of the world from which our ancestors came. As time grew nearer to my trip to New York, my wife, Dixie, decided to accompany me. We took a train to New York, registered in our hotel, The Plaza, and I set off to make a purchase at Sak's Fifth Avenue. I told the clerk that I had, in years past, had credit at the store, but did not know if I had an account now.

In a short time, a gentleman approached me and introduced himself as the credit manager of Sak's Fifth Avenue. I was a country boy. I told him my name, Fred Whitaker, a country lawyer from Carthage, Texas.

"Are you the same man," he asked, "who sold oil and gas properties to the DuPonts last month?"

It came to me as an overwhelming surprise that he knew something about a sale that J.C. Trahan and I had made for three million and three hundred thousand dollars to the DuPonts on some production we owned in Carthage. The credit manager said that this oil deal had appeared on the front page of the *New York Times* business section, and had appeared in a prominent place in the *Wall Street Journal.*

I then began to realize that I had received a little identity and publicity before I made the trip. He told me to simply charge anything I wanted in the store.

At that time, the money the DuPonts had invested was a great deal of money. It would have had to have been at least a hundred million dollars today to make the same impression that three million, three hundred thousand made. I left the store walking on air, thinking how lucky I would be if I could now actually make contacts to form a group of investors for the purpose of drilling and producing oil and gas properties in a successful manner for the investors and myself.

The next day, we signed in and obtained our badges at the Plaza Hotel, the headquarters hotel for the American Bar convention. That evening we attended a dance and an evening of entertainment arranged for us by the American Bar Association. Throughout the evening, different attorneys came to our table to discuss the large oil and gas deal I had just made before this convention started. How and in what manner other lawyers found out about this transaction, I will never know.

On the last day of the convention in New York, we visited the United Nations. After the meeting in New York, we boarded the Queen Elizabeth for our journey to London for the next meeting of the Bar Association. Our luggage was brought on board the ship and we proceeded to what would be our living quarter for the next few days.

Within twenty-four hours after we had left New York and said good-bye to the Statue of Liberty, we began to get acquainted with other lawyers and judges and their wives on board ship. Hundreds of lawyers, several circuit judges, United States district judges, and appellate judges from throughout the nation sailed with us to London.

We received engraved invitations to parties given by law firms, individuals and politicians. Among those we met were Mr. and Mrs. Maurice Koodish. Maurice would later play an important part in introducing me to oil investors. Each afternoon around five o'clock, others invited Dixie and myself to cocktails. Since this was an English ship, scotch became the preferred drink. I learned to drink scotch without drinking too much liquor by ordering a "scotch mist," crushed ice with a small amount of scotch sprayed on top. After the cocktail hour, the private parties began. Some evenings, we attended two or three different parties. The several-day trip became something of a continuous party.

Others on board came to know Dixie and me as Texans, and knew me as a lawyer who had traveled to other states and had a reputation as a successful lawyer. At the time, I loved to fight for the underdog, the underprivileged.

I realized during these several days that the wonderful eating and the few drinks I enjoyed would cause me to gain weight. In order to compensate for this, and to prevent myself from gaining too much weight,

I began walking, taking fast walks on the deck each day, and swimming for about one hour in the pool provided for us. I did gain a little weight, but I felt wonderful and refreshed which, I'm sure, came from a combination of the entertainment we enjoyed and breathing the fresh air from the sea, and basking under the sun.

We arrived in Southampton, England, on July 18, 1957. We kidded the English lawyers, asking them why they hadn't celebrated the Fourth of July. From Southampton we boarded a train to London. When we arrived, a tour guide met us and took us to the Park Lane Hotel where we had confirmed reservations. However, the hotel clerk informed us that there had been some mix-up and that, in fact, we did not have reservations. He referred us to another hotel, saying it would be attractive and well-located. We took a cab to the other hotel where we found the dirtiest hotel imaginable.

We took a cab back to the Park Lane Hotel and, during that short ride, I tried to think of what tactics I could pursue in order to get our rooms. I felt tempted to grab the clerk by the collar and give him a good shake, but I decided I might reach him by another method that I knew had oftentimes worked. I took a twenty dollar bill out of my wallet, shook hands with the clerk and asked him if he could somehow find us a room at the Park Lane. The twenty dollars got us a beautiful room where we enjoyed our stay in London before going on to Europe.

We next enjoyed a cocktail at the American Bar, then took a cab to the Savoy Hotel where we sat in the bar watching the British gather for cocktails. Before taking our train, a sleeper, to Glasgow, Scotland for the weekend, we stopped for dinner at a restaurant that catered to the theater crowd. After a scenic ride to Glasgow, we checked into the Hotel Central.

The bell captain immediately arranged a golf game for me that afternoon and the next afternoon on a municipal golf course. For the first time, I played golf where the game originated. I played with two young gentlemen who took great delight in showing me the difference in the way they played golf and the way we were accustomed to playing it in the States.

The heather grass on the fairway always provided us with a good lie. The golf balls were somewhat smaller than the golf balls we were accustomed to in Texas. At some points, more than one green was combined, one side being played for one hole and the other side being played for another hole. One of the greens was located at least fifty feet higher than the fairway. We first had to hit a ball on a plateau, then hit a second ball on another plateau on which the green had been placed.

I knew that in order to get a good loft to the ball, I would need to stand behind with the iron opened to get the ball high enough to reach the next level. This I accomplished with very little difficulty, but it was a whale of a lot different from what I'd been accustomed to playing before this game.

By train and by bus and boat, we toured Scotland and then worked our way back into London where the tour guide dropped us off at the Park Lane Hotel.

Before the American Bar Association met in New York, we had completed forms listing our preferred activities in England. We decided that we would like to spend two or three days in the home of an English solicitor and get to know the English people. On a Saturday morning in London, we left by bus for Maidstone where Mr. Jeffrey Day met us and drove us to their seventeenth century home. Jeffrey showed us around their four hundred-year-old home and explained how, in previous time, the English had cooked on this fireplace now used for warmth and decorative appearance.

We walked the narrow roads and met a small man on a bicycle who approached us from the rear. He wore a collar usually worn by priests, or persons of the catholic church. Jeffrey explained that the man belonged to High Church and, as he approached, he smiled a friendly grin and asked if we were the couple from America visiting in the community over the weekend. We felt such a welcome.

Jeffrey then showed us the remains of a decayed castle located about one or two hundred feet from his home. Most of the castle walls had fallen throughout the centuries from the time it had been erected, about eight hundred years prior to this. Jeffrey told me how he and his wife had prepared to attend the garden party to be held at Buckingham Palace to honor the American Bar Association members. If we had not decided to stay in the Days' home over the weekend, they would not have been invited. All of the members of the American Bar Association had been invited to the garden party and, as our hosts, the Days had been invited.

Jeffrey said he had been trying on clothes for the past thirty days, trying to decide how he would dress for the occasion. It had never occurred to me that the people in England were not given the opportunity to visit their

Queen's palace but that I, as a stranger and tourist, could be invited into the palace to meet the Queen.

On the day of the garden party, we drove about two hours along narrow, winding roads, past Winston Churchill's stately summer home, and into London. It was a beautiful day, and flowers filled the Buckingham Palace grounds. I was simply enthralled when the Queen, with her husband, Prince Philip, started slowly marching down one of the paths to the garden. We did shake their hands.

The next day, the meeting between lawyers of the United States and Great Britain commenced with a speech made in the House of Commons. The speaker explained the history of English law and the administration of the courts. When complaints were made, the king heard evidence based on grievances made by his people. The king heard the grievances in Westminster Abbey or any other place he designated for such hearings.

The complaints, or grievances, grew as the population grew, and the king appointed different people to hear the complaints because he simply could not take care of all the complaints brought to him. In the early days of these hearings, England had no provision for a jury to be impaneled to try the cases. The courts grew from this.

In time, the courts held forth in places that did not look or appear as our courthouses do in the United States. The buildings, without any particular look, were usually called Inns, or Court Inns. One evening we adjourned for entertainment at the Grey Inns. We attended at least one meeting in a building named after Francis Bacon, an English attorney general, philosopher and writer in the 1600s. I had known of him only as a writer whom I recalled from having taken sophomore English in college.

After attending lectures during the day, we adjourned for dinner provided by caterers. Dinner usually started by passing a loving cup for each to take a small drink. When the cup reached an Englishman, he drank, saying, "Long live the Queen." Not to be outdone, we Americans said, before taking a drink, "Long live President Eisenhower."

A woman judge, Judge Plunkett, who sat next to me insisted that I take a second drink and, I obliged her. Before dinner, it appeared to me that we were somewhat inebriated. Judge Plunkett and I fell into a discussion of the average English lawyer's practice and that of American lawyers.

Guides took us on sightseeing tours where we saw where Washington would have been beheaded had we not won the Revolutionary War. We saw the crown jewels of England. We cruised on the Thames River, which I had always thought of as a large river, but now found much smaller than I expected. As luck would have it, someone selected my small group to cruise on the Queen's yacht. As we boarded this private ship for our cruise, an Englishman in a very loud voice announced our arrival. "Hear ye, hear ye: Mr. Fred Whitaker and his wife, Mary Elizabeth Whitaker, now board this ship," which made us feel quite important.

The American Bar Association meeting came to an end and we joined several other couples, who had attended, and took a steamer to Holland. We remained two days, seeing the tulips, visiting dairy farms where part of the farmer's home provided shelter for cattle during the winter months. They immaculately maintained the barns which gave very little odor from the droppings. Of course, we bought cheeses and shipped them to our friends in the States.

From Holland, we traveled to Bonn, Germany and took a bus trip through the Black Forest. In Bonn we discovered a casino used for gambling which we had read about. The casino housed more than gambling, though, and we enjoyed outstanding music where we could dance as late as we cared to do so.

From Bonn we traveled to Cologne, and boarded a steamship for an all-day trip up the Rhine River to Wiesbaden. From the Rhine, we viewed vineyards on the hillsides and castles well placed along the banks. That night we stayed in a luxurious hotel in Wiesbaden.

The next day we took an all-day bus trip to Switzerland. As we drove through the countryside, our guide advised us that the size of the manure pile in front of the house gave evidence of the wealth and success of the farmer. In the early part of the evening when we finally arrived at our hotel in Switzerland, the hotel had overbooked. They provided us transportation to a little-known hotel located high in the mountains, about thirty minutes from the original hotel. We did not feel cheated, because the new hotel had, at one time, been the summer home of Queen Victoria of England.

We rode cable cars up and down the mountainside, purchased a Rolex watch for myself and a beautiful diamond for Dixie. We stayed in the German part of Switzerland where, some twenty years later, I would own a home after a new marriage, and spend a great deal of time in Montana-Crans near Geneva in the French part of Switzerland. The beautiful scenery and quiet people may have played some part in my purchasing a home here.

Of course, no one can visit Europe without going to Venice, the city that should, or could, never have been since it is constructed entirely in water. We traveled by bus to Milan, Italy then on to Venice where we immediately got on a small boat, that acted as a taxicab, and took us to our hotel.

In Venice, we visited the glass factory, as everyone does while in Venice, and took boat rides during the day and late into the evening. It is in the evening, when the lights go on, that Venice becomes its most beautiful and romantic. On one gondola trip, we took our own refreshments: a bottle of wine, loaf of bread, cheese, and small sausages. The gondolier sang beautiful and delightful Italian songs on the trip that lasted about two hours. We regretted that the excursion came to an end.

While in Florence, we traveled by car one particular day. By coincidence, I saw a lady driving a sports car and recognized her as Eleanor Naylor Dana, a woman who now lived in New York, but had grown up with me in Carthage and whose father owned Naylor Dry Goods Store. We made arrangements to have lunch together. It seemed like such a small world. Eleanor Dana had, when she left Carthage, married Charles Dana of New York, one of the most outstanding and wealthiest men in the world. In the years to come, Eleanor Dana and I renewed our friendship.

From Venice, we traveled to Florence, and on to Rome. A person's education is never complete, in my opinion, until he has been to St. Peters Cathedral in Rome. While staying at the Excelsior Hotel in Rome, we became acquainted with the director and actors making a motion picture in the studios located in Rome. The director invited us to go on the set where we met Ester Williams and Jeff Chandler. We found this interesting and exciting, and then spent several hours on the set where we had an informal lunch with the crew.

The people with whom we traveled seemed quite interested in the fact that we had toured the motion picture set and visited with actors and crew. We found ourselves wanting to meet more and more people. We sat at the bar, which gave us a better opportunity to meet people, drinking Campari and soda for twenty-five cents per drink. Dixie and I tried to make new acquaintances throughout the trip. We particularly became well-acquainted with the Koodishes.

When Mr. Koodish learned of my interest in investors for oil and gas operations in East Texas, he immediately informed me that his client, Fred Ziv, produced more television programs than anyone else in Hollywood. His very success caused him to pay an enormous income tax each year. Mr. Koodish thought Mr. Ziv would be interested in investments that would be to his tax advantage, since the oil business afforded an investor an attractive tax advantage.

From Rome, we traveled to Genoa, Nice, and Monte Carlo before arriving at the ultimate climax of our tour of the continent: Paris. There we met up with Maurice and Sara Koodish during lunch at the Eiffel Tower. They had received from friends clippings from the *New York Times* that contained our pictures. We had no idea that two people from Carthage would have their pictures spread on the society page of the *Times.*

We resumed our trip with the Koodishes. Maurice and I spent one full day in the art district of this great city. Through Maurice, I later became acquainted in New York with David Baird who expressed an interest in investments, but first wanted to know more about me and my operations. Dixie and I stayed in the George V Hotel, a beautiful hotel, and visited other hotels such as the Plaza Athenée. We went to the Follies Bergere and the Lido, the night club where beautiful girls remove ninety-eight percent of their clothes. While in Paris, we stopped at sidewalk cafes and dined on gourmet food which we found delightful. It caused me to wonder if the type of food that we had eaten in Texas all our lives was as good as we thought. The meals were made more delightful with a glass of wine, which was very different from anything I had experienced in Texas. We were not entirely without wine or champagne in Texas on special occasions, but it appeared to us that wine with meals was a daily occasion in France. Finally, we boarded the Queen Mary to return to the States.

Hollywood mixes with New York investors

The following month after our return to Carthage, the Koodishes visited with us for a long weekend. They stayed in the Cherokee Club, where we held membership, located at Lake Cherokee near Longview, Texas. This afforded them a nice vacation and, on one occasion, they spent the night in the guest room of our beautiful home that had a private golf course around the grounds.

But my law offices where I maintained a very active law practice, and the oil and gas operations just being started in the Carthage gas field, impressed Maurice Koodish the most. I had never met a man with a keener mind than Maurice Koodish. Even though he was not familiar with the oil and gas business, he followed the program which I had already initiated. We wanted to obtain permits from the Railroad Commission to drill additional wells in the Carthage Field. This would necessarily have to be a permit to drill as an exception from rules already promulgated for the large Carthage gas field.

I assumed that Maurice Koodish made a favorable report to his friend and associate, David Baird. As soon as possible, I finished working out a program to start drilling. I had at least ten times as much money raised through these two people than I had attractive deals in which to put them.

From time to time I made new acquaintances, mainly in New York. The very mention of David Baird caused everyone to relax and ask to be in our drilling program because they knew he was a very conservative investor, and only dealt with people with whom he had confidence. At this stage in the oil and gas business, outstanding people participated in the program.

The lure of the St. Regis Hotel

In the 1960s, I'd go to New York two or three times a year and stay at the St. Regis Hotel for two weeks at a time. I stayed there because the people who invested in oil usually liked the amenities found at the St. Regis, including the King Cole bar.

Colonel John Jacob Astor IV built the St. Regis in 1904 and his son, Vincent, carried on his father's tradition maintaining the St. Regis as a gracious hotel. Brooke Astor, Vincent's wife, described in the October 1991 *Town and Country* what attracted the powerful and rich, Broadway producers, publishers and media owners such as Bill Paley and the Cowles, and such entertainers as Grace Kelly, Mary Martin, and Henry Fonda.

Eddie Duchin, whose orchestras provided the music to many events I attended, served as St. Regis musical director in the 1960s.

"On every floor," Brooke Astor wrote, "a service pantry stood open twenty-four hours a day. Two men were always on duty, the same rotation of men, so that the guests could get to know them and depend on them to serve an egg just the way they wanted or to provide the champagne or vintage wine they preferred. On each floor young housekeepers did the flowers for the suites and counted the monogrammed linen sheets. There were also four older housekeepers and the head housekeeper, who examined the rooms to see if a chair needed upholstering or a curtain sagged."

At that time, it seemed to me that the St. Regis hotel room costs ran unusually high, though I could understand why. I sometimes would walk down the street and have a hamburger instead of eating at the hotel. I stayed there, though, because it provided the best place to entertain investors. The man who headed the oil department of the Chase Manhattan Bank used to meet me at the King Cole bar, and James Cromwell, the Ambassador to Canada under Roosevelt, used to bring his wife and meet me at the same bar.

Town and Country writer Jerry Patterson best describes this famous gathering place. Legends have been gathered about "the King Cole Room, in which hung the most famous bar painting in the history of American conviviality: Maxfield Parrish's *Old King Cole*. The work was originally painted for the Astors' Knickerbocker Hotel." When the Knickerbocker closed, Vincent hung onto the painting which he later hung in the St. Regis in 1935. The painting consists of three panels that depict the monarch beaming down from above the bar. I had been told and Patterson writes, "King Cole regulars explained the monarch's merriment: the king, having unexpectedly broken wind, elects not to stand on his dignity and instead chuckles along with his retainers."

I first met Salvador Dali, the great surrealist painter, in the King Cole bar, though at the time I didn't know what he painted. I later learned that Salvador Dali lived at the St. Regis for several weeks or months when he came to New York to visit.

Salvador Dali and I would meet in the King Cole bar at about six o'clock in the evening for drinks. He always brought with him four or five very young women, and he always expected me to join his party. We would have drinks and talk, sometimes for hours. At first, I wondered how he could drink so much, then I begin to notice that he didn't drink much at all.

Other investors I met in more traditional places, but even those meetings brought surprises. I first met the Gabors through Ben Zwick of the Chemical Bank of New York & Trust Company, in the oil department in about 1960. Ben knew I was looking for oil investors. At that time Dick Brown had a large deposit at the bank. When Ben invited me to have lunch with him and Dick Brown at the bank, even Ben didn't know that Dick Brown was married to Eva Gabor.

Dick Brown said he was interested in making investments with me in the oil business, and that Zsa Zsa and Eva would be interested, too. I hurriedly set up a deal in Arkansas and I think they, combined, invested something like forty thousand dollars. The well, which had good geology, came in dry. So I put them in another well near Texarkana, Texas and that also came in dry. This so disappointed Dick Brown that he ignored his bills when we sent them to him. It became necessary later that I file suit. In filing suit, I didn't realize that if you sue someone like the Gabors it will hit the newspapers. The news of my suit appeared in newspapers all over the country. Just before the case was tried, we reached an amicable settlement because by that time I was fed up with the publicity I was getting. I knew that if the case was tried the coverage would get worse, so I settled for about half of what they owed.

Other investors during this period included Fred Ziv, the largest producer of television shows in the world, who invested with me for twenty years; Frank Pace, Jr., the former cabinet member under President Truman who served the papers to General MacArthur to fire the General; Robert Anderson, Secretary of the Treasury under President Eisenhower; Mr. Latimore, president of Magnolia Petroleum Company which later merged with Exxon; Louis Mayer of Metro-Goldwyn-Mayer.

During this time I bought a one thousand acre cattle ranch near Longview with investors. I went to Fort Worth to arrange financing of one hundred thousand dollars to buy cattle. When I applied for the loan with the president of the Continental National Bank, Gus Holmstrom, he looked at me and said, "Certainly we'll make the loan with people like that on the note. How in the hell do you know people like that? How do you get acquainted with them in the first place, then get them to invest with you in a ranch? I'd give my right arm to meet Frank Pace, Jr. because all through the years he's been president of General Dynamics and done business with the other two large Fort Worth banks, but he's never done business with us."

"Would you like to meet Frank Pace, Jr.?" I asked. "Yes, definitely," he said.

"Arrange to be in New York the next time I'm there and I'll introduce you to him."

The next time I went to New York, Mr. Holmstrom arranged to meet me. I made plans for us to meet with Frank Pace, and during the meeting Mr. Holmstrom got an account from General Dynamics, equal to that of the other two Fort Worth banks, with Frank Pace. Mr. Holmstrom told me confidentially this amounted to the biggest day in his career as a banker. After the meeting, we immediately went to eat lunch at a French restaurant. When the bill came, as bankers always do, he allowed me to pay the bill.

The beauty of David Baird's charity

I sometimes felt intimidated in the presence of David Baird because of his tremendous wealth. At that time, he gave more money away to charity than any other person in the United States. He purchased a building in New York and converted it into a small hotel where about two to three hundred elderly people could maintain residence on a permanent basis. He deeded the building to Bishop Sheen, in trust for the occupants of the building who lived there without having to pay rent. It was at that time the largest gift ever given to charity. I was overwhelmed by the many gifts he made.

When I realized how David Baird used his wealth to help others, I just had to see the residence. It became one of the most touching experiences I've ever had when I toured the medium-sized hotel David Baird had purchased for older men and women. And, believe it or not, the occupants of the building were allowed to have a cocktail hour. But, it was provided that they pay ten cents per drink. This way they could enjoy what they had probably enjoyed earlier in life.

David bought another hotel just off Washington Square in Greenwich Village. It provided a residence for every woman released from jail in the city and county of New York. They lived there without expense in a residence so that they might be rehabilitated at Mr. Baird's expense.

A wardrobe was provided for each individual, and all things necessary for residents to apply for jobs, and to enjoy a new way of life. It was shown that only a small portion of the people who were benefitted in this way resumed their previous way of life. Many of these people given a chance became very successful people, enjoying a place in society without further cost to the state.

When one of Mr. Baird's assistants took me through this hotel, I was so impressed and touched that tears came in my eyes. I could recall the days when I was state's attorney, convicting in many instances, people who were incarcerated in jails and the state penitentiary. Once released, they usually did not have proper clothes, enough to live on, a place to stay, and enough to eat. When applying for a job with a history of previous conviction of crime, the chances of their making a place in society was very slim, resulting in a large percentage going back to crime.

It is my hope that the legislatures in various states may make provisions and provide some means for persons released from imprisonment to at least have a fighting opportunity to become law-abiding citizens.

For the ensuing twenty years after making these contacts and acquaintances during and after the American Bar Association meetings, I drilled more wells than any other independent or major oil company in the Arkla-Tex area. A greater portion of our activity was in East Texas, northwest Louisiana, and a small amount in the southern part of Arkansas.

In the 1960s, I sold, or merged, my production, with International Helium of Toronto, Canada. It seemed the right time to sell, and I decided I would prefer a practice of law rather than going further with oil and gas operations. I had not stopped practicing law altogether, but in going back into the law practice on a full-time basis, I considered my options.

Percy Foreman calls

Percy Foreman, of Houston, offered me a fifty/fifty partnership and guaranteed my portion of the partnership to be at least two hundred and fifty thousand, and later two and a half million dollars per year. I had never made anything like this in the practice of law in Carthage, and it was tempting to accept this proposition. Finally, I decided I would not move to Houston for the purpose of practicing law. I would remain in Carthage.

Chapter Fourteen

Mixing Banking, Oil and Law

As I looked around for investments to add to a much lesser income from law practice, I decided to buy controlling interest in a bank as an investment. I decided buying control of a bank would not only be a prestigious thing to do but would provide additional earnings up and above my law practice.

Someone called my attention to Farmers State Bank in Center, Texas, twenty-eight miles south of Carthage, which might be for sale. Allen Shivers, former Governor of Texas, then living in Austin, owned control of the stock in this bank and he made it known he would be interested in selling his stock at twice its book value. I went to Austin and talked with Governor Shivers. At this time he explained to me that there was a group in Center trying to raise the money to buy the bank; but they had not done so. If I was ready right then to make the purchase, he would sell me control of Farmers State Bank.

While I was negotiating for a loan, the group that had been working on raising the money got together and said, "No way will we allow Fred Whitaker from out of town to come in and control one of our local banks." They didn't think it would be good for the community. Before I could provide the money to buy the bank, they beat me to it by about forty-eight hours.

I had arranged for financing through Continental National Bank in Fort Worth that had examined the bank. I had copies of the last two or three bank examiners' reports. Continental made the loan available to me, but we didn't have time to close on the loan before the group in Center completed their purchase. I wasn't able to buy Farmers State Bank, which resulted in a great disappointment.

Within about two or three days after this occurred, I received a telephone call from Mr. Sanders who owned control of First National Bank in Center. This was not a very large bank. It was quite a bit smaller than the Farmers State Bank, but it had a beautiful building that had just been built to house the bank. We had a conference with Mr. Sanders about my buying the bank. The price he was asking was extremely high and he wanted three times book value.

In the examining of the bank, or conditions of the bank, I noticed that it was under capitalized. The bank examiners had been calling for new capital in the bank. I took all the information I needed, went back to Fort Worth, talked to Mr. Holmstrom, President of Continental National Bank, and so again he said, "If you really want to buy a bank, this would be a good buy. It's not as bad as you think because I'm going to loan you enough money to increase the capital and if you increase the capital at book value then that dilutes what you're paying for the bank." In effect, I was buying the bank at almost twice its book value.

Center is a good community and everything looked good so I decided to go ahead and buy the bank, and did buy the bank in 1966. The bank examiners came to see us on Monday after we closed the deal on Friday. For someone who didn't have banking experience, it felt a little frightening to have bank examiners coming into your bank. They come in and they take charge of the bank. They take the keys to the vault. You're not allowed to go into the vault while they're there examining the bank. They took over my office. I thought, "well, gosh, this is a little different from what I expected."

The bank was examined by the bank examiners, and nothing was found of a serious nature. That still didn't satisfy me. Here I was, a country lawyer from Carthage, taking on new things generally to become a banker overnight. I had assumed when I bought the bank that I'd continue my law practice full-time. I later learned that this would not be just an investment that allowed me to maintain as active a law practice as I had anticipated.

Learning banking rules and regulations

When bank examiners came for that first time after I purchased the bank, I decided then that being a lawyer didn't necessarily make a banker out of me. I found out that bank examiners called any violations of the rules and regulations, however minor they might be, a violation of the law. To me, a <u>violation</u> of the law was a violation of the law as we know it in the law practice and the penal codes in the state of Texas. I had to get used to bank examiners making a big to-do about any minor violations of any rules and regulations, whether or not they were good for the bank. If I couldn't fight them on this, I decided I had better learn something about their thinking.

I talked with some friends, and they suggested that I enroll at Southern Methodist University Southwestern School of Banking for three summers and learn something about the banking industry. So, hurriedly, I enrolled. This was a smart move. The knowledge I acquired helped me with not just the bank, but in all my businesses throughout my life. It was tantamount to having a Master's degree in finance or economics. I benefited greatly. As soon as I got into the school that was made available to those in the banking industry, I worked the problems, studied the banking rules, learned new terms. We covered a great deal of study in only two weeks each summer. While we weren't in school, we were working what we called, "Problems," a kind of correspondence course. We actually went to school for three years.

This proved to be a very valuable course. I'd always felt that one can not get enough business schooling for his work. I had taken one course in accounting at TCU and I had taken one course in economics. I felt a little deficient in that regard.

I took the information I learned and applied it to the bank. I finally developed into a fairly good banker. I knew when to turn down a loan, when to make a loan. Our loan losses were very low.

The principles of banking apply whether it's a large bank or a small country bank like the one I bought. I'd like to comment on certain of these principles. In case of a loan in default, the loan officer should never make it hard on the borrower, but he should work with the borrower to repay the loan, even if sometimes reducing the rate of interest. On some occasions, he might renew and extend the loan so that the borrower can meet the payments thereby not losing the assets of the bank. The loss of a loan is taken out of the capital. You simply don't have that amount of the loan that is charged off as capital in your bank as long as the loan is delinquent or charged off.

I devised means of my own to collect delinquent loans. I first wrote a very friendly letter to the person who was in arrears. The borrowers received this letter from me, written on attorney-at-law stationery instead of the bank's letterhead. The letter called the borrower's attention to the problem and made the person realize this was a serious matter. I explained in the letter that we did not want to make it difficult for them to meet their obligations. I explained how important it was for them that we preserve their credit rating. If they did not fulfill their obligations, they might not be able to obtain a loan again, not only in this bank, but in any other bank. After the borrower received this letter, almost everyone came into the bank to discuss their loan with a banking officer. At that time we would, if necessary, renew and extend, and in some instances, reduce the rate of interest. By reasoning and discussing like this, we were able to keep our loan losses to a minimum.

On each banking examination, we'd have some charge offs just as every bank has. But the collections were so well done that by the time the bank examiners came in the next year or two, it sometimes seemed an unnecessary effort to see the bank examiners charge off loans when the borrowers were temporarily behind in their payments. We did an excellent job of making recovery.

I did something in the bank that I'm very proud of. I formed a loan and discount committee, which is a committee appointed out of the board of directors to act as a committee in passing on loans. I gave myself authority to prevent any loan from being made, if I so desired. Since I owned control of the bank I had more or less veto power. I read a lot of guidelines for loan discount committees to act upon. Then I rewrote one guideline in condensed form for our own bank. One person may see a loan, or the application for a loan, favorably or unfavorably. But when a committee acts together, somehow in the discussion very few loans are made that shouldn't have been made. If there's a doubt, don't make the loan.

The profits in the bank were not all that good. Banking is, more or less, a way of making a living and trying to get returns on your investment. I would have made more money during the ten years I owned the bank if I'd devoted myself to the full-time practice of law in Carthage. But I got wide experience in the financial world that I hadn't had.

Farmers State Bank had twice as many loans in the community as the First National Bank at the time I purchased the bank. They even had gifted loan officers. Farmers had a loan officer by the name of Shine Fleming. He would loan money to people we wouldn't even think about loaning money to because, in the past, they'd had an automobile repossessed and did not have a good credit rating. Loans to these people were not according to good banking practices, but Shine Fleming had a way of not only making this type of loan but in collecting it. Farmers Bank made a great many loans; their delinquents were sometimes bad, but the State Board of Bank Examiners examined Farmers and we thought the state examiners were not quite as strict as the federal bank examiners who examined our bank.

Competitive banking

Farmers State Bank was the most competitive bank that anyone could have in the community. In order to get new accounts, it would always become necessary that the owner of the bank take part in the community. I did go to the Chamber of Commerce's annual meetings, but I simply did not have time to take an active part in the community to build up the personal touch necessary to obtain customers.

If I had decided to move to Center, which I wasn't about to do, I could have gotten busy and within two or three years caused my bank to be very competitive and it might have grown to be equal in size to Farmers State Bank. The bank needed a lot of work. I still carried on a law practice, and I didn't have the time nor inclination to become a full-time banker.

The earnings of the bank were fairly good. I was able to pay myself a salary in excess of fifty thousand dollars a year. At that time we wrote credit life insurance on loans that were made from time to time. If the recipient of the loan died, the insurance paid the loan and relieved the heirs of the burden. It was usually a good thing for the borrower and the bank. The commissions on the premiums that were paid, if you had your license to sell insurance, went to the owner of the bank. It was a custom to sell this kind of insurance at that time, although the practice of allowing the banker-owner to collect the commission was later prohibited. My income from the bank was in excess of one hundred thousand dollars a year with these commissions. But even that didn't quite replace the earnings I had in the practice of law. Quite naturally, when I started spending some of my time in the bank, I couldn't spend as much time practicing law. Therefore, the income from my law practice declined.

When I first bought the bank, I thought I'd hire good loan officers, elect someone president of the bank, and elect myself as chairman of the board. Thus I would not have to go to the bank except occasionally, and to the board of directors meeting once a month. But I found out this couldn't be done. There were too many loan officers who might have relaxed the rules and regulations, such as loaning money to friends, usually known as brother-in-law loans.

I owned the bank for ten years. One of the greatest benefits I got from the bank was the acquaintance and close relationship I developed with Ed Clark who served as chairman of the board at that time. At the time I bought the bank, Ambassador Clark immediately asked me if I didn't want him to resign so that I could elect a new slate of officers for the bank and a new board of directors. I told him that I preferred not to and that I would name myself as vice chairman of the board and let him remain. He said, "Do that."

Later, he thought I should take the honor and distinction of being chairman of the board. Right after I bought the bank, he attended one board of directors' meeting. He came back from Australia to attend that meeting. Ed Clark, today, was one of the outstanding businessmen and lawyers in the state of Texas. He was a personal friend of Lyndon Johnson's at the time Johnson was elected President of the United States. President Johnson immediately inquired of Ed Clark what he would like to have in Johnson's administration. Johnson told Clark he could serve as a cabinet member, an ambassador, or whatever he chose.

Ed Clark wasn't too demanding. He had earned many honors in the state of Texas. He settled for being ambassador to Australia. He said that the more he read about Australia the more it appeared to be like Texas. We had a party in honor of Ed Clark and his wife. Toward the end of the event, we asked him if he would talk about Australia. It became one of the most interesting talks I've ever heard. Ed Clark was a large man, slightly overweight, and he had a low, soft voice. We gathered around him in a conversational group and, before we realized it, found that the time was after one A.M.

Ed Clark stayed on as chairman of the board for about two years. Farmer's State Bank had former governor Allen Shivers as their chairman of the board. These men do lend prestige and recognition for your bank. You will notice that, from time to time, former Presidents are elected to bank boards.

One morning the telephone awakened me about 6 o'clock. To my surprise, I found Ed Clark calling from Australia. He said that he wanted to sell his stock in the bank. He owned more than qualifying shares. He owned five to ten percent. We agreed on a price. I asked him if he would draw a draft on me for the purchase price of the bank stock, with the stock attached. He said, "I don't have to draw a draft on you at all. I'll mail you the stock, and when you get the stock, you send me a check."

My reputation as a competent banker caused Mr. Martin, a large stockholder of the First National Bank in Dallas to call me. Martin, who had originally come from Marshall, Texas, said he wanted someone who was a lawyer, someone who knew banking, could improve the bank's assets, and whom banking examiners and the FDIC respected.

Martin said he wanted me to serve as president of the First National Bank in Oak Cliff and a small bank in downtown Dallas. I wanted to own those banks because I planned to work hard and make them prominent, make them grow, and create inducement for people to use the bank in downtown Dallas as an oil bank.

However, Mr. Martin refused to sell me the banks, after I made them profitable, except at a price so excessive that I had no inducement. They wanted to give me a mere fifty thousand dollars a year salary, which was the going price. I wasn't interested in that. They offered to obtain for me membership in the Dallas Country Club, which I found attractive, but hardly worth it. I had my law practice which provided me more income than that. Bankers get good salaries but they don't get big salaries.

I decided to sell the bank in Center in 1976. It had always been difficult to take time to drive to Center for the board meetings. I had also decided to move to Dallas where I would live part-time. As a result, this made it difficult for me to drive from Dallas to Center. I placed the bank on the market. I sold the bank to Bill Rudd of Waskom, Mr. Woods of Marshall, and Jack Strong of Longview. The bank was in excellent condition. It had been showing a nice profit from year to year. I was able to get a little more than two and a half times book value of the bank. I made a profit of about one million dollars. And, I had already received more than one million dollars out of the bank during the time I owned the bank. I sold the bank just at the right time and just prior to banks becoming less attractive as an investment. If I had kept the bank another year or two I'm sure I would not have received nearly as much profit. For it to be a smooth transfer, I spent a great deal of time with the new owners advising them on different loans and administrative matters.

Incompetent bankers

Years later, my knowledge of banking helped me to negotiate a settlement with a large bank in Dallas. My knowledge enabled me to see inside the Dallas bank and know what they were doing and what I should do in order to settle the claim I had against the bank. They had forced me to sign an unreasonable loan agreement in order to get a renewal and extension of an oil and gas loan I had which was not in default.

The loan agreement, which I considered unreasonable, stated that they had to pass on every business transaction I made over ten thousand dollars. They put a twenty-six-year-old man in charge of my loan. Other than a job in the oil field one summer while in school, he had no experience in the oil and gas industry. He absolutely did not know anything about the oil and gas industry. Every time we arranged to rework a well, to drill an offset which would be profitable, he refused to agree on anything. When I had the money to drill one well in the Carthage Gas Field, he refused to allow me to drill. Most of these refusals were done orally, but I did persuade him to write me a letter saying that I couldn't and wouldn't be allowed to drill this well. This well, which I did not drill, would have generated in excess of one million dollars over a period of years and with very little expense and with little, if any, gamble because it was between two producing wells at that time.

I threatened to sue the bank. The man who headed the oil and gas loan department was not only arrogant but not knowledgeable about my business. The first time I met this manager, he had called and asked me to have lunch with him. I said that would be fine, that I'd have lunch with him, just as I had had lunch with other officers of his bank who had invited me. As we called for a menu, he looked at me and he said he was going to call my loan unless I agreed to place additional collateral, such as real estate, with the bank. My loan was not in default. I was so dumbfounded when he related this to me that I could hardly speak.

I knew that in the banking industry the bank has such an advantage over the borrower that the bank can do almost anything the banking officers choose to do. The manager acted as though my loan was in default. To persuade me to place additional collateral, he said they would be able to go along with me in creating enough operating cost to maintain the wells. Every oilman knows that this must be done. I did in fact give additional collateral, such as real estate near Carthage. In preparing the papers in the beginning, the only way they made the renewal was for me to assign one hundred percent runs so that they had all the money and all the income. I had to go to them as a child must go to his parents in order to get an allowable to maintain and produce the properties. What had been a good loan for the bank and for myself was reduced to a nonperforming loan due entirely to the fault of the bank.

Then one day I went to a Dallas Bar Association meeting and the speaker, a member of the Robert Strauss law firm, talked on what the banks had gotten themselves into by requiring these loan agreement and not living up to them. I knew I had to have a remedy. When I heard this talk, he cited some cases. I read the cases. I found I did have a remedy. After I approached the bank manager, it took me about two months to get into his office because he was so important and arrogant. Finally, I asked to talk to the president of the bank. After being forced to wait about three or four months, I did see the president of the bank. By this time, I had prepared a petition to sue the bank for about sixty million dollars, which I might have collected both for actual damages and for punitive damages if I were successful in trying the case.

While I was negotiating, one party in Texas sued this same bank and actually recovered around sixty million dollars. When I talked to the president, I knew my time in that office was very limited. I told him I had a claim, a lawsuit, that I was going to file if they would like to read the petition. Or, I wanted my damages which would only be forgiveness of the balance due on my loan which was less than two million at that time.

I got their attention. They did not want this lawsuit filed. At the same time, I didn't want to file this lawsuit. I just wanted out from under the clutches of this bank and to go on my way. We talked and we talked. Finally, the matter was resolved. Then I went on my way and did for myself what I could have been doing all along for the bank and myself.

Recognizing reputable bankers

Compare the attitudes of these bankers with John Scott who worked in the oil and gas department of Dallas' Republic National bank in the 1960s. On one occasion, I had allowed my accounts payable to increase to about three hundred thousand dollars. In order to make payment of these accounts, taking a two percent discount, it was necessary that I make a short term loan. I had known John Scott with the oil department at the Republic National Bank since I had obtained a loan for five hundred thousand dollars when I bought oil and gas properties owned by someone in Longview, Texas.

I had never attempted to borrow large sums of money without giving collateral to obtain the loan and guarantee the payment of it. On this occasion, just prior to going into the bank, I bought a book, *My Life in Court,* by Louis Nizer. I happened to think that John Scott, a lawyer, might be interested in reading this book. As we sat down to discuss the loan I needed, I asked him if he had read Louis Nizer's book. He said he had not, but he had read about it and wanted to read the book. I laid the book on his desk. Then I told him I had allowed my accounts payable to get in the arrears, and that I needed the money for only about ninety days.

He asked me how much I needed. I said, about three hundred thousand. He called his secretary and asked her to prepare a note, due and payable in ninety days. I signed it and he handed me a deposit slip so I had the money. I walked out of the bank, and walked for about a block before I turned around and looked at the tall beautiful Republic Bank building. I reviewed what I had just done which was to receive a loan that was unsecured. It was a very touching experience. I could actually go into a bank with a good credit rating and borrow that much money without collateral. I stood there on the sidewalk; tears filled my eyes and spilled down my face.

My experience in banking developed so that it became my number one avocation. I learned, however, that I just simply didn't want to be a banker. When I sold the bank at a nice profit, the oil and gas operations began to become more attractive as an investment.

At the time I sold the bank I again considered moving to Houston because Percy Foreman continued to insist I join his firm. I did have lunch with Percy Foreman, and he insisted that I come to Houston to practice law with him. I decided not to join Percy's firm because I always thought that Carthage afforded a better life whether or not it was financially to my advantage to remain in Carthage.

Many Texas lawyers then generally conceded that Percy Foreman and Fred Whitaker ranked as the number one criminal lawyers in Texas. However, a greater portion of the work he did, and I did, was in civil practice. But the news stories caused the public to think that our practices might be mainly criminal practices.

The following case that dealt with Workman's Compensation illustrates the kind of civil case that generated so much publicity that added to my reputation as a trial attorney.

The man who got caught working

This lawsuit was filed in Federal Court in Tyler. In about 1960, I represented Troy Jones from Carthage in a claim for Workman's Compensation. An appeal was taken from the ruling of the Industrial Accidents Board for the state of Texas. A lawsuit had been filed in the State District Court of Panola County, Texas but since there was a diversity of citizenship and grounds for removal, the case was removed to the Federal Court in Tyler. The defendant was represented by Earl Sharp, a very capable attorney from Longview, known in this part of Texas for representing insurance companies.

The defendant, a company that Mr. Jones had worked for at the time of injury, became little-known after the suit was filed. Instead, the defense was made entirely by the insurance company that carried the Workman's Compensation for the employer. The lawyer for the insurance company, Earl Sharp, had responsibility for the outcome of this case. Because he had been a judge at one time, we sometimes called him Judge Sharp.

The claimant, Troy Jones, and his wife rode with me from Carthage to Tyler each morning as I drove my car to appear in court at nine o'clock. On the second morning, as we were driving to Tyler, I informed Mr. Jones that there was something unusual about this case and I just wondered if he had told me everything. I said, "For instance, have you been working on another job even though you claim to be disabled?"

"Oh, no," he said, "I have not been working."

We went ahead in the trial of the case. The following morning, as we approached Tyler, Mrs. Jones, said, "Mr. Whitaker, my husband hasn't told you the truth. He has been working."

"I wish you had told me about this in the beginning," I said. "We could have avoided a very embarrassing situation. You know, as lawyers, we can admonish our clients to tell the truth, but we can't get all over them. After all, they are human beings. It's not the place of the lawyer to tear someone up for doing something that he shouldn't have done."

As we walked into the courtroom, I had a very sinking feeling. Mr. Sharp had been in the courtroom prior to my arrival and had asked the court attendants to lower all the shades. This could only be for the purpose of showing pictures of this man while working which would refute almost all the claims that he had for benefits under Workman's Compensation. Then we proceeded. Mr. Sharp asked Judge Sheehy, the judge at that time, if he could be allowed to show some tapes. This was granted by the court. The screen was placed so that the jury could see it. In fact, we could all see it because it was a very large screen. At one point, it showed Troy Jones rolling a big rock that weighed two or three hundred pounds out of the place where he was operating heavy equipment and moving dirt, preparing for construction of some type of building to be erected after the ground was prepared.

There he was, just as plain as if we were looking at him at the time. He was doing this work and some other heavy type of work that showed entirely that this man was not disabled as he had claimed.

I sat there. As this picture was being shown, I lowered my voice and talked with my client. I put some words in his mouth. Whether they were true or not, we'll never know.

"Why did you do this?" I asked. "Did you do it because you had to work to support your children? Was it approaching school time? Did your children not have any shoes?"

"Yes, yes," he said.

When I spoke to the jury, I said, "This company refused to pay what they lawfully owed. Instead, they resorted to this thing which is so low. If you would compare what they have done to what my client has done, they've done so much more. They've resorted to tactics that are unheard of. They've sneaked around undercover, and taken a man's picture invading his privacy. Now they want you to go along with this sort of thing. But you, ladies and gentlemen of the jury, are not going to allow that. You're going to let them know that is a low, horrible way to prepare a defense for a case in this court of justice."

One man in particular kept looking at me, and I could tell he was agreeing with me entirely. All the other people on the jury were so impressed with this kind of defense; that is, with this poor working man's condition, until I noticed tears were in some of their eyes. They were genuine people who understood what goes on in the world. Then I concluded my argument. I asked the jury to give this man his dues.

By this time, I was emotionally involved. The plea I made must have been very effective. I challenged Judge Sharp to explain why he had done all of this.

"He's going to address you in a few minutes," I told the jury, "and I want him to explain it to you."

I looked at Judge Sharp, and said, "Judge Sharp, will you kindly explain to this jury why you did all of this?"

I turned back to the jury and said, "He's not going to explain anything to you because there's no explanation. He's going to evade it. He's not even going to talk to you about it because he doesn't like it now anymore than we do. Go on and do your duty and give us what we're entitled to."

When Judge Sharp made his address to the jury, he again did exactly what I said he'd do. He didn't talk about it. That made it worse.

Finally the jury retired to the jury room to deliberate the case. They came back within a short time and not only did they answer every question in our favor, but gave total and permanent disability, which I doubt today if we were entitled to according to our own testimony.

The man in the jury box, who had paid a lot of attention to me, when court adjourned came to me and shook hands with me and told me he felt like they had rendered the right verdict. He said, "I like what you've done in this case. I like the fight you made for your client. I'd like to buy your lunch."

"I don't know if that's appropriate," I said, "but I appreciate it."

Then I went outside the courtroom for a minute and I saw Henry Strasburger. I had known Henry Strasburger for years. I had tried cases wherein he represented the opposition. I knew he was a great lawyer, one of the most capable lawyers I had known. He said he wanted to talk with me a minute. This is what he told me.

"Fred, I felt so sorry for you when those pictures were shown on the screen. As a matter of fact, I've never, never had any greater feeling for anyone than I did for you because I knew you didn't know your own client had been working. I want to tell you something further. I've never had any more admiration for any lawyer since I've been practicing law for the great comeback you made in overcoming their defense and then taking the affirmative in the case. You're to be congratulated. You did a great job."

Henry Strasburger died several years ago. He lived in Dallas and built one of the finest law firms in Dallas that still carries his name. He was such a great lawyer that his comment meant so much to me.

Henry Strasburger, as a defense lawyer who represented insurance companies, wouldn't have done what Earl Sharp did. If Earl Sharp had thought further about the case, he would have known that this was one way of defending his client. But if it didn't work, it could backfire on him and hit him right in the face, which it did. He had such strong evidence until he felt confident this would be the end of the case, that we would probably ask for a nonsuit and walk out of the courthouse.

I tried a great many cases in Tyler in Federal Court because when the defendant had reason for petitioning the cases in Federal Court they would bring them to Tyler. If you didn't have a strong case you should not have been over there because they were very strict.

As I tried cases in the courthouse in Tyler, I caused some of the people who lived in Tyler to notice me. A very successful oilman in Dallas, Bill Rudman who would later come to my assistance, said that when he noticed that I was in Tyler, he would oftentimes go to the courthouse and hear me try a case. He said he liked the way I walked into the courtroom. He said I would walk into the courtroom rather fast and with a great deal of confidence. Throughout the trial of the case, even though I was courteous to the court, I tried to be the type of lawyer who was an advocate of the law.

When I made an argument in a case, I sometimes raised my voice so that it could be heard distances beyond the courtroom. Then I would lower my voice to a whisper. This type of argument to the jury is not used so much today.

Why, so many people have asked, did I enjoy such an outstanding law practice? My success went beyond any lucrative income. I feel that I could have made at least ten times as much had I moved to Houston or to Dallas instead of living in a small town in East Texas.

The principles, however, that I followed as a lawyer still apply to successful lawyers today.

Ten maxims for a successful law practice

<u>One.</u> It is imperative that a lawyer allow the interests of the client to come first. After employment starts and continues, commence and continue to do a good job regardless of whether you are adequately paid.

<u>Two.</u> Maintain professional dignity at all times. If a client paid me in cash or by check, this payment remained on my desk unless or until my secretary accepted the payment with a proper receipt given the client for the payment made in order to maintain professional dignity at all times. I made every effort possible to understand the problems that might be undertaken in each case in which I became engaged.

<u>Three</u>: The actions and conduct of the lawyer should demand respect throughout the relationship of attorney-client. Even though some problems have more or less a humorous side, it shouldn't ever be known by the client that you see a certain amount of humor in the situation in which he relates to you about the problems. A lawyer should remember that the client's problems are very, very serious to him, or he wouldn't be in the office in the first place.

<u>Four</u>: The attorney should at all time be dressed properly, and never at any time wear flashy clothes. Before I was thirty years of age, I made a trip to Neiman-Marcus in Dallas. I was fortunate enough to have an opportunity to talk with Stanley Marcus, whom I think everybody agrees is a genius in his field of endeavor.

I told Mr. Marcus that I wanted his advise about how to be dressed. He was delighted. From that time on, I wore no clothes except those that were made by Oxford. Either all, or a greater part of the suits and accessories I purchased, I purchased in the downtown store at Neiman-Marcus.

<u>Five</u>: A proper weight should be maintained at all times. If the temptation to eat too much occurs, then with a certain amount of discipline and exercise, you can usually correct the situation that all of us sometimes experience to some degree.

<u>Six</u>: The lawyer should engage in ethical behavior at all times. Then the lawyer should rejoice along with his client with the success that results from a lot of hard work and dedication. It is often said that lawyers "sell out to the other side." In my opinion, this is brought about by the slovenly

sort of work that is done by lawyers, rather than by actual dishonesty, as the public might believe.

It has been stated to me by one of the trustees of the tremendous Texas Christian University that he some day would be in favor of having a law school. Some day I would like to contribute and help in some way to finally add the law school to the other departments, a greater portion of which are in the fine arts. If this is done, and should I have influence, each law student should be required to study ethics, with as much emphasis on the study of this subject as the school places on corporate law, civil law, and other subjects of the law.

In adding to this study of ethics, it might not only benefit the students, but have far-reaching influence throughout this great nation that we have a privilege of being a part.

The relationship between attorney and client today is deplorable in too many instances. It is now the exception instead of the norm to have the feeling that clients do not respect their attorneys after the work that they are engaged in is concluded. Such a course at Texas Christian University would bring back the self-respect that the legal profession once enjoyed, and the respect that people should have for the legal profession.

Seven: Take over the client's burden. I could see the worry and concern that clients showed in their general demeanor when they came to me. First we reviewed the facts; then if the client employed me, before the client left the office, I told him to go home, and dismiss all this worry from his mind. He could now let his lawyer do the worrying, because everything was going to be done that was necessary to see that he had his day in court. It is a pleasure for a lawyer to see the immediate relief that his client has when this is explained to him.

Eight: Avoid working with prospective clients who lie to their lawyers. There are times that employment might be available to the attorney, but somehow he has a sense that the facts being told to him are either false or exaggerated. The attorney should tactfully refuse to take this case, but might recommend or suggest that the prospective client see other lawyers who might be able to take on his problems.

Nine: One of the most important things that a lawyer can ever do in the practice of law is to advise with a client as to whether or not he should file suit, even though the merits may be in his favor.

The best illustration of the above is a man by the name of C.B. Duke, formerly of Carthage, Texas. When he was about forty years old, he accepted employment by the First National Bank in Atlanta, Texas as president of the bank. Mr. Duke was a very likable man, and would often make loans without adequate collateral. When he was in Carthage, he had so many friends that almost everybody without exception repaid him whether or not he forced them to do so.

As time developed in the First National Bank in Atlanta, Texas, a large percentage of the loans became delinquent, and the bank examiners threatened to require additional capital to support a large percentage of losses. Finally, the board of directors of that small bank dismissed C.B.Duke, and he was no longer an employee of the financial institution.

I received a telephone call from Mr. Duke a short time after his dismissal, and he took great delight in telling me what he was going to do against the bank and the directors in charge of maintaining and overseeing that the bank was properly operated. I had a feeling that this enthusiasm by Mr. Duke was not justified. I asked him why he had not come to see me before he had instituted his lawsuit through another lawyer. He replied that he was of the opinion that I would not have taken the case because I owned control of another bank in Texas, and might not be as sympathetic to his position.

Then I slowly but emphatically asked him if I wouldn't be the best lawyer he knew to first tell him whether he had a lawsuit or not, and determine if he was taking on more than he could chew? This suit would add troubles to the difficulties he was having at this time. I believe today that I could have prevented him from filing suit. Not only that, I could have saved his life.

Within thirty days after this telephone conversation, he could then see the handwriting on the wall, and attempted suicide. Within the next twelve months after that time, he died either from a self-inflicted wound, or by the impossible situation he had placed himself as a result of this litigation.

Ten: In my opinion, desist, if possible to do so, in taking employment on an hourly basis. A large percentage of the lawyers today take employment in this manner, and keep their own time. If a ditch digger was employed in this manner, that is, kept his own time, I am sure he would exercise more honesty in turning in his work by the hour than the average lawyer does if he has an opportunity to gut his own client.

Lawyers know the average amount of time it takes to prepare a case for trial or do the work required in a given case. But the average client doesn't know, and, instead, relies upon the lawyer's integrity. To eliminate overcharging a client, it might be advisable to handle litigation on a fixed-fee basis as I did in almost every case I handled throughout my law practice. An hourly fee basis, as practiced today, is used oftentimes by a lawyer to steal money from his own client.

It should be proper and it should be encouraged for lawyers, that is adverse lawyers in each case, to maintain a friendly relationship through-out the duration of the controversy. The friendly relationship between adverse lawyers I refer to is not the same kind of relationship that has developed in Dallas between lawyers and judges that allows them to continue a case when it's not necessary. These continuances just add to the time in which lawyers extort some two hundred or two hundred and fifty dollars an hour from their client.

It appears in some instances that the judges get in on the same act, especially in domestic relations, or family law cases. Whether or not the judge directly receives any of the proceeds of the case, he causes it to appear he just might receive some lucrative campaign contributions.

If you have any doubt that this goes on, then you should talk with some of the litigants, especially in divorce cases that have been pending in Dallas, and perhaps in other parts of the state, especially in Longview where similar questions have been raised. It appears that some lawyers just simply should not be practicing law because they sometimes do not have the temperament to do so.

In February of 1990, the *Dallas Times Herald* newspaper carried a front page news story that quoted Federal Judge Buckmeyer's opinion about lawyers. The story expresses, to a large extent, my opinion of today's lawyers. They have degraded themselves to such an extent that a Federal Judge would admonish lawyers in an open statement.

The *Dallas Times Herald* headline read: "Think Lawyers Are A Joke? Tell It To The Judge." Judge Buckmeyer is quoted, "I don't want to waste my time saying how marvelous lawyers and judges are because no one is going to believe you."

At the time I obtained my license to practice law, I felt so proud of being a lawyer that I sometimes volunteered to others that I was an attorney. However, during the last fifteen or twenty years that I practiced law, I lost a great deal of respect for lawyers. Too many lawyers today look only to the fee that they might collect rather than to think about the services they might render for a client who had engaged them to represent them in legal matters.

I no longer feel proud that I am an attorney. In 1991, the State Bar of Texas received about six thousand complaints, more complaints than any other licensing agency in Texas. That same year, eighty-seven victims of lawyers' schemes and dishonesty received four hundred thousand five hundred forty-nine dollars from the State Bar's Client Security Fund. The Bar reported twenty-five percent more disciplinary actions against lawyers than the total for the thirty-three years between 1939 and 1972. The figures speak for themselves.

The wonderful education a lawyer has as a background should enable him or her to go out into the world using this background to great success.

The value of an education

Through the years I have encouraged young people to continue their education. At one time, a young black man worked as a janitor in my building in Carthage. I told him, "You can become a lawyer."

"Oh no, Mr. Whitaker," he said. "I couldn't go to law school because my parents are very poor."

"You can do it if I did," I challenged him. We continued to talk about this from time to time.

One day as I sat in Joe's Cafe in Carthage, this young man's mother came up to me and shook hands with me. She said, "Now my son is a lawyer. Don't you remember?" she asked. "He was your janitor. He said the only reason he's a lawyer is because you told him he could be a lawyer. He gives you a lot of credit."

"How wonderful," I said.

"In fact, he's in Dallas now. He works for the Attorney General's office." She told me where he worked.

"I'll make it a point to go see him," I told her.

The next time I went to downtown Dallas, I walked a few blocks to his office and looked him up. I recognized him and shook hands with him. He again told me how much he appreciated the encouragement I'd given him. He was so happy he had gone to school and could make a good living.

He's now with a large law firm in Dallas and doing quite well. I get a lot of satisfaction out of that.

In my own case, I know that without my education and my legal background I would not have been as successful, or would not have enjoyed the success I have had in the oil and gas industry. The knowledge a person acquires in law school and in the practice of law provides him with knowledge of the business world, of reading contracts, and of learning the nature of man and why he acts against certain stimuli. It's a great education that is provided and I'm sure the background I have had enabled me to become a successful oil and gas producer.

Chapter Fifteen

The *ABC's* of Oil Financing

My skills as a lawyer not only helped me protect my investments in oil and gas properties, they helped me right certain wrongs in law. In the process, one of my suits set new precedent in law.

A gentleman by the name of Weeks, of Wichita Falls, Texas, worked out a system to finance purchases of oil and gas properties eliminating or amortizing the income taxes that would be paid over the period of time in which the loan or purchase price would be repaid.

This method allowed the seller to retain an oil payment in favor of a third party, and then later the bank that was actually financing the property would purchase this oil payment at a discount, and assignment of the oil runs would go directly to the bank in repayment of the loan. The weak point in this transaction could develop if the bank required a personal guarantee, and the bank always did, from the purchaser so that if, for any reason, the oil payment did not repay the loan, then the borrower would be required to repay the amount of the advancement made by the bank, together with accrued interest if there was any deficiency while the oil payment was being made.

I purchased some oil and gas properties from F.R. Jackson of Longview, Texas in the sum of five hundred thousand dollars. John Scott, head of the oil department of the Republic National Bank of Dallas, did the financing and, in the instrument of conveyance, F. R. Jackson retained, or carved out, the amount of the purchase price in favor of the Howard Corporation, a corporation owned and controlled by the Republic National Bank of Dallas.

In a subsequent transaction, unrelated to the five hundred thousand dollar loan, a group of investors and myself decided to purchase oil and gas producing properties located in Starr County, Texas near the Mexican border. A Mr. Ginsburg of Fort Worth, Texas decided to make a commitment to furnish the finances through the Able Finance Company, a corporation he owned. Mr. Ginsburg used the financing formula developed by Mr. Weeks. There developed a dispute between Able Finance Company and the debtors. We refused to pay the excessive rate of interest the finance company was attempting to charge. Mr. Ginsburg threatened to sue us.

It was arranged for Mr. Ginsburg to meet me in Longview, wherein he would fly in his private plane to discuss a settlement of the dispute in question. As the plane landed in Longview, the flight attendants actually laid out a red carpet for the wealthy Mr. Ginsburg to walk upon while coming into the airport for a friendly discussion of the entire controversy.

Mr. Ginsburg's shoes were so well-polished that they appeared to be finished in patent leather, the kind of shiny shoes that people wear only with formal attire at social gatherings. Mr. Ginsburg not only had a diamond ring on his finger, he had diamonds in his stickpin attached to his tie. You might be able to picture this gentleman more if you compared him to very rich oil people from Saudia Arabia or Iran after they became so wealthy that only the best of everything surrounded their very existence.

The contemplation of a lawsuit against Fred Whitaker and the other purchasers of the oil properties was not settled at this meeting in Longview. Mr. Ginsburg left in a huff, but did inform me that he would file suit even though I had pointed out to him that the rate of interest he was charging was usurious and excessive. We would be glad to pay him the amount of the loan at a legal rate of interest; that is, not to exceed the ten percent he could lawfully collect under the laws of the state of Texas at that time.

A lawsuit was filed later in Carthage, Panola County, Texas against Fred Whitaker and the other purchasers of these oil properties. Little did Mr. Ginsburg know that a defense would be imposed wherein it might be shown that the entire transaction would be held as void since the financing of these properties might be shown to be an avoidance of income tax imposed by the federal government. This would be an illegal contract.

The case was tried before the court and it was held that this contract could not be enforced because it was an illegal transaction not enforceable in the state of Texas. For example, a gambling debt cannot be enforced in Texas. The banks, oil companies, independent oil and gas operators were aware of this lawsuit then pending in Carthage, Panola County, Texas and were waiting for the outcome since it would affect large sums of money that might be used in the purchase of oil and gas properties.

Within a few hours after the decision was made by the court, I received a telephone call from John Scott of the Republic National Bank in Dallas. He asked me in this telephone conversation if I would come by his bank on my next trip to Dallas. I knew that in all probability he desired to discuss this Able Finance Company case with me. As I recall, I had no urgent reason to be in Dallas, but arranged to be there a short time after this telephone call with Mr. Scott.

Mr. Scott was a lawyer, even though he did not practice his profession. When we met in the office in the bank, he immediately wanted to discuss with me how and in what manner we successfully defended this lawsuit against Able Finance Company. I explained to him that the avoidance of income tax was illegal. The evasion of income tax was not only illegal but could be coupled with a violation of law and would be subject to criminal prosecution by the U.S. government. Mr. Scott said that, in his opinion, we were correct in that his bank would not thereafter finance the purchase of oil and gas properties in what was known as the ABC Route.

The public would ordinarily expect this sort of case to be overturned in a court located in one of the large cities of Texas. But the law is the same no matter what the size of the city. This method of financing was corrected in the 123rd Judicial District in Panola County, Texas in the small town of Carthage.

The amount of this loan and lawful rate of interest was ultimately paid to Mr. Ginsburg and his company. An appeal was not perfected. Even though overturning this law was never written in the legal reports, it nevertheless was known throughout the oil and gas section of the country. It's not likely that this form of financing was ever used after this time in financing the purchase price of oil and gas properties.

The gas deal that got away

A short time after I started dabbling in the oil business in a small way, I learned the hard way how courts can be skewed to favor persons with influence.

One day, I received a telephone call from Gus Holmstrom, who had moved from Continental National Bank to president of the First National Bank in Fort Worth. He informed me that he knew of a purchase deal on an oil and gas property that he would recommend that I take if I could finance it. The property had a purchase price of seven million dollars.

This was shallow gas property, located in Moore County, just north of Amarillo near the Oklahoma border. I arranged immediately to drive to Fort Worth from my office in East Texas and meet with the officer of the bank. I learned that an evaluation report had been prepared by Mr. White of Houston. Mr. White had an outstanding reputation in evaluating oil and gas properties. It appeared that by purchasing the property it would produce enough cash to recover purchase price, together with interest, over a period of about six years. Thereafter, it would have tremendous reserves that would produce for many, many years.

The sale of gas was then three cents per MCF, per thousand cubic feet. Somehow, the Anadarko Pipeline Company that owned the property had been able to prevail upon the Federal Power Commission to increase the price of this gas from three cents to ten cents per MCF. As a result, this enhanced the value of these properties many times over.

However, there were some political manipulations going on in Washington, D.C. that caused Anadarko to have misgivings about this price. Those misgivings had caused them to decide to sell the property, take the money and get out of any future repercussions.

I had become acquainted with an engineer in the First National Bank in Fort Worth who evaluated oil and gas properties. I decided that I should get a second opinion; that is, one in addition to Mr. White's of Houston. I did employ the Fort Worth man. He immediately informed me that Mr. White's report weighed on the conservative side. He would give the property a greater evaluation.

At this time, I decided to go to New York to try to close the deal with Mr. MacGuire who was then president of Anadarko Pipeline Corporation. I called Mr. MacGuire and he said he wanted to see me immediately. He invited me to lunch the following day at the bank. As I went into the dining room I was immediately introduced to Henry Morgenthau, Jr. who had represented Anadarko in Washington to get the ten-cent price increase.

I immediately told them that I would pay the seven million dollars, that we could start closing the deal. However, I did not have a loan commitment covering this amount at this time. I felt confident that I could secure the loan. The following day, I saw Ben Zwick with the Chemical Bank of New York & Trust Company. Ben looked at the reports I had and said his bank didn't make long-term financing like that but he knew a place that would be glad to make this loan.

He called the man who headed the General Electric Employee Pension Fund. They had about fifty-five million dollars on deposit at the bank where I had been negotiating for this loan. As we walked into this place, I was immediately introduced to this gentleman. He looked over the reports, asked Ben what kind of credit reputation I had. Ben told him I had a Triple A rating with Dunn and Bradstreet.

He said, "If this bears out, we will make the loan provided we have someone to service the loan."

I spoke up and asked Ben, "Why don't you and your bank service the loan for the benefit of the Pension Fund?" They agreed upon this. In a short time I had a loan commitment for seven million dollars and I was walking on air. This was the first large deal I had tried to make.

In the meantime, in Fort Worth, the engineer working for the First National Bank had been talking with me about paying him a fee for the First National Bank of Fort Worth forwarding this deal to me in the first place. I had halfway promised to pay him a fee, which would have been in conflict with the work he had been doing with the bank. I felt reluctant to get involved in this sort of thing. He resented my not making him a firm agreement of what he would receive. He had wanted fifty thousand dollars.

I received a telephone call from Mr. MacGuire two days later while I stayed in the St. Regis Hotel in New York. He said he wanted to talk with me because he had had another offer for these properties. This came as a shock. I learned later that the engineer at the Fort Worth bank had called the deal to the attention of Allen Shivers, former Governor of Texas. Shivers had contacted Mr. MacGuire and offered one million more for the properties. Mr. MacGuire told me, in effect, that my deal was off.

I felt so enraged about the dealing I had received from a major oil company, that I decided that I might dwell upon some of their weak points. I called Ralph Yarborough, a United States Senator from Texas and good friend of mine, and arranged to meet him in Washington. I told him exactly what had happened to me. He said he was familiar with the fact that some manipulation had been occurring. Ralph had just been appointed to investigate what had happened with the ten-cent price increase.

Ralph felt somewhat reluctant to get involved. I suggested that he get involved in an indirect way. I asked him why he couldn't have his secretary call the Federal Power Commission and have all the original papers brought to his office for his study.

I went back to New York, knowing that the next morning the papers would be brought to Ralph's office, and that Mr. MacGuire and others might learn that there would be an investigation of what they had done. I hoped that this would stimulate the Anadarko Company to go ahead and do business with me even though we did not have a written agreement.

I then called at Mr. MacGuire's office but his secretary at first refused to let me see Mr. MacGuire. I sat and waited two hours. Finally, I got up and walked back to his office, opened the door and walked in. There he sat alone. I simply told him that I had gone to all the expense and trouble of getting this loan and that I'd like for him to honor his agreement with me and close the deal.

He smirked and called his shoeshine man in and told him to give him a shine while I talked. I did get his attention. I told him he wouldn't enjoy what he was doing because I was going back to my office in Carthage and file a lawsuit against him for specific performance of a contract that he had entered into with me.

I went back to Texas and hired a lawyer in Oklahoma City, who had been a district attorney in Oklahoma City, to work with me on the case. He was an aggressive lawyer. Suit was filed. He found an old case in the Oklahoma state courts that said a contract to sell real estate, even though it was not in writing, if it had gone too far then it was enforceable. We had a case supporting us.

The federal judge made two preliminary rulings in our favor. We were getting along in this lawsuit until Senator Bob Kerr of Oklahoma got involved. From that time on, the judge ruled every time in favor of Anadarko. My attorney in Oklahoma City told me that Senator Kerr, who had served as United States Senator when this man had been appointed judge, talked with the judge about our case.

We decided that since we had nothing in writing, we would not try the case. All of a sudden, without any knowledge of why, Anadarko wanted to talk with me further. I received a call from Henry Morgenthau, Jr., attorney for Anadarko. I went to New York immediately and met with Henry Morgenthau, Jr. whom I found very charming and capable. We discussed the kind of practice I had in Carthage. He suggested that I go back to Texas, locate some people with contracts in Texas who were not obtaining a reasonable price for gas, and suggest we represent them in Washington, D.C. However, I did not wish to engage in this kind of law practice.

We settled the case against Anadarko during this discussion. At that time I knew that it would be next to impossible to win this case in the courts in Oklahoma. Mr. Morgenthau recommended that his client pay me the sum of eighty thousand dollars. This was a great amount of money at that time. It somewhat soothed my outrage that I had been kicked around in a way that no one with any principle would have done. The suit ended in this manner.

Anadarko kept the property. These properties generated so much money that it staggered my imagination. However, I did not have the right influence or clout to acquire the property.

Over the years since this happened to me, I've wondered if I made the wrong decision in not working with Henry Morganthau, Jr. I could have made a tremendous amount of money. But, I made the right decision. I still have no regrets.

Chapter Sixteen

Love and Loss

While many people marvel at my successes as a trial lawyer and a few envy my wealth garnered as an oil and gas operator, I admire those who can make mistakes in their personal lives, forgive, and hold tight the love of their families.

My banking career might have lasted longer had I not made a major change in my life: divorce. That upheaval caused me to lose almost all of my estate, my immediately family, and to move to Dallas on a part-time basis with the hope that I might start over. I knew the unhappy consequences of a marriage-gone-wrong when I married the first time at a too-young age. That marriage produced a lovely daughter and brilliant son, now a physician.

My second marriage, I had hoped, would work. I certainly hadn't anticipated meeting a future wife when I met a trucker, Haskell Rogers, who operated a truckline under the name of Rogers Truckline. Shortly after I started practicing law, I met Haskell Rogers of Kilgore, Texas. One of their trucks, while hauling oil field equipment to Indiana, had side-swiped a man in a pickup. This resulted in the driver of the pickup losing his left arm while driving with his left hand and arm on the arm rest of the pickup truck door. The man filed a lawsuit in Henderson, Kentucky against Rogers Truckline.

Even though the truckline had liability insurance coverage, Mr. Rogers found it advisable to hire me to assist the lawyer of the insurance company in defending this lawsuit. As I recall, the insurance policy had limited coverage, and it might have been possible that the jury, if they decided in favor of the plaintiff, would assess damages in excess of the insurance coverage. Then it would become incumbent upon the defendant to pay any deficiency that might occur.

I arrived in Henderson, Kentucky and the lawsuit was settled just prior to the time it was called to trial. The lawyer, Mr. Ralph Chauser, who represented the insurance company, was leaving for Chicago some two hundred miles north. I decided to accompany him and his wife and spend a couple of days in Chicago to see the big city before I returned to my offices in Carthage.

Mr. Chauser drove a Plymouth, or Dodge sedan, and I started the trip by riding in the back seat of the car. Within a very short time, we all became so cold that we decided that we might give each other some warmth and support if we all rode in the front seat. I had only a light topcoat and by the time we arrived at the Sheraton Hotel in Chicago, I was almost frozen. We learned why we had had such an uncomfortable ride when they told us in the hotel it was twenty below zero.

The room assigned to me seemed to have a draft. I called downstairs, and they sent an engineer to check the room since it seemed almost as cold in the room as outside. The engineer simply closed one window in a firm way and, all of a sudden, the room began to warm up until it reached a comfortable temperature of about seventy-two degrees.

Mr. Chauser arranged for me to have a date with his secretary, a Miss Bobette Boyson, for the following evening. But Bobette Boyson called me later that day and advised me that she would like for me to date her roommate instead of having a date with her. That didn't make any difference to me because it was more or less a blind date. I had not, of course, known either of them before this time.

The date with Elizabeth Simpson, Miss Boyson's roommate, started with our going to Christie's, a famous place known for its steaks, located on a second floor of a building in the heart of the big city. We made reservations for the following evening at the Palmer House for dinner and dancing. Eddie Duchin provided the music.

On the third date, we saw the play, *Life with Father,* performed with the original cast. At lunchtime the following day, she invited me to lunch at a private club called The Chicago Farmer's. Mary Elizabeth, or Dixie as we called her, was not only secretary at The Chicago Farmer's, but she edited a magazine mailed to each member monthly. The president of The Chicago Farmer's was Rockefeller Printess, a first cousin of the former Governor of the state of New York, Nelson Rockefeller.

Later that same day I boarded a train to make my return to Texas. There would not have been too much interest in making my trip to Chicago if it had not been for the fact that Mary Elizabeth and I carried on a correspondence, talked by telephone, and finally, in June, I met her in Taylorville, Illinois, where her parents resided. We became engaged to be married and proceeded back by automobile to Carthage and married on June 10, 1941.

We settled down in Carthage after we made a trip by automobile to Mexico City for our honeymoon. Our daughter, Melinda, was born about fifteen months after we married. Then came Jennifer, Deborah and our son, Mark.

The paradox of Sid Turner

A long-time Carthage lawyer, Sid Turner, who became my Nemesis in a way, played a part in where we eventually lived. Sid Baker Turner served as County Attorney for four years prior to the time I was elected County Attorney in Panola County. For various reasons, he was unable to establish himself as a successful lawyer.

It was necessary that we appear in court from time to time on opposite sides of a case. On some occasions, he would stand up before a jury, the papers in his hands shaking, because of a bad hangover that he had from drinking excessively the night before. Of course, I took advantage of this situation. After we had tried cases like this for four or five years, he refused to go to the courthouse to try a case with me because it was a losing proposition for him every time he did so.

Sid Turner did things like this. On occasion during the trial of a case, even though he had other lawyers who worked with him, he would get up, probably to go get a drink, and leave the courthouse while the case was being tried. In the argument of the case, when he wasn't at the counsel table, I'd ask the jury, "Where is Sid Turner?"

Then I'd make a remark, such as, "I know why he left. The proof he had in the case was a little obnoxious even to him. He didn't want to hear it either." Finally, he wouldn't try a case against me. Eventually he quit going to the courthouse. He developed a hatred for Fred Whitaker that was beyond belief. He had wealth, but he couldn't go to the courthouse and practice his profession.

Then later, much later from our young days in Carthage, he filed suit for a divorce against his wife, Norma. There was one child, Theresa, involved. The consequences over the custody of the child were enormous.

At the time just prior to the divorce's being filed, Sid Turner became a chronic alcoholic and, through the years, his wife also became addicted to alcohol. On one occasion, Norma's mother came to Carthage from Brownwood, Texas and picked up her daughter, Norma, and took her to a hospital in Brownwood. Norma's mother did this so hurriedly that they did not take the child with them. A lawyer from Dallas was engaged to represent Mrs. Turner and the main issue of this divorce became the custody of the child.

Mrs. Turner's Dallas lawyer came to my office and attempted to engage me as local counsel to work with him to try to get custody of the Turner child. I told him I might take the position of advising with him from time to time without pay, but it was my better judgment that I should not take the case because there was so much animosity between Sid Turner and myself. In the past, I had somehow or another caused Sid Turner to back down when things got really tense. I knew that he was so involved with his child, and that he cared too much for his daughter. He would stop at nothing to maintain custody. I did advise and talk with Mrs. Turner's lawyer, but never accepted employment as such.

What ensued from that time on would be difficult for anyone to know. First, we had in our possession letters Theresa wrote to her father, with whom she lived but rarely saw. In the letters she begged him to come home, and wrote that she disliked living in a home by herself, with a black man, who had been a devoted servant for the Turners for many years. The father stayed out nights drinking and sometimes he stayed away days from the house. These sad and pitiful letters were finally destroyed. They showed the neglect and abuse that parents sometimes put upon their children without knowing what they have done.

Mr. Turner was able to get a continuance of this case from time to time. On one occasion a visiting judge came to Carthage to go forward with the trial. But Sid Turner put the fear of God in the judge and created such a disturbance that the judge went back to his home in Dallas. Sid Turner held meetings with his friend from time to time about what procedures he might take.

Sid Turner, in desperation, resorted to everything at his command to win this case and get custody of his daughter. Judge Sanders, who was a capable and lovable judge, had been a judge for years and was still the judge in the case, although he had an illness that affected his mind. He and his wife had accepted invitations to have dinner with Sid Turner in his big and beautiful two-story home. It is, of course, unethical for a judge to be drinking and socializing with any litigant who might appear in his court.

One day I received a call from Sam LaGrone in Deadwood, who said, "I know you're not in the Sid Turner case, but I want to tell you about something that's going on. You might be interested. Mrs. Sanders, the wife of Judge Sanders, is taking money from Sid Turner to influence her husband in this case."

I said, "I'll pass that on to the lawyer in Dallas who represents Mrs. Turner." I did. Then the case was actually tried. A man from Deadwood served on the jury.

Sam LaGrone came to me and said, "Look, something else is going on in the Sid Turner case. They paid this man to decide the case. He told me all about it." I passed that on to the lawyers in Dallas. After the case was tried, the jury was hung by this one man. A mistrial was declared. This went on for about four years. The greater the desperation that Sid Turner felt in handling this case, the more he resorted to drink.

One day, while under the influence of an excessive amount of alcohol, Sid called Dr. Johnson who came to Sid Turner's residence to attend him. Dr. Johnson informed Sid Turner that there was one thing wrong with him and that was drinking. He told Sid he had one choice. He could either continue to drink and die within a short time, or he could stop drinking and get well. Sid Turner replied to Dr. Johnson, "What the hell. I don't care one way or the other." He continued to drink.

At one time, I saw this poor man in his office before he finally died. His waistline had increased in size to almost double. His face was bloated. I hardly recognized him. Sid Turner died before the case was tried. This enabled his wife to take custody of the daughter.

At the early age of about fifty-two years when he died, Sid Turner had a will that named his aunt, Mrs. Woolworth, executor of his estate. His mother, Mrs. Ruth Turner, survived him, but he did not place her in charge of his property.

Judge Woolworth, the lawyer who had written a recommendation for me to the Texas Bar examiners enabling me to take the Bar examination, was Sid Turner's uncle by marriage. Judge Woolworth served as chief counsel for Magnolia Oil Company, and was one of the most capable lawyers that Texas had. Judge Woolworth had no children, and he and his wife were very devoted to Sid Turner, their nephew. They sent Sid to law school at Baylor University, and when Sid graduated, they gave him a Packard convertible. Sid was a good looking man himself.

Certainly Sid Turner had everything to live for. No one I've ever known has had such a beautiful life handed to him without any effort on his part. Judge Woolworth's wealth was ultimately passed on to the Sid Turner estate. Here's what I believe really killed Sid Turner: he never learned to develop any confidence.

Mrs. Woolworth was interested in disposing of this beautiful home that had been built by Sid Turner about ten or fifteen years prior to his death. Mrs. Woolworth sought advice from a friend, Herman Jacobs, of the First National Bank in Carthage. I called Mr. Jacobs and told him I'd be interested in buying this property, which consisted of about a five-thousand-square-foot home together with twenty-five acres of land within the city limits of Carthage. We negotiated on a price and finally reached an agreement, but Mr. Jacobs said he had one condition outside the very attractive price we had agreed upon.

He stipulated, but did not put in writing, and I agreed that I would not take a case against the Turner estate or against him personally at any time in the future. The additional requirement that I never represent the sawmill company did not affect me because, as a lawyer, I'm not required to take any case. Mr. Jacobs told me at that time he wanted this stipulation because he and Sid Turner had made or obtained six hundred thousand dollars in cash from the Lewis-Werner Sawmill Company that owned a lot of land in Panola County. Sid Turner had been put on a retainer's fee by Lewis-Werner Sawmill Company. He was in a position to influence the sale of timber on this land owned by Lewis-Werner Sawmill Company. He prevailed upon a gentleman, who was in his eighties in charge of the Lewis-Werner estate and lived in Shreveport, to sell this timber at a price for much less than it was worth.

Sid Turner and the banker were able to get a six hundred thousand dollar kickback that, divided two ways, amounted to three hundred thousand dollars each. Sid Turner had more worries on his mind, besides his divorce, that caused his untimely death. He had to wonder whether he would be apprehended for taking this money unlawfully. The bank president wanted to make sure I didn't represent the Lewis-Werner Sawmill Company. Lewis-Werner Sawmill Company did not use me as their attorney after Sid Turner's death. They used someone else. Another sawmill company that had bought the below-valued timber had given Sid Turner the kickback to persuade the owner of the estate to sell his timber at an undervalued price.

I talked with the contractor on the Sid Turner house and he told me that the greater part of the money paid to him was paid in cash. They hid a lot of illicit money, money not reported for income tax purposes, in this house. It is a very well built house. The foundation is good enough for a commercial building several stories high. It has a life-time slate roof and copper decking on the balcony. So I bought the property. I paid cash. I paid only fifty-six thousand dollars for the house even though it cost over one hundred thousand to build. Hot money is a funny thing. You can't put it in the bank and it becomes hot in your hand. You don't know what to do with it.

Sid Turner's mother provided a chapel to be erected on the campus of Panola Junior College in Carthage that carries the name of Sid Turner. His name will be there perpetually. It's a beautiful chapel.

Divorce ends my marriage

Forty years later, my own marriage crumbled and I, too, vacated the Sid Turner house.

After the divorce was granted between Fred Whitaker and Mary Elizabeth, the estate was in such condition that it might have gone into bankruptcy because of the way the judge had divided the property, giving Mrs. Whitaker one half of the property. He imposed on me the duty of paying three million dollars in community debts. The property division reduced the collateral I had used to secure these debts. It also reduced the income the property had been generating.

This was a condition impossible to overcome. A lawyer friend in

Carthage advised me to take bankruptcy and not only wipe out the debts I owed but cause the properties set aside for Mrs. Whitaker to be sold in payment of the debts. It is generally known that when you go into bankruptcy, the properties never bring what they are worth. The divorce division created such a condition of chaos.

Another lawyer in Carthage advised me to take bankruptcy. My own attorney in Longview, Earl Sharp, said he didn't see any way I could pay the debts.

I talked with the bankers and they said that I might start liquidating and see if I could pay the debts. I might start all over again. At that time, I knew the oil business forward and backwards. Hurriedly, I generated and obtained one hundred thousand dollars in cash. I was afraid to leave that in the bank because I was afraid a lawsuit would be filed against me and the bank account would be garnisheed and tied up.

So I took this one hundred thousand dollars and my son, Mark, went with me to Dallas. I rented a lock box in the Republic National bank where I placed this cash. As most people know, the law requires that if you move a certain amount of money, you must report it so this information is available to the Internal Revenue Service or any other interested party in knowing the movement of cash.

After I placed this money in the bank, I decided I would take a gamble and start buying leases in Panola County in the Carthage Gas Field. The leases were available for me to buy at ten dollars per acre. When I spent the hundred thousand for leases, I ran out of money. I tried and tried to get help from different people in buying the balance of the acreage that I wanted to lease.

No one would agree to join me even though I offered to give the people one half of the property if they would put up another one hundred thousand dollars for me to finish buying the block of leases.

One of the people I talked with was Grace Stemmons of Dallas, an extremely wealthy woman. I asked her if she would be interested in joining me in obtaining this lease block. After she talked with her accountant and other advisors, she decided she wasn't interested in pursuing this venture with me.

After I could not find anyone to join me, I decided to go ahead and buy new leases on properties and try to farm it out to other people for development. I had no money to develop it.

I farmed it out, part of it to Delta Drilling Company in Tyler, and another to Arkla Gas Company of Shreveport, Louisiana. This proved to be the best route that I could have taken. In doing this, I wound out owning about one third of the property that had been developed and become very valuable. About eight thousand acres with tremendous reserves of more than one hundred million dollars became my part of the portion of the leases that I still owned.

No one thought this could be done. I advised with my lawyer friends in Carthage. I told them I wasn't about to take bankruptcy. I was going to work this thing out. I did work it out.

I said to myself, two miracles have happened in my life. It was a miracle that I got my license to practice law. It was certainly a miracle that I survived the divorce judgment rendered by Judge K. Baker who tried my divorce case; and that I could take this small amount of property with a minimum amount of capital and build it up to immense wealth as I have done in the past ten to fifteen years.

My relationship with Mary Elizabeth Whitaker is friendly, and we occasionally get together with our four children and our six adorable grandchildren, Brandy, David, Tracy, Brett, Jeff and Neil. Mary Elizabeth still lives in Carthage where she has built a new home adjacent to the Sid Turner house. Even though her house is only recently built, it was built to look like an old Texas farm house. She is an avid bridge player and enjoys entertaining friends in her home. She even boasts of having the only Bed and Breakfast in Carthage. It occupies a former horse stable which she named The Best Little Horse House in Texas.

Much to everyone's surprise, she made the national news a few years after our divorce. The incident began on one quiet evening as she watched television in the old Sid Turner house that had a swimming pool in the backyard. She heard a huge splash and ran to see who had jumped into the pool. To her horror, she saw her prize Brown-Swiss bull swimming frantically, trying to climb out of the pool.

She hurridly called the Volunteer Fire Department. As luck would have it, they were meeting that very evening. By this time, the bull had gotten tired and looked as if he might sink to the bottom. She lay beside the pool and grabbed one of his ears to keep him afloat. When the fire fighters arrived, they found Mary Elizabeth face down holding on to the bull for dear life. They rescued her and the bull. The national news media loved the story which they saw as another rich Texan tall tale.

As I've said, I believe so strongly in education. I sent all of my children to college. I have provided since my children's high school days more than thirty years of college education. My youngest son, Mark, attended college in Huntsville, and received a degree in Business Finance and Agriculture. He lives in Carthage and works with me in the oil and gas operations. Melinda, my oldest daughter with Dixie, lives in Houston and works for Rice University. She attended Monticello College and SMU. Both Debbie and Jennifer attended Texas Christian University in Fort Worth and Stephen F. Austin University in Nacogdoches. Jennifer still lives in Carthage, and Debbie lives in Mansfield, Texas.

Father of the year

One of my fondest memories stems from Melinda's college days. In 1961, I received a formal invitation to visit Monticello College in Godfrey, Illinois for Father's Day. Melinda had decided to attend this girls' school because it had been so highly recommended by members of her mother's family. After receiving this invitation, I had to make a business trip to New York.

I decided that rather than return to Texas from New York, I would go to Illinois directly from New York. Before leaving New York, I called Melinda and told her that we should make this a beautiful weekend. I asked her if she would reserve a suite of rooms in a Godfrey hotel, and rent a car for us. She asked me what kind of car.

"Why don't you rent a convertible? It's spring. We can put the top down." She rented a red convertible, a very sporty car.

After spending the first night in the hotel, I received a telephone call from Melinda, who preferred to stay with her girlfriends, asking me if I would like to attend breakfast with her at the school cafeteria. After we had breakfast, I went into the lounge to relax and read the paper. I found that this was not the place to relax. Young ladies came to me from time to time to engage me in conversation. They asked me all about myself, what I did, what I liked in the way of entertainment. I must have met and talked with twenty or thirty students.

The following night, on a Saturday, we went to a dance where a ten-piece orchestra played excellent, sometimes fast, dance music. Lo and behold, the president of the school played the drums. He was rather young, maybe in his thirties. About fifty fathers attended with about one hundred young ladies dressed in evening clothes. We danced and we had fun with the young ladies. I had not wanted Melinda to go to a girls' school, and had insisted that she attend a school in Texas. But, for the first time, I decided this was the place for her to attend for one or two years. They were all so happy.

About eleven o'clock in the evening, the music stopped, then the orchestra struck some cords to signal some important event. The president of the college said they had an important announcement to make. The girls had selected the most outstanding father: the father whom the girls would most like to spend the weekend with. They were naughty little devils. The man they had selected was Fred Whitaker. That floored me.

That might be the most thrilling moment of my life. Then we all danced. I must have danced with every young lady there. Then I admonished Melinda, "You knew what was going on all along. That's why I had so many interviews."

"Daddy," she said, "I knew nothing about it until you did."

To this day, I don't know if she knew. I do believe that her being such an attractive and sweet girl, whom they all liked, might have influenced the others to select Melinda's father.

The two children by my first wife include my daughter, Suzanne, who lives in Los Angeles, California. We don't get to see each other as often as we would like, but we have a very warm relationship. My son, John, from my first marriage came to me in Carthage after he graduated at the top of his high school class in Tocoma, Washington. He told me he wanted to become a doctor. I sent him to the University of Texas where he graduated at the top of his class. He had the opportunity of going to any medical school in the country, but he chose Southwestern Medical School in Dallas, then chose to take a residency in psychiatry.

Suzanne's and John's mother, Florence Slaterly of Shreveport, Louisiana, also believed in education. She obtained her degree from LSU; then got a Master's degree in education. I met her in Shreveport in 1934 when I first started practicing law. I was young and inexperienced.

Who knows? If I had not had these reverses in my life, I might not have done as well. My financial problems caused me to take better care of my health because I knew that I had vast undertakings to meet.

The return to oil

The surge in leasing that had started again in Carthage and Panola County began in the mid 1970s. The operators produced gas from the Petit Formation, and from Travis Peak Formation, at a depth between six and seven thousand feet. This production had become marginal in some instances and a large, or substantial, part of the leases had simply expired for lack of production.

I used a large part of the money realized in the selling of the bank to buy new leases, and did purchase, on an average of twenty-five dollars per acre, eight thousand acres of leases in the Carthage Gas Field. We were then expecting to obtain production from the Cotton Valley Formation at a depth of about ten thousand feet.

The cost of drilling and completing wells in the Cotton Valley Formation was approximately one million four hundred thousand dollars. In order to drill, complete and develop the acreage I had, it would have been necessary that I go in debt for a very large amount of money. I finally decided that I would have investors to share in this enormous and expensive operation.

In visiting people in New York, this sort of money had kind of dried out. I then took a trip to California and did make one contact with Tom Dahlgren, a banker who had financed the making of the motion picture, *The Godfather.* He became interested in what I was doing, and finally Francis Ford Coppola, who was doing business with Mr. Dahlgren at his bank, committed verbally to develop these properties over the next two or three years.

In the late 1970s, when I had the money available, drilling rigs became scarce, and I could not get drilling contractors to contract for this work. There simply were not enough drilling rigs available at that time. So I contacted people who had drilling rigs. One of the largest drilling rig contractors in the United States was Delta Drilling Company in Tyler, Texas.

They first informed us that they would not be interested in this deal, but when I was next in Dallas, I ran into Bill Rudman of Rudman Resources, whom I had known for many, many years. In conversation I told him about the deal, but that Delta Drilling Company had refused and was not interested.

He suggested that I might go back and see them and tell them that he would take whatever percentage of the deal that they did not retain. Bill Rudman, known more often as Duke Rudman, is a colorful sort of person, and is financially able to do almost anything that the major oil companies can do.

Just before the price of oil dropped from thirty dollars a barrel to ten dollars a barrel, he sold a sizeable portion of his production, or oil reserves, for a hundred and seventy-five million dollars. That, among other operations that he pursues, gives us great respect for the astute way in which he has made his fortune.

The same day that Mr. Rudman made his commitment, I saw Fred Meyer, former president of U.S. Steel Company, in Dallas. His son, Fred Meyer, Jr., headed the Republican Party in Texas. Mr. Meyer told me that if Delta Drilling Company would do the drilling and become the operator, he would take one-fourth of this deal.

With these two tremendous backers, I went back to Delta Drilling Company and argued with them and asked them, "Why not take this deal, since I have this tremendous backing? The charges that you will make for the drilling of these wells will be rather attractive."

We finally reached an agreement with Delta Drilling Company. It is interesting to note that they liked the deal so well that they did not send a portion of this deal to Duke Rudman, or to Fred Meyer. They kept it all, other than the portion which I had, one-third interest that I retained on this acreage and still own.

At or during the time the deal was made with Delta Drilling Company, I owned a block of leases located about nine miles east of Carthage, just off the Shreveport Highway in Panola County. At the time, this farm-out acreage was made to Arkla Exploration Company in Shreveport, Louisiana, leases were selling for more than one hundred dollars per acre. It was difficult for anyone to obtain a lease without its being heavily burdened by overrides, ownerships by other people carved out of the leasehold estate which is usually a seven-eighths interest, in addition to the lease cost.

The deal was made with Arkla Exploration, but they refused to take me on as a partner, but offered me one-quarter override. This was rather attractive since it would not cost me anything by way of operating costs, and the override would be of tremendous value as the property was developed.

Through the years, Arkla refused to develop this property as it should have been developed. They drilled only about six or eight wells, and because I wouldn't renegotiate and reduce my override, they simply refused to drill and produce this property, resulting in my filing suit against them in the United States District Court in Tyler, Texas.

We planned to show that we had been damaged at least fifty million dollars in future income. We finally reached an out-of-court settlement.

It gives me a great deal of pleasure to know that through the years, and with hard work and dedication, I have accumulated tremendous reserves, a greater portion of which are in the Carthage Gas Field. In speaking of reserves, it doesn't necessarily mean that I can sell reserves for nearly as much as I expect to receive over a period of ten to twenty years or longer. The discounted dollar comes in so that it might take as much as one hundred million dollars in the future to obtain a sales price of twenty million dollars or less.

There were only a few investors who were disappointed in the outcome of oil and gas ventures they invested with me. Occasionally, it became very difficult for them to take their losses, which is always inevitable if you're engaged in oil and gas operations.

The attorney Louis Nizer of New York has very ably expressed that this situation befalls an investor if he cannot cope with losses that are incurred. In his book, *Reflection Without Mirror,* he writes, "One can lie and wait to see how risky enterprises turn out and then announce that he was a partner all the time. The courts are full with many such cases, particularly in mining where millions may be lost or won."

"One judge expressed this age-old principal in colloquial terms: 'Heads I win and tails you lose, cannot, I fancy, be the basis of an equity.'"

In *Allens v. Occidental,* Louis Nizer wrote, "The Allens sought the best of two worlds. If the oil was struck they claim a 25 percent profit in the point venture; if it turns out to be a dry hole, it could disavow liability for 25 percent of the loss. The Allens cannot have it both ways. *Allens v. Occidental,* Court of Appeals affirmed the judgment."

Chapter Seventeen

An Advocate of the Law

I n 1972, when I decided to move to Dallas on a part-time basis, I rented a three-bedroom apartment on Turtle Creek. Eventually, I made my residence in Dallas and my life took me into two more marriages, both with women of European roots. While these marriages introduced me to a different view of Europe, they helped me evaluate my own roots and rediscover the real values in my life: my family and friends in Carthage, the rewards received from following my mother's advice and teachings to use the law to right wrongs.

I return to Carthage regularly and each time I walk from my law office to the courthouse square and other parts of town, memories of the many people who shaped and enriched my life, who taught me the value of living, flood my mind.

As I've said, I've always tried to be the type of lawyer who was an advocate of the law. I can still see Mrs. Anderson, a cousin of mine, coming into my office shortly after I began practicing law in Carthage as a young lawyer in the 1930's. Mrs. Anderson informed me she felt so pleased that I had become a lawyer and come back to Carthage because a great injustice had been done. She told me about the Robert Thomas family who had been forced to leave their home many years ago. In fact, Mrs. Anderson said, the property had been stolen from this family around the turn of the century.

This case involved knowing a great deal of land law, which I'd learned in law school, but had had no actual practice in doing this type of litigation. I started working on the case immediately, but the more I got into it, the more it appeared to me I would not be able to get this property back to the rightful owners.

About twenty years later, after I had tried many lawsuits involving land titles and disputes, the children of the family forced off the property came to my office. At that time, the oldest son, Robert Thomas, and his brothers and sisters told me the same facts that Mrs. Anderson had told me, and then the children gave me more details. The oldest son had been living at the time the family had been living on their property in question. One evening, someone had thrown a rock into their home. The rock had a note tied to it with the message, "You niggers better leave if you care anything about your lives."

The Thomas family left their home, which consisted of about two hundred acres of land located about ten miles east of Carthage near the Sabine River, that they had bought and paid for. Two white men, one by the name of Bounds and the other by the name of Holt, who lived in the nearby community, had forced the Thomases off their property because the white men didn't want black people as neighbors.

This property then remained in the family of the Bounds. At the time the Robert Thomas family came into my office, a grandson, Jimbo Bounds, had possession of the property.

I started working. I looked up the title and found that at the turn of the century, the title of the land had gone into the Robert Thomas family. In the next conference I had with the Thomas family, I informed them that the statute of limitations had run and that they likely would not, under any circumstances after some fifty years, be able to recover property that had been occupied and used by the people living on it.

I explained to them very carefully what the statute of limitations meant: other people had taken the land, put it under fence, used it to the exclusion, underline exclusion, of anyone else. I asked them if they knew of anyone who had used this property in any way, such as easements others might have used going to and from or across this property.

All of a sudden, one of the heirs said, "I know something. Did you know that this property has been used as a public burial ground for all these many years?"

In talking with them further, they explained the reason it had been used for a public burial ground. Many bodies had been found floating in the Sabine River. When someone found one of the bodies, people would take the body out of the river and give the person a proper burial. That had been done for these many years.

I decided I could break this statute of limitations that enabled people so many times to steal property instead of rightfully own it. With this favorable information, I decided to accept employment and drew up a contract on a contingency fee basis whereby I would receive fifty percent of all the property I recovered for them. I made my percentage high because I knew I would have a lot of difficulty in winning this lawsuit for them even though we did have enough facts to go to a jury.

It occurred to me that it would be an unpopular case for me to take and it would take so much time that I would be almost making a career out of this one lawsuit.

When I took the case, the Thomas children felt very happy that they could do what their mother and father had asked them to do. I immediately filed a lawsuit against Jimbo Bounds, with whom I had gone to high school and liked personally, alleging the property belonged to the Thomases and we were suing for the title and possession of property that was rightfully theirs.

The defendant hired the law firm of Long and Strong that had a lot of experience in trying land suit matters. I received a telephone call from Judge Strong advising me that I had a lot of nerve to try to recover land that had been out of possession of the record title owners and had been used and occupied by other people for almost one-half century.

I informed him I had a few facts that might be an exception to the general rule. We went forward, the case was set for trial before a jury. After we introduced our record title, we rested. But, the defendant showed that without any question the property belonged to him because the adverse possession was perfected just about as well as could be done.

For the rebuttal, we put fifteen or twenty people on the witness stand who were familiar with the fact that this property had been used as a public burial ground. About forty people had been buried there, either bodies found floating down the Sabine River or bodies of paupers who had no place to be buried. A few small tombstones showed the dates.

We tried the case, and made out the case to show that the Thomases were the rightful owners of the property. The jury deliberated several hours and came back to answer all the questions in our favor. The property was recovered for these people.

Several years later, this property proved to be oil producing property which benefited the Thomases. The fee I received, which I had no idea would be worth anything, became one of the best fees I'd ever been paid in representing people in Carthage. However, the fee I received had little value compared to the good feeling I've had all these years in doing work in a community so that justice finally prevailed, although sometimes it seemed that justice would never come to pass.

The old courthouse, built in 1881, in Carthage where I tried this case is gone now. I do miss that wonderful old courthouse with its straight-backed chairs, the seats covered with cowhide. And I miss the offices, some of which had wood-burning fireplaces. When I first started practicing law, if we didn't have enough jurors to try a case, the sheriff would go into the streets of Carthage and call men to come serve on the jury.

Many years later, when the county decided to tear down our classic courthouse, I worked with our local historical society to try to save it. Unfortunately, I lost that case.

However, the home that belonged to my great grandfather, John Whitaker, still stands and, just as I promised my dad, I've never sold the original home.

I always stay in that home when I return to Carthage. My son, Mark, and I have improved the old homestead so that it is a comfortable home while, at the same time, it retains the authenticity of the house built by Great-grandfather Whitaker who came to Carthage in a covered wagon two years after the Civil War. I know Mama and Papa would feel proud of my success at holding on to the family homestead.

I have had friends and acquaintances to ask me from time to time how I attribute my success in law. If I look back and review what I have done since finishing high school in Carthage, I would say the first hurdle had been getting a license to practice law. I enjoyed working long hours, attending school at Texas Christian University in Fort Worth, and later at Cumberland University in Tennessee where I obtained a law degree.

As I told my daughter Jennifer, I truly enjoyed practicing law. I heard other lawyers complaining about Monday mornings, but I looked forward to them. It was a genuine pleasure for me. I even had fun with the jury. They wanted to see me win.

Sometimes I do wish I could live my life over and not fight so much. In those bygone days, though, if someone questioned your honor, or called you a derogatory name, you had to fight even if you got the hell beat out of you. Otherwise, we were taught, you didn't have any honor. I still remember what happened the day Carthage's newspaper editor called me a sonovabitch.

Handling the press

Today people complain about the media mishandling them. Many years ago in small towns, we had our own ways of resolving differences with the media.

In the late 1930s, people in Carthage gathered in the evenings in Moore's Drugstore where we discussed everything. One evening, in walked Neil Estes who not only owned the *Panola Watchman*. but edited the newspaper. For some reason, he had had a few drinks and was in a belligerent mood. He started making remarks about me, what I would have to do if I expected to be elected county attorney and succeed Sid Turner, then serving a four-year term as county attorney.

The discussion went on for some time. The more we talked, the more belligerent Neil Estes became. Suddenly he called me a sonovabitch. I turned around and hit him very hard right between the eyes. He was taken to a doctor to see if he had any severe injuries, which he did not have.

When I next saw Neil Estes, I decided that maybe I'd done something that I might regret for a long time because he did own the newspaper and I could have favorable kind of publicity or negative publicity in establishing myself as a country lawyer in Carthage.

As we talked again, he referred to our ruckus in a light manner. He told me that whatever had happened was all his fault and I should think nothing of it. We later became very good friends. For about twenty-four hours, though, I felt very concerned about what I'd done so far as the media in Carthage was concerned.

Fighting for clients

Around the same time as my fight with Neil Estes, I got into a fist fight with Ross Duran, an attorney who was never very popular, and who represented the opposing side in a case I was trying. In the course of the trial, he kept making disparaging remarks about me personally and about my client. On one occasion, he said one of these remarks one time too many.

I got up from the counsel table, walked to where he stood, and hit him so hard I broke his jaw right in front of Judge Sanders and the jury. Judge Sanders left the bench, came over to separate us, got back on the bench, and fined us ten dollars each for fighting in the courtroom. I signed the check right then for the fine and I signed in a way you'd never know I'd been excited.

Once again my conscience told me my hot temper might have done something that was detrimental to me. I had second thoughts. I went home, washed the blood off, changed shirts, and went back to my office.

Then people started talking about me, saying Fred Whitaker was a fighter; if he couldn't win a lawsuit one way he'd do it another. People who had hard feelings against someone they had a claim against began coming into my office to ask me to represent them. I had difficulty living down that reputation that I'd win cases one way or another as a fighter. I wasn't proud of that.

I did learn that beating the hell out of an unpopular lawyer was rather popular. That had its problems though.

About a year later, I had another encounter with the Ross Duran family. A relative decided to take up the fight. He called me on the telephone and said he had a gun and was going to come to see me and kill me.

I didn't have a gun in my office, so I hurriedly went home and got a .32 caliber pistol, put it under my belt, and went back to my office to wait until he got there.

He never made his appearance. I'm so glad to this day. What pleasure could anyone have in killing another man? I didn't want to be known as a fighter, but as an advocate of the law.

And, as I walk around the square in Carthage on the returns I often make, I reminisce and recall back to the time long ago that I had dreams of becoming a lawyer, a very successful lawyer. Little did I dream that these visions would come true and maybe, just maybe, they exceeded the dreams. What a wonderful world!